AGGRESSIVE CAPITALISM

The Overleveraging of America's Wealth, Integrity, and Dollar

---

Claude V. Chang

University Press of America,® Inc.
Lanham · Boulder · New York · Toronto · Plymouth, UK

⊖™ The paper used in this publication meets the minimum
requirements of American National Standard for Information
Sciences—Permanence of Paper for Printed Library Materials,
ANSI Z39.48-1992

This book is dedicated to those who have endured the indignity of poverty and inequality, institutionalized.

Contents

Figures		vii
Tables		ix
Preface		xi
Acknowledgement		xiii
Chapter 1	Introduction	1
Chapter 2	Economic Quagmire: The Impossible Trinity of Mounting Debt, Balanced-trade, and a Strong Dollar	7
Chapter 3	Free-market Capitalism in Terminal Crisis	25
Chapter 4	The 1990s: American Triumphalism on Steroids	47
Chapter 5	The Confluence of Rationality, Reductionism and Existentialism	61
Chapter 6	The Abiding Tension between Capitalism and Equality	89
Chapter 7	China on the World Stage	109
Chapter 8	Targeted Revaluation: A Double-edged Sword?	137
Chapter 9	Biting the Bullet: A Concluding Perspective	153
Bibliography		173
Index		179

Figures

Figure 4.1   Average Annual GDP Growth Rates: 1965-1989   59

Figure 6.1   Percentage of Total US Household Income
By 1/5 Segments and Top 5%   93

Figure 6.2   US GINI Coefficient: 1970-2006   94

Figure 6.3   GINI Income Distribution (Highest & Lowest 10%
of Income Earners): 1990-2000   96

Figure 6.4   GINI Income Distribution: 1990-2000
By 1/5 Segments and Highest 10 %   97

Figure 9.1   Students Leaving W/out First Degree in
Tertiary Education: 2005   166

Tables

Table 6.1   Percentage of Total US Household Income
By 1/5 Segments and Top 5%   93

Preface

This book seeks to fill the void that exists between erudite but discrete perspectives of the 2007–8 financial and economic crises, on the one hand, and causality rooted in a value-system informed by the confluence of rationality, reductionism, and existentialism, on the other hand. It argues that since the late 1960s, this confluence manifested increasingly in economic and business models constructed in the beliefs that there is "virtue in selfishness", "winning is the only thing" and "Greed is good"; that such beliefs have not only guided America's domestic socioeconomic and political policies in the late twentieth and early twenty-first centuries but also informed its foreign policy approaches; and that, in consequence, wealth accumulation in America became increasingly premised on military power and on the added belief that there has to be some advantage to being the sole superpower after the collapse of the Soviet Union in 1991.

The unbridled pursuit of wealth, it is further argued, is not without costs; it has resulted in the abandonment of societal norms, with trust and integrity replaced with the "fine print" as defining legal and moral responsibility. Moreover, in addition to the overleveraging of America's assets, the pursuit of wealth accumulation by the highest 10 percent of US income-earners has resulted in greater income inequality in the US since the 1970s; it has also resulted in the overleveraging of America's integrity with the wider world and the latter's trust in the US dollar.

It is further contended that, as a result of this focus on wealth accumulation and the abandonment of basic moral values, the US has squandered the moral authority it enjoyed with the wider world since the end of World War Two (WWII). Therefore, whereas the US was able to recover from the consequences of over-extending itself financially in the past with help from its friends—as evidenced by the switch to a gold exchange standard in 1934, and the agreement to floating exchange rates in 1972—on this occasion, it is likely to find itself having to effect fundamental changes to its geo-economic and geopolitical models as conditions precedent to continued forbearance and support from its international trading partners.

It is further argued that the 2007–8 financial and economic crises have served to highlight fundamental weaknesses in free-market capitalism as a viable world economic system; indeed, that it took unprecedented government intervention to prevent total collapse in 2008 suggests that free-market capitalism as we know it is in terminal crisis and is unlikely to exist at the end of this decade. Moreover, unlike economic downturns of the past, the collapse of the US financial system and its reverberations to the broder economy have placed the US at the crossroads of greatness, on one hand, and fortress nation, on the other hand, and this must be of great concern to the wider world, in particular China, given America's chronic discomfort, if not intolerance, with the slow process of international diplomacy (see Chang, 2008).

Finally, this book, to borrow from Arnold Toynbee (1948: v), "has, in the writer's mind, a unity of outlook, aim, and idea which, he hopes, will be felt by his readers." To this end, the common aim of the nine chapters is not only to bring some gleam of insight into the meaning of society, but also to share with readers some of the unspoken consequences of fostering a culture of selfishness and greed.

Claude V. Chang
North Miami, Florida
April 30, 2010

Acknowledgements

In a work of this kind, the writer is often given to his or her own fears, prejudices, and ignorance. Hence, to moderate these unconscious limitations, there is a cadre of friends, colleagues, and relatives who give of themselves unstintingly in the form of comments, suggestions, and the all-important editing; therefore, they are as much contributors as the author; their contributions are thus gratefully acknowledged.

Of such contributors, first and foremost, I am deeply indebted to my colleague, Petas Bonaparte, of Johnson & Wales University; her professionalism as editor is matched only by her unwavering enthusiasm, patience, and support for this project; I am indeed, fortunate. I am also thankful to my other colleagues at Johnson & Wales, Teresa Crew and Michael Moskwa, for unreservedly sharing their insights with me; I have benefitted greatly from them, and I believe this manuscript is all the better for their inputs.

Chapter Seven is essentially a combination of "The Dragon Awakes" and "Is an Emerging China America's Dilemma?" taken either in whole or in part from *Territoriality and the Westernization Imperative: Antecedents and Consequences*, copyrighted in 2008 by University Press of America, Lanham, Maryland. The writer and the publishers therefore take this opportunity to thank University Press of America for their courteous permission to reprint them in this book.

Finally, I would be remiss if I did not acknowledge the contribution of Bebe: spouse, disciplinarian, critic, and librarian. As a professional librarian, her insights, research skills, and facility with information-sourcing on the web have been invaluable to this project; so too were her enthusiasm and encouragement.

Chapter One

Introduction

Contrary to initial denials and later rationalizations, the world economy was thrown into economic chaos in 2008 in consequence of aggressive capitalism premised on the overleveraging of America's wealth, integrity, and the Dollar: a uniquely American risk management model that transferred risk onto unsuspecting Americans and the wider world.

Such was the certainty in the edifice of risk management, its proponents boldly proclaimed it as the model of all models, one that secures the twenty-first century as the American century; it was heralded by the then Chairman of the Federal Reserve System (FED), Alan Greenspan, as portending the end to economic downturns. However, as played out, its framework of financial market liberalization was nothing less than the construct of decades of increasing self-interest pursued by America's intellectual capitalist class, and was designed to access the savings from a largely trusting and unsuspecting world.[1]

The quest by this class for greater wealth and power outpaced the American housing market's ability to support its falsely-based models and the world's capacity to absorb the over-pricing of the increasingly large quantities of collateralized debt obligations (CDO) and Credit Default Swaps (CDS), the latter an insurance-based product that covers for risky sub-prime mortgage investments by seeking to narrow the standard deviation. As a consequence, the "capitalist world-economy" as currently constructed, and America's standing as its leader, have both been called into question. To be sure, the global financial system has in effect collapsed under the weight of the greed that pervaded Wall Street, London, and, to a lesser extent, other major financial capitals around the world.

Even if both—the capitalist world-system and America's standing as its leader—survived the current crisis, as most observers expect them to do, they are likely to emerge weaker, not stronger than before. That this should be so is perhaps because the lessons of history, rather than used as a navigator's chart by which to steer a course between charted rocks and reefs, were cast aside in deference to intellectualism for much of the last quarter of the twentieth century and since. Moreover, the pharisaical notion that the new economic model, that spun the illusion of well-being during the late 1990s and the first eight years of the twenty-first century, exempted the US from the possibility of falling into those mistakes and mishaps that have been the ruin of so many societies and empires, gained momentum from the collapse of the Soviet Union in the 1991.

In light of the above, this decade will, I believe, be a period of great challenges, some opportunities, and much uncertainty—what the ancient Chinese refer to as "interesting times"—not just for Americans but for the world as a whole. This perspective rests on four premises which are argued in this book. The first is that the United States of America (US) is in an economic quagmire. Its mounting debt burden and escalating budget deficit are primarily the result of an overleveraged currency, manifesting in a state of perpetual saving-investment imbalance, and, therefore, balance of payments imbalance on current account. These are fully discussed in Chapter Two. The second premise arising from the first and argued in Chapters Three and Four, is that unregulated capitalism or free-market capitalism is in terminal crisis—having been progressed in the last quarter of the twentieth century on the mistaken belief in the certainty of intellectual capitalism—and is unlikely to exist as the dominant economic model for growth and development at the end of the decade.

As contends in Chapter Four, financial market liberalization was aggressively pursued in the US and abroad after 1980 pursuant maximization of self-fulfillment, and, therefore, must be seen as either feeding into or resulting in the excesses that have come to define the intellectual edifices of an essentially aggressive capitalist system. Evidence of this was clearly discernable in the shift in the US's position on the Chinese currency issue in 2005. According to the then Secretary of the Treasury, John Snow, "moving toward a truly flexible exchange rate regime requires quite a large number of steps. . . . We recognize that will take some time."[2] Days earlier, Secretary Snow was trying to persuade the Chinese toward greater "financial modernization" and "to let American companies own a controlling stake in financial firms in China."[3] At the same time, American banks have been expanding their investment banking operations in Europe. According to Bank of America, "if we don't continue our product differentiation internationally, it is going to impair our business domestically."[4]

As further argued, the collapse of the global financial system brings into closer scrutiny, as indeed it must, not just the edifice of risk management that, before the 1980s had been premised on a pricing mechanism of unquestionable integrity, but also the motivation of the architects of the new economic model. To this latter end, to the extent that human rationality and the reductionist ethos are seen as informing many of the central themes in economics, philosophy, and the social sciences, they bear scrutiny for their contributions to the resultant economic chaos; thus, they form part of the critique in Chapter Four.

The third premise is that a sociopolitical and economic system founded on greed—or the "relentless maximization of self-interest" as defined by Amartya Sen, (2002:4)—is necessarily short-term in horizon, unsustainable, and, ultimately, destructive as argued in Chapters Five and Six. As we have witnessed in the last two decades and detailed in this book, the outcomes from the aggressive pursuit of wealth have served to render Norman Rockwell's perception of Americana an American utopia in the twenty-first century.

Furthermore, given that the first ten years in the twenty-first century have been mired in disruption for the world, in addition to critiquing the collapse of the US financial system in 2008 from the perspective of its implications for the capitalist world-economy, this book seeks to treat with rationality, reductionism, and existentialism as among the basic ideas informing our present value-system towards greater perversity. Hence, these concepts are approached in Chapter Five not from their theoretical constructs but rather as ideas that informed game-theoretic models, the pinnacle of American intellectualism. In this approach, it seeks to tease out a causal relationship between a value-system that has undergone fundamental changes since the 1960s culminating in the collapse of free-market capitalism in 2008. To this end, the discussion in Chapter Five seeks to convey a perspective largely informed by the evidence—albeit selected—resulting from aggressive wealth accumulation and other manifestations of self-interest that are clearly informed by rationalism, reductionism, and existentialism, either as discrete influences or in concert with one another.

Clearly, in taking this approach, I am suggesting that outcomes in the twenty-first century to date, have indeed manifested "the relentless maximization of self-interest"—in keeping with Max Weber's substantive rationality—to the exclusion of societal norms, to wit the invasion of Iraq and the collapse of the global financial system; that the "rational fool", as defined by Amartya Sen (2002: 7), is more real than theoretical in consequence of the widening income inequality gap as measured by the GINI coefficient, and the erosion of holism; and that, since Kenneth Arrow's 1951 contribution to the literature, upon which social choice theory turns, rationality—substantive rationality—has become indistinguishable from the existential ethos of self-fulfillment.

This is not to deny the importance of Amartya Sen's (2002:4) conception of rationality—subjecting one's choice to "reasoned scrutiny"—to knowledge and the broader discourse. His arguments are persuasive from a theoretical perspective and in the right place and at the right time would be difficult to dispute. However, in context of twenty-first century reality, which demands an evaluative framework premised on evidence rather than on theoretical arguments, the self-interest of the intellectual capitalist class is inescapably visible and, in consequence, gives substance to the notion of rational fool. Indeed, as will be discerned from the discussion in Chapter Five, the rational fool is a constant in the intellectual capitalist model of the twenty-first century; it manifests in the *fine print* of every economic transaction; it validates the long-held perception that greed has its own punishment: the hunger for more. Hence, the fourth premise is that, having moved far from social and economic equilibrium, the US finds itself compelled to make fundamental changes to its value system within the framework of a changing geopolitical and geo-economic world order that must necessarily be premised on restoration of trust and integrity; and this it must do not just to fall in line with the wider world but also with the demands of its public.

Whilst getting to this point of disequilibrium was easy pursuant a model of high consumption, trade imbalances, budget deficits, and easy access to the world's savings within an accommodating global political and economic framework, getting back to equilibrium would be much more challenging than most envisaged. Indeed, how, when, and in what form the US emerges from this quagmire, and its eventual place in the emerging world order depends crucially upon its national and political will to undertake fundamental economic and geopolitical changes as outlined in Chapter Nine. With respect to the latter point, of concern must be America's attitude to the wider world since WWII; for a country that has not only grown accustomed to living beyond its means but also to the idea of omnipotence and dominance, the outcomes from these changes are at the very least clouded in uncertainty for the rest of the world.

From a domestic perspective, in seeking to reform health care and the financial and regulatory frameworks, the Obama administration has taken critical first steps in the face of unprecedented opposition. Moreover, in abandoning the strictures of free-market economics from focusing on preventing a total collapse of the economy through fiscal and monetary interventions, the Obama administration has clearly put the welfare of Americans ahead of ideology; it has also taken a crucial first step to building substantive social cohesion in a polarized America.

From an international relations perspective, as Americans and the world have recently learned, it is a narrow and arrogant policy to suppose that political and social changes can be achieved at the sharp end of the sword— not dissimilar to imposition of a *Pax Romana*, if you will—and that this country or that is to be singled out as the perpetual enemy of America, to paraphrase the nineteenth century British Statesman, Lord Palmerston. It is thus with foresight that the Nobel Committee has seen it fit to award the 2009 Nobel Peace Prize to President Obama, whose approach is clearly to give recognition to "Other" and to deny fear and intimidation a substantive place in his administration's foreign policy. Also, in giving cognizance to the increasing roles of Brazil, Russia, India, and China (BRIC) as purveyors of global economic and social development outside the center-periphery framework established by the industrialized countries after World War Two, the Obama administration has taken the crucial first step to rebuilding the trust the US once enjoyed with the developing world. These are crucial first steps; they could be the catalyst for lifting the US out of the economic quagmire it is in currently; but to be effective they require presidential strength and focus not seen since the Great Depression.

In addition to the above, I have included a chapter (Chapter Seven) on the emergence of China on the world stage not only because of its enhanced role but also because such enhancement came sooner than expected; it clearly took China out of its comfort zone. Also, given this expanded role of China in international relations and in the capitalist world-economy since 2008, the US needs to move beyond animus and accept the outstretched hand of friendship, even from a communist country, in keeping with Lord Palmerston's take on not holding steadfastly to the idea of perpetual enemies. But, the US can only do so by first seeking to understand China from a perspective other than as a threat, the prevailing American perception of China; hence the inclusion of Chapter Seven.

As should be discerned from the chapter themes, this book seeks to expand upon, and supports many of the ideas expressed in *Territoriality and the West-ernization Imperative* (Chang, 2008). It does, for example, support the contention that game-theoretic models premised on the certainty of outcomes are inherently unreliable as tools in arriving at truth—both within and outside their cultural underpinnings—if only because Westernization is still a work in progress (Huntington, 1996; Toynbee, 1948); also because of the egocentric needs of their architects to ascribe successful outcomes to them. In this regard, as the costly misadventure in Iraq and the collapse of the American financial system evidence, the certainty of an American-centric world order in the twenty-first century since the demise of communism in 1989 is anything but certain. Instead, they lend credence to Immanuel Wallerstein's (1999: 1) determinist observations that "the first half of the twenty-first century will be far more difficult, more unsettling, and yet more open than anything we have known in the twentieth century;" and that the modern world system "has entered into a terminal crisis and is unlikely to exist in fifty years;" and, furthermore, that the period of transition to another system or systems "will be a terrible time of troubles, since the stakes of the transition are so high, the outcome so uncertain, and the ability of small inputs to affect the outcome so great."

Since the current financial and economic crises began to manifest in the middle of 2007, the Federal Reserve System (FED), the Bush administration, and the Republican-led Congress soon found themselves rationalizing the unintended consequences of misguided policies, in the hope for, if not certainty of, a quick recovery in 2008. However, given their inability to orchestrate the world to an esoteric value-system premised on greed that has become America's, rather than confident and secured in its presumptive role as the bastion of the capitalist world-economy, the US finds itself in a weakened, vulnerable, and highly defensive position at the closing of the first decade of the twenty-first century, with far fewer options than it had at the turn of the century. Indeed, the options available to the US in this decade have been narrowed considerably; the result of its own making, unintended, to be sure, but arguably in consequence of triumphalism and certainty with which it entered the twenty-first century as discussed in Chapter Four.

Ironically, the choice the US makes in this decade must necessarily be an existential one, having relied upon the existential ethos as the pathway to supremacy for most of the latter half of the twentieth century. But whatever the choice, the US will be locked in to it for generations to come and to another place in history: in the end, either as a truly great world power for good—by example of international cooperation and goodwill—or as a dysfunctional fortress nation plagued by both external and internal strife of one sort and another. For the latter reason and from the perspective of the world, the narrowing of choices has come too quickly to a society of enormous military power and capability that continues to evidence the birth pangs of nation-building while exhibiting chronic discomfort, if not intolerance, with the slow process of international diplomacy. Hence, how the US addresses itself to the domestic and international challenges confronting it in the next decade and beyond must be of great concern to both Americans and the wider world. Clearly, staving off the disastrous denouement of liberalization by force, as evidenced by the invasion of Iraq in 2003 under the banner of freedom and democracy, must be the singularly most important priority for all if we were to avoid validating history as deterministic.

NOTES

1. See Secretary Henry Paulson's interview with Jim Lehrer on News Hour, *PBS.org*, May 17, 2007
2. Andrews, E. L., "Snow Shifts His Demands on China", *The New York Times*, October 17, 2005
3. Andrews, E., "Snow Urges Consumerism on China Trip" *The New York Times*, October 14, 2005, C1
4. Timmons, H., "For Bank of America, Next Target is Europe", *The New Your Times*, September 23, 2005, C7

Chapter Two

Economic Quagmire:
The Impossible Trinity of Mounting Debt,
Balanced-trade and a Strong Dollar

Given: a) a hidden debt obligation approaching levels normally found in mismanaged developing countries and decried by the multilateral financial institutions—International Monetary Fund (IMF) and World Bank—as untenable; b) growing federal and state fiscal budget deficits that, again, are approaching levels found in grossly-mismanaged countries the servicing of which takes away from private investment; and c), a currency that has lost its luster, the US is arguably in an economic quagmire.

We could, of course, depending upon the extent of our programming, deny these observations by flogging our minds to accepting President George Bush's contention that "it would a terrible mistake to allow a few months of crisis to undermine 60 years of success"[1] or that it was those greedy investors in Shanghai and Dubai that were responsible for the crisis, as the then Senator Hillary Clinton pronounced in her campaign rhetoric. Alternatively, we could for the sake of our children and grandchildren ask the unimagined question and learn to accept the unwelcome answer, as the Librarian of Congress, James Billington, entreated us to do. While the latter would be the obvious choice for most, Americans brought up in the belief of a Manifest Destiny would find it difficult to question America's omnipotence; indeed, choosing the latter requires us to, again, as James Billington exhorts, "get back into developing the qualities of judgment, wisdom, and imagination that are internally generated and not defined by somebody else's picture on the screen."[2] Therefore, how well we are able to manage the challenges of this new decade depends crucially upon our individual and collective willingness to inform ourselves of the facts, however unwelcomed or inconvenient they might be.

Debt and Consequences

Despite disclaimers to the contrary, America's hidden debt obligations are its Achilles heel and the world's responsibility. They comprise not only the recognized portion of the national debt—estimated by the Congressional Budget Office to reach US$17.1 trillion in the next ten years, but also unfunded obligations of social security and Medicare—a domestic issue that is beginning to expose the falsely-premised approach to funding the federal budget—and, more significantly for the wider world, the unaccounted stock of US dollars in the coffers of foreign governments and private institutions and individuals.

The smoke and mirror approach to funding the federal budget has been revealed by the expected collection-payment imbalance in Social Security for 2010. As reported by Stephen Ohlemacher, *Associated Press,* the social security retirement program is projected to pay out an estimated US$29.0 billion more in benefits than it collects in taxes in 2010.[3] As a result, it is expected to cash in the IOUs the government issued to it—approximately US$2.5 trillion—which the federal government issued to the Social Security Administration partly in lieu of foreign financing of the federal budget. The effect of this is to add to the budget deficit and to the public debt in the coming years.

With respect to the unaccounted stock of US dollars in foreign hands, for decades the US dollar served as a safe haven from the reach of corrupt foreign governments and the ravages of unstable currencies. Its reputation as a store of value and as the leading reserve currency was built upon the trust and confidence placed in it over time. Unfortunately, that trust and confidence have been overleveraged in recent years in consequence of aggressive capitalism that defined the American economic experience since the mid 1980s.

Premised on the belief in the certainty of the American economy's ability to grow *ad infinitum,* and the unassailable status of the Dollar—ergo "the dollar is our money but their problem," according the then Secretary of the Treasury, John Connolly[4] in the hay day of the Dollar—the printing press at the FED was placed in overdrive; funding at-will America's access to the world's resources and products, in the belief that foreigners will continue to hold US dollars *ad infinitum.* In consequence, one of the greatest geopolitical and geo-economic challenges facing the US, indeed the world, in this decade is a coordinated move away from the Dollar as the primary means to settlement of international debt obligations and as the principal reserve currency. Therefore, discussed below are two scenarios that could confront the US as well as the wider world in this decade.

Worst Case

As a worst case, any precipitous move away from the dollar, I believe, would be catastrophic not just for the US but also for the world economy, despite the prevailing perception that the US economy "has never been stronger" and thus would be able to weather such an occurrence. For those who do not remember, the British economy was once thought to be invincible in the hay day of empire, and the price of gold traded at US$ 35.00 per ounce before floating exchange rates were introduced in 1972.

For the US, then, the challenge would be in the timing of such an occurrence, and the in tempering economic and foreign policies in reaction, in the interest of coexistence in an atmosphere of mutual respect in a pluralist world order. Expanding on this idea, as of today the US would be hard pressed to increase the absorptive capacity of the domestic economy to handle the flow-back of Dollars without triggering asset bubbles or hyperinflation as Americans and foreigners seek to convert dollars to tangible assets. Such a flow-back in today's environment would be in effect the equivalent to monetizing the budget deficit *ex-post*, but without the funding benefits usually expected to be derived from *ex-ante* monetization tied to the growth rate of the economy (see Fischer & Easterly, 1990). Moreover, the flow back would come at a time when foreign borrowing over the recent past has made the US less competitive as reflected in the external imbalance on current account.

For the wider world, a flight out of Dollar to hard assets—commodities, gold, and other currencies such as the Swiss Franc, Yen, and Euro—would also have implications for economic stability and growth. One such implication would be to make exports from the major exporting countries more expensive, thereby further reducing international trade and world output. Some might argue that the latter would give the world a well-deserved breathing space to regenerate; nonetheless, a reduction in world economic welfare and an increase in international conflict would be the likely consequences. The challenge under such conditions, then, is to recognize that any flight out of the US dollar is nothing more than a self-correcting market mechanism in the absence of an official devaluation of the US currency, and to react to it as such; furthermore, that a flow back of Dollars would allow, forced if you will, the US economy to regain competitiveness by reducing imports and increasing exports, as discussed below.

At the same time, the price of gold would undoubtedly be pushed to levels once thought unrealistic; it is highly likely that both Americans and foreigners would simply prefer to convert Dollars to gold rather than hold Treasury bills as a flight to safety becomes the "new normal" in an environment of high inflation. However, this demand for gold should allow the FED to absorb some of the currency flow-back by selling part of its gold reserves at the inflated price: another form of sterilization, and yet another opportunity to transfer its debt obligations as it did in 1934 and again in 1971. It is thus instructive that both India and China reportedly are increasing their holdings of gold as opposed to adding to their holdings of US dollar. While this would undoubtedly push the price of gold to new highs, it provides a semblance of management to the flow-back, assuming that the sale of gold would be by the US government and residents.

The recent experience of Greece suggests that US treasuries would have to be steeply discounted to have any significant play in the bond market in this environment of a flight to safety; how steep a discount depends on purchasers' perception of the US government's ability to effect a quick reversal to the economic quandary; hence, in the absence of confidence, the deeper would be the discount, and the larger the public debt if government expenditure were maintained at current levels. However, the deep discount for treasuries would act as a market mechanism; it should force the government to balance its budget as the market price for foreign borrowing would be prohibitively high. In addition to Greece, there are numerous examples of this play-out to be found among the highly-indebted poor countries (HIPC) of the developing countries, or Third World, as they were once fondly labeled.

Concurrent to high interest rates, high tariffs and quantitative restrictions would be imposed on imported goods on a scale reminiscent of the 1930s in abrogation of World Trade Organization (WTO) rules as the US resorts to unilateralism in seeking to punish those whom it now finds convenient to blame for its predicament. History tells us this knee-jerk reaction is indeed the single most dangerous action the US could take. Such a move would undoubtedly add to global instability and would certainly trigger super if not hyperinflation in the US as prices skyrocket to reflect self-inflicted shortages of goods and raw materials. In addition, any idea of a controlled flow-back of Dollars would be thrown out the window, and any access to foreign savings would be rendered extremely difficult if not impossible in retaliation.

Again, as history tells us, the global economy, as it is currently constructed, would be severely if not irreparably damaged in the short term from a repeat of the "beggar thy neighbor" policy of the 1930s; export-oriented economies would be the worst for the pull-back in international trade. In this connection, the major Asian economies would likely experience a drastic decline in their gross domestic production (GDP), to the extent of their exports to the US and EU, which by this time would have become fortress economies. Similarly, commodity-exporting countries in Africa and elsewhere would also experience a decline in the demand for their products; the major exporting countries in the EU would likely withdraw support to the weaker states; governments around the world would be forced by their respective publics to redress the situation by whatever means, with the stronger industrialized countries resorting to unilateralism, discarding the lessons of history, but which, if used intelligently and courageously, would serve as a means to avoiding past mistakes.

For the Asians, Africans, and South Americans, the pain, I believe, would be likely less severe, and short lived; the formation of regional trading blocs over the years would offer a floor, as would the internal growth of the emerging economies in these regions; also, their cultural underpinnings would allow them to adapt more readily to shortages. For Americans and Europeans who have become steeped in values inculcated since and in consequence of the Enlightenment, on the other hand, adjustments to the "new normal" would be a greater challenge; history tells us that they are likely to pursue their own self-interest at the cost of high-minded notions of multiculturalism and pluralism, manifesting in social disruption and in racial and ethnic violence.

In times of irrational behavior, then, which this period is likely to be, it is highly probable that the dominant members of the Organization for Economic Cooperation and Development (OECD) would be tempted to join the US in closing ranks against whomever or whatever the US fingers as *causa causan* or *casus belli*. It is not novel. The containment of the Japanese economy in the late 1980s and early 1990s was achieved by a combination of US unilateral trade policies—for example, Super 301 as embodied in its Trade and Tariff Act, 1974—voluntary exports restraints, and other trade-restricting practices, such as "rules of origin," and local content imposed in concert with the Europeans (see Finger, 1992; Hamilton, et. al, 1992; Bhagwati & Patrick, 1990; Goto, 1989; and Bhagwati 1988). These mechanisms have not disappeared over time; rather, they have been supplemented by more subtle instruments. For example, the US and Europe have been able to incorporate social and environmental regulations as aspects of their respective trade policies with emerging economies, not entirely because of concern for human rights, but also because doing so serves their economic interests. In addition, targeting a trading partner's currency has been added to the tool box of options since the late 1980s.

With respect to the latter, the efforts of the US, backed by the EU and the IMF, to seek a revaluation of the Chinese currency speak in large measure to targeted revaluation as the preferred tool in managing external imbalances on current account. By targeting a currency for revaluation—a form of devaluation of the domestic currency nonetheless, if surgically so—the US avoids an increase in the general price level that would have resulted had it simply devalued the Dollar. The arguments advanced for targeted revaluation, as was the case with Japan in the late 1980s and early 1990s, and now with China in the twenty-first century, are existential; the US needs to correct increasing trade deficit arising from its high domestic consumption without disadvantaging itself with respect to imports of essential raw materials and other commodities, such as oil, which are priced in Dollars and which would reflect in an increase in the general price level from any devaluation of the Dollar. Moreover, devaluation of the Dollar would not only have negative implications for foreign investments and for foreign borrowing to fund the budget deficits but also for the holding of dollar-denominated assets in general as recognized by the FED chairman,[5] and as discussed below.

Absent America's reductionist and existential approach to balance of payments economics, the Chinese Yuan is not as grossly undervalued as claimed by the US, EU, and now by the IMF in concert; rather, the US dollar is substantially overvalued relative to America's consistent external imbalances on current account since 1980s together with its burgeoning national debt—which is off the scales—and its dependency of foreign oil. Moreover, the IMF, given its composition,[6] could hardly claim impartiality on this issue; its miss-diagnosis and intervention in the 1997–8 Asian financial crisis speak to this contention (see Chang 2006: 41–45).

As evidenced by the data, aided by an overvalued currency derived from the trust and confidence of the world, the US, to be sure, has been feasting on the world resources and savings on the presumption that it will always be able to grow into its obligations; and, equally significant, that it will always be in a dominant position vis-à-vis other international economic actors. Hence, both Treasury Secretary Paulson and FED chairman, Ben Bernanke, had no hesitation in predicting that a fiscal budget surplus would be achieved by 2012.

Targeted revaluation also has geopolitical and geo-economics implications that are downplayed in analyses; in addition to making imports from the targeted country more expensive, revaluation, were it to be successful, would essentially render the targeted country less competitive in third markets and to limit its ability to influence development in third countries. This, however, is yet another manifestation of seeking to rescue the US economy and the capitalist world-system; targeted revaluation would limit the geopolitical reach of the country whose currency is targeted, especially its ability to effect changes to the workings of the Bretton Woods institutions that were designed to perpetuate the capitalist world -system.

Despite the clamor for targeted revaluation of the Chinese currency, as is well exemplified in the case of the automobiles and consumer electronics industries in the US, the theory behind targeted revaluation is falsely-premised and does very little to correct external imbalances either substantially or sustainably. Squeezing the Japanese auto and electronics industries in the 1980s and 1990s as a means to controlling Japanese exports simply provided others—South Korea, China, India, and Taiwan, for example—with the opportunity to fill the void in response to economic profits that exist in a consumption-driven economy, and to the inability of US manufactures to be cost-effective in a competitive global economy: ergo, the collapse of the traditional US auto industry and the infiltration of foreign-made consumer electronics at the expense of domestic manufacturers.

Target revaluation is thus a short-term tool with the economic costs likely to exceed the benefits in the medium to long term. Indeed, with a US$800.0 billion annual trade deficit of which about 25 percent is with China, targeting the Chinese Yuan is a weak attempt to exert influence over the direction of the Chinese economy and China's geopolitical and geo-economic influence. Hence, apart from being a play-out of a pre-conceived foreign policy strategy, its value lies mainly in what it can buy in the domestic political arena. This is especially so when there is still a lot of animosity towards China, as discussed in Chapter Seven, coupled with the failure to bring the supply of Middle East oil under Western, specifically US control.

At this stage, as the absolute worst case and only an absolute worst case notwithstanding that some might point to the ease with which Iraq was invaded, the US could find itself tempted to resort to its enormous military capability in keeping with its long-held notion of safeguarding its national and security interests. The attempt by the Bush administration at unification of the world by force—the familiar method of the forcible imposition of a *Pax Romana*—as the path of least resistance for the resolution of the formidable geopolitical and geo-economics forces facing the US in the twenty-first century is always a possibility, a *Pax Americana*, if you will. Samuel Huntington's *Clash of Civilization* (1996) speaks to this assertion as a possibility. Indeed, lest it be missed, the acronym of "Operation Iraqi Liberation" is OIL; such was the certainty of outcome with which the invasion of Iraq was planned.

Given the outcome of the 2003 invasion, my sense is that the US needs time to recover and to forget the mistake of invading Iraq. Be that as it may, I am reminded of the remarks of Harvard University's Bryan Hehir, in 2007: "When you have a superpower of enormous capability, it is not a bad idea to place it in a framework of law and policy, moral argument and legal argument and force it to justify what it should do." The challenge to the rest of the world, then, would be to stand firm for such a framework in the interest of world peace. Whether or not this is possible depends crucially upon the extent to which the major developed and developing countries have been damaged; it also depends on whether some see opportunity in weakness.

Too Big to Fail

The worst case scenario painted above should not be allowed to become a reality. Indeed, if American International Group (AIG) was appropriately regarded as "too big to fail" in context of the American economy, then the US economy is most certainly too big to fail in context of the global economy; the reverberations would not only be felt in every corner of the world but also would present the greatest challenge to mankind in modern economic history, with possible implications far greater than those discussed above.

To prevent the worst case scenario from becoming a reality, as the experiences of the HIPC in the 1980s and 1990s tell us, the US central bank would have to engage in the classic IMF prescription of mopping-up excess liquidity by flooding the market with treasury bills and other government-issued instruments or be forced to sell its gold reserves. But, this process is not without consequences. At the very least, as discussed above, Treasury bills or other debt instruments would have to be significantly discounted to attract buyers as US public debt load approaches untenable levels; this in turn raises the real interest rates and thus the cost of absorbing the flow-back of Dollars; it also raises the cost of private investment which would reflect in lower private investment as marginal firms seek alternative investment opportunities elsewhere; not to mention its manifestation in higher prices.

Therefore, like the highly-indebted developing countries that have gone before it, the US would be in need of a lender (or lenders) of last resort which, again, as history tells us, comes at a price: As any student of development economics knows only too well, while the HIPC had the IMF and World Bank as just such lenders, access to funding from them came at a steep price in terms of sovereignty, pride, and dignity. But, accepting structural adjustment and a realistic GDP level, and thus a lower standard of living, does not come easy, as the 2010 Greece experience evidences. It is thus instructive that Treasury Secretary Geithner sought to reassure the Gulf Arab states that the "U.S. dollar assets they hold in large quantities remain a strong investment."[7] Be that as it may, the US is finding that foreigners are less than enthusiastic about adding to their stock of US Treasuries.

Apart from the clear indication of a closing of ranks by the Western economies to a perceived threat to the capitalist world system—the Japanese experience of the late 1980s and 1990s discussed above speaks to this contention—there is, arguably, no country more acutely aware of this than China. I say this not because China on the surface has more to lose in terms of its exports; to be sure, a shortsighted perspective of those who would impose trade restrictions on Chinese goods. Rather, I say this because China, more than any other country, has much more to gain from ensuring that the US economy does not fail, lest there be a domino effect, triggering the worst case scenario discussed above. It is, therefore, not accidental that China continues to help finance the US fiscal budget deficit even when to do so puts its foreign reserves in potential jeopardy. Moreover, by increasing its stock of gold, China is effectively directing inflation away from domestic consumption—which is contrary to US expectation—while at the same time helping the US to limit growth of its huge debt burden, estimated at US$14.0 trillion in 2010, by buying gold from the US central bank.

As a geopolitical strategy, increasing its holdings of US government-issued debt is one way, perhaps the opportunistic way just now, for China to convey to the American people that "yellow peril" is a figment of the imagination of fiction writers. Indeed, China has the opportunity to dispel any notion of a potential "clash" between the two giants. To understand this, one needs to look deeper into the checkered relationship between the two countries since 1949, and the opportunity presented by this crisis, as discussed more fully in Chapter Seven.

It is further instructive that China has, at this time of global economic uncertainty, taken steps to phase-in a policy of encouraging greater domestic consumption while seeking to de-emphasize exports as its main economic driver. Indeed, for China, the timing is propitious as the US and the EU take steps to curb Chinese exports not only to their respective markets but also to third markets primarily by seeking a revaluation of the Chinese currency as discussed above and in Chapter Eight. Additionally, China's "no-strings" policy of development aid to South America and Africa is being criticized as fostering corruption in recipient countries, notwithstanding that such criticisms come from those who have long benefitted from pursuing a "center-periphery" relationship with developing countries, and whose development-aid programs have been regarded by some foreign governments as providing opportunities for subversive activities.

The Depreciating Dollar: *Casus Belli*

Despite attempts at "talking up" the Dollar, of concern must be the growing consciousness of the emerging economies over the inherent weakness of the US
dollar, that it is not as good as gold; and that it is only as good as the trust and
confidence placed in it by others which, in turn, depend crucially upon the underlying US economy and the integrity of the US government and institutions
such as the FED. This uneasiness of the emerging economies with the inherent
weaknesses of the US dollar is reflected in the declining value of the Dollar vis-
à-vis other currencies that have proven more stable since the turn of the century,
more especially since the invasion of Iraq and the collapse of the American financial system in 2008. To be sure, the Swiss Franc, Canadian Dollar, the Euro,
and the Pound Sterling have seen unprecedented appreciation vis-à-vis the US
dollar; in the case of the Pound and the Euro, such appreciation is achieved despite the weakened state of their respective economies. With respect to the Japanese Yen, while it has been appreciating against the dollar, it is primarily for
reasons discussed above, that is, the Japanese economy is still a threat to the US
economy; this is even more so, in light of the current economic crisis.

While the US dollar has deservedly enjoyed unprecedented trust and confidence from international actors over the decades, it has, arguably, suffered ir-
reparable harm since the unilateral invasion of Iraq in 2003 and the collapse of
the US financial system in 2008. Both, and in particular the reverberations from
the latter, have left the world in a state of insecurity and uncertainty for the fore-
seeable future. Indeed, replacing trust and integrity as the underlying basis for
international financial transactions with legally-contrived "fine print"—an essential American innovation—which the former Chairman of the FED, Alan
Greenspan, sought to justify, has served to take integrity and trust in American
institutions to a level that gives pause to many holders of dollar-denominated
assets, and the Dollar as the reserve currency.[8] It is thus instructive that foreign
demand for US treasury bills is waning in the light of the increased risks associated with holding dollar-denominated assets.[9] As observed by Monica Malik,
"there is already likely to have been a diversification of GCC [Gulf Cooperation
Council] reserves in terms of currencies over the last few years given the dollar
weakness and the expanding trade with Asia and Europe."[10] In terms of the fall-
out from the invasion of Iraq, the resort to the doctrine of preemption after September 11, 2001 (9/11), coupled with a demonstrated preference for dominance
over diplomacy—evidence of a *Pax Romana* syndrome—by the Bush administration, controlled as it were by the "Vulcan" element within it, have caused
many of America's would-be friends to place "warming relations" and military
build-down on a cautious footing, with obvious economic consequences. Tellingly, is this observation by the then president of Russia, Vladimir Putin:

> Nations are witnessing an almost uncontained use of force in international rela-
> tions. . . . One state, the United States, has overstepped its national borders in

every way. . . . This is very dangerous. Nobody feels secure anymore because
nobody can hide behind international laws.[11]

Equally telling, is the then British Prime Minister, Tony Blair's, declared foreign
policy change to include the use of hard power in international relations at a
time when others were chastised for reacting to the changing military equation.

In addition, Israel's embrace of preemptive military strikes as paramount in
its relations with its neighbors adds to the change in the military equation and to
the need for military build-up of friends and foes alike. Indeed, Israel's dependency on a strong military supported, arguably, by the US in a *quid pro quo* arrangement as its staunchest ally pursuant the Westernization of the region
(Chang 2008; Toynbee, 1948), places an added financial strain on a faltering US
economy (see Mearsheimer & Walt, 2007). For example, the approval of a
US$30.0 billion aid package for Israel by Congress in 2008 includes 25 percent
for military purposes and comes at a time when development aid to Latin America was being reduced.[12]

At the same time, Iran, by its belligerency and implicit threat of a nuclear
weapons program, further keeps military expenditure in the US at abnormally
high levels as does the modernization of China's military and its space program.
Hence, the US military budget for 2011 is expected to exceed US$708 billion,
including US$$33.0 billion for the increased troop levels in Afghanistan and
continuing the war in Iraq[13] at a time of increasing fiscal budget deficits in an
economy in crisis. It is a scenario not unlike that that brought down the Soviet
Union, and should give pause to those who believe that the US is exempted from
history.

Clearly, the resort to military intervention in international disputes and in
seeking control over resources in foreign lands has ignited undeclared rearma-
ment by both foes and friends alike. For the US, this comes at a time when re-
sources would be better employed addressing the growing income inequality in
an increasingly-polarized country and faltering economy as it seeks to respond
in kind. Hence, the US is undoubtedly further disadvantaged when the economic
cost of fighting terrorism is factored into the equation. In this connection, it is
instructive that the former Soviet Union collapsed under the weight of its en-
hanced military program, which it undertook in response to Ronald Reagan's
"Star War" initiative at a time when it could have ill afford to do so.

In the light of the Soviet Union's experience, it is possible that the US could
spend itself further into decline pursuant military goals; such a possibility is in
keeping with history. Increasing budget deficit in pursuit of geopolitical objec-
tives poses a very real risk to a timely recovery from this economic dilemma,
which, as contends in this book, arises not from the play out of what many char-
acterized as the trough of a business cycle but rather from an overleveraging of
assets, goodwill, and the Dollar, manifested in the sudden collapse of the finan-
cial system in 2008.

Asleep at the Wheel, or Belief in Certainty?

With respect to the collapse of the financial markets in 2008, the US has been clearly indulgent if not derelict in its management of the financial sector since the 1990s. Despite the evidence of substantial risks associated with speculative capital flows and the attendant moral hazards (see Chang 2006: 41-42; Fischer, 2000; Mohamed, 1998; Tobin, 1998; Helleiner, 1997; and Chunan, et al, 1996), the US, in particular the FED, whose finger supposedly was on the pulse, had chosen to ignore them. In this connection, consider this observation offered by then FED chairman, Alan Greenspan, on the 1997-8 Asian financial crisis: "That episode of investor behavior fright has largely dissipated. But left unanswered is the question of why such episodes erupt in the first place."[14]

The issue of moral hazard was clearly one the FED Chairman was not prepared to address, especially since the hedge fund, Long Term Capital Management (LTCM), as the leading edge of America's intellectual capitalism, was involved. Nonetheless, as was quite evident at the time, moral hazard would arise if the expectation of bailout induced hedge funds and deregulated financial institutions to pursue otherwise risky transactions on the basis of the rational calculation that the potential bailout made such risks economically advantageous. Hence, in contrast to Greenspan's observation, consider the earlier observations of Malaysia's Governor of the IMF and World Bank, Dato Mustapa Mohamed (1998; 134-36), in response to the same crisis:

> "There are also rising concerns on the *destabilizing activities of hedge funds and other institutional investors and the lack of regulation over their activities.* . . . The belief that globalization and liberalization of markets and the unfettered workings of the market, especially the financial market, can only bring benefits is flawed. . . . In recent times, it has been shown that *rating agencies have failed to make objective assessments*, despite being provided with comprehensive information [emphases added]."

Clearly, the FED and US policymakers paid little heed to the observations of the IMF and World Bank, either because they consider themselves outside the influence of these institutions or because, as later observed by Nobel Laureate, Joseph Stiglitz, "there was a party going on, and many of their friends were attending; and they didn't want to be a party pooper."[15] Joseph Stiglitz was clearly referring to the reluctance of then Secretary of the Treasury, Henry Paulson, and to FED Chairman, Ben Bernanke, to reign in Wall Street, more precisely, the hedge funds that dominated investment banking institutions the likes of Bear Sterns, Goldman Sachs & Company, Lehman Brothers (an archrival of Goldman), Citi Group, and others.

The apparent lack of concern by the appropriate US policy-making and regulatory bodies can best be attributed to a belief in the certainty of the American model of risk management and to market triumphalism, especially after the 1997-8 Asian financial crisis which was heralded as the triumph of the American model over the Asian economic model (see Tobin 1998). Moreover, the US has in the past been able to rationalize its debt obligations simply by moving away from the gold standard to a gold exchange standard—as it did in 1934, which inflated the price of gold and thus the value of its stock of it—and again in 1972 by having a floating exchange rate system adopted by its major trading partners. In both instances, it was able to eliminate its debt obligations almost overnight, and in the twinkling of an eye moved from being the greatest debtor nation in the world to the greatest creditor nation in the world. Furthermore, had the Bush administration been able to bring the Iraqi oil reserves under US control as planned before 9/11, not only would fiscal deficit have become a thing of the past but also the US dominance in the twenty-first century, as envisaged by the self-styled "Vulcans," would have been assured; the Middle East would have been brought under Western control, with Israel as integral to the process (Chang 2008).

However, the reality at the start of 2010 is quite different from 2001. It is, to be sure, a humbling experience for the US to be seen assuring lender-countries—once regarded with disdain and as irrelevant in the larger geopolitical and geo-economics scheme of things—of its credibility and ability to overcome its current financial and economic crises. Those developing countries that were exposed to the strictures of conditionality-lending of the IMF and World Bank—premised on the Washington Consensus—can relate only too well to the experience.

Fiscal Budget Deficits,
Foreign Investment and Trade

As observed, by the former Comptroller General of the US, David Walker:

> The most serious threat to the United States is not someone hiding in a cave in Afghanistan or Pakistan but our own fiscal irresponsibility. . . . We suffer from a fiscal cancer; it is growing within us and if we do not treat it, it could have catastrophic consequences for our country.[16]

Since this observation by David Walker in 2007, the US fiscal budget has more than doubled and has assumed a significant role in the US economic policy playbook since 2008. For example, excluding the cost of the wars in Afghanistan and Iraq, the budget deficit reached US$1.4 trillion in 2009. It is in the words of Martin Crutsinger: "It's more than the total national debt for the first 200 years of the Republic, more than the entire economy of India, almost as much as Canada's, and more than $4,700 for every man, woman and child in the United States."[17] On the heel of the 2009 deficit, the Congressional Budget Office is estimating a deficit of US$1.35 trillion for 2010 and is projected to increase to US$6.0 trillion in the next ten years. Hence, fiscal budget deficits do matter, especially when they are increasing largely as a result of government support to the private sector, the moral hazard effect of bailouts if you will.

Rising fiscal budget deficits in the US have rightly become a concern not only for Americans but also for foreign investors. Indeed, at a projected US$3.0 trillion over the next decade, the US fiscal budget deficit is approaching Third World levels, the prescription for which has been a healthy dose of fiscal discipline and structural adjustment. Hence, the growing US fiscal budget deficit is examined in context of the macroeconomic implications of financing a government budget deficit.

As observed by Blejer & Cheasty (1991): "When the public sector runs a [budget] deficit it must be financed by the private sector or by the rest of the world." As such, the macroeconomic effects of financing fiscal budget deficits upon the economy and upon trading relations with other countries will in large measure depend upon the method of financing such deficits. Stanley Fischer and W. Easterly (1990) identified four basic methods of financing a budget deficit: monetization (*seignorage*); use of existing foreign exchange reserves; domestic borrowing; and foreign borrowing.

To understand the implications of each of the four methods, we need first to have a basic understanding of national income identities, thusly:

$$C + S + T = C + I + G \qquad (1) \text{ where:}$$

C = private consumption; S = private savings; T = taxes; I = private investments; and G = government expenditure. And, since C is common to both, the expression could be rewritten as:

$$S + T = I + G \qquad (2) \text{ or as:}$$
$$S = I + (G - T) \qquad (3)$$

From expression (3), it is clear that in a closed economy, that is, one not open to foreign trade, savings (S) must equal private sector investment (I), plus the government budget as represented by $(G - T)$. It follows that, if government expenditure exceeds tax collection, private investments will be reduced correspondingly as suggested by Blejer & Cheasty, so that:

$$G > T = I < S \qquad (4)$$

If one were to incorporate foreign trade in keeping with the *New Cambridge* approach that identifies government budget deficits (surpluses) with balance of payment deficits (surpluses) on current account by applying the concept of "zero sum of sector balances," then in equilibrium:

$$S + T + M = I + G + X \qquad (5) \text{ where:}$$

M = imports and X = exports which can be rewritten as:

$$(T - G) + (S - I) + (X - M) = 0 \qquad (6)$$

Expression (6) assumes that what is not consumed is invested, and surplus of one sector becomes the liability of the other sectors which when added together should equal zero in equilibrium. Hence, any government budget deficit (surplus) must be reflected as an imbalance in either of the two sectors or both, that is:

$$(G > T) - (S - I) + (M - X) \qquad (7)$$

This last expression indicates that where there is a budget deficit (G > T), there must be an offsetting surplus in the sum of the other two sectors, thereby revealing the role of imports (M), that is, either savings (S) must be greater than private investment (I) or imports (M) must be greater than exports (X) or a combination of both.

The Consumption Factor and Aggressive Trade Policy

Recent American experience is for both government expenditure to exceed tax collection, and private investment to exceed private savings—the saving-investment imbalance—resulting in both being partly funded by external borrowings. For example, in 2005, savings (S) in America was negative. By definition, then, both private investment (I) and government expenditure (G) had to be financed from accessing prior savings (living on capital) or from foreign borrowings (M), the latter reflected in a negative balance of payment on current account. Moreover, with consumption (C) remaining constant, again by definition, imports must be greater than exports, and would have very little to do with the trade practices of America's trading partners and everything to do with excesses in private consumption, private investment, and government expenditure in the US. Indeed, what has been omitted from these expressions is the role of consumption which has become the economic driver of the US economy and the target of policy and business plans.

A policy prescription for IMF and World Bank bailouts, is that external imbalance on current account should be addressed first by a reduction in foreign borrowings so as to restore lost competitiveness. But for the US to reduce foreign borrowings, it must change the terms of trade through expenditure-switching measures; this require depreciating the nominal exchange rate, the objective being to increase the competitiveness of the export sector, and hence its production, while simultaneously reduce imports. But given that the US is a high-cost producer for most manufactured goods, many of which are sheltered from competition by subsidies, tariffs, and non-tariff barriers, it must also reduce the domestic cost of production in all sectors. As is well recognized, the major source of such costs is labor related, and like Greece in 2010, any attempt to reduce wages or benefits in the US would be strongly resisted.

Clearly, if expenditure-switching is effected through the exchange rate, it is essential that a real devaluation takes place with all its implications for the domestic economy, including suffering a higher than normal unemployment rate and resisting an accommodating monetary policy, neither of which the US seems positioned, let alone willing, to pursue. Indeed, the US is not only getting deeper into debt by its stimulative fiscal polices, it is also pursuing an accommodating monetary policy, the likes of which has never been seen before now, which is likely to manifest in high inflation if the theory holds. In pursuing such policies, the US is clearly in denial of the domestic economic reality and the need for it to make the necessary internal adjustments. Moreover, the absence of responsible fiscal and monetary policies must give pause necessarily to those who are willing to lend a hand within a framework of international economic cooperation.

In light of the above, the notion that America's "new normal" means less import from China or from the emerging economies is specious at best. Moreover, increasing budget deficits coupled with a dependency on foreign investments, which have been in decline since 2005[18] because of waning confidence in the US economy, and thus the Dollar, necessarily translates to an aggressive posture in international trade relations. In other words, the current US trade policy is to reduce its balance of payment deficits on current account, not by curbing its inordinate domestic consumption—manifestation of the American dream according to one US analyst—but rather by pursuing target revaluation, when convenient, concurrent with seeking to bring the cost of imported energy down through the control of Middle East oil production and reserves (see Chang, 2008). This posture of the US must give pause not only to its foes but also to friends and allies alike; recall, there are no eternal allies in a capitalist world-system, only national interests.

The American experience and expectations in trade are not dissimilar to that of many of the African, Caribbean and Pacific (ACP) countries that signed on to the EU's ACP sugar protocol in 1974. For the ACP countries, it was the benefits derived from the promise of guaranteed prices well above the domestic cost of production and world market price; it matters not that such prices were conditioned on a restricted quantity of their sugar exports to the EU (Chang, 2006; Borrell & Duncan, 1992). For the US, on the other hand, it was, and still is, the benefits derived from its seemingly at will right to resort to unilateral restrictions and sanctions against countries that posed a competitive threat to US domestic producers (Bhagwati & Patrick, 1990).

Both the ACP Sugar Protocol and US unilateral trade policy manifest in perverse incentives to domestic producers and consumers alike, albeit from different perspectives. For several of the ACP countries, the ACP sugar protocol translated into inefficiency in production and a dependency on price subsidies to EU sugar farmers. The sugar industry became the main source of employment and the center for social development for these countries. For the US, American domestic producers became reliant on the government to exact concessions from competing countries or to imposed tariffs and other quantitative restrictions as deemed necessary. For example, in the case of sugar, the imposition of quotas on the Caribbean Basin Initiative (CBI) countries in 1988 saw an 84 percent across the board decrease in sugar exports from the CBI to the US (Krueger, 1993).

Sugar is only one area targeted by American trade policy. Voluntary export restraints (VER) were negotiated bilaterally, mainly with Japan, South Korea, Thailand, Malaysia, Taiwan, and Hong Kong, to restrict exports to OECD countries. In addition, anti-dumping and countervailing duties were imposed mainly as "tactical devices to soften up one's foreign rivals and propel them and their governments into negotiating voluntary restrictions on exports" (Bhagwati,

1988: 53). As a countermeasure, the major Japanese, and now Korean car manu-facturers, have established manufacturing plants in the US and other OECD countries under threat of CVD proceedings as a form of *quid pro quo* direct for-eign investment; they have established themselves as domestic producers and in the process, have gained market share at the expense of homegrown icons that were never weaned of government intervention of one kind or another in their behalf.

Since the early 1980s, therefore, American industries and consumers have enjoyed the benefits of an aggressive trade policy pursued by the US govern-ment. More significantly, they have become reliant on unilateral trade sanctions whenever domestic consumption and or production are threatened; and this is notwithstanding that the threat comes from within through the perverse incen-tives implicit in a regime of trade restrictions discussed above.

Not surprisingly, therefore, faced with increasing budget deficits, a peren-nial saving-investment imbalance, the chairman of the FED, Ben Bernanke, should encourage greater private consumption while seeking to find savings in the public sector: "the most direct way to address savings is to try and improve savings in the government sector."[19] Bernanke's answer clearly must rest in his certainty of America's capacity to grow its economy and to access needed re-sources, imports generally, in a framework of dominance. Indeed, as noted ear-lier, the FED chairman along with the then Secretary of the Treasury, Henry Paulson, was confident that the US would experience a budget surplus in 2012, and that the answer to America's economic woes rests in creating more markets for American goods and services, that is, universalizing consumerism (Chang, 2008: 123); a posture that resonated with a Republican administration and Con-gress.

The notion that America's growth is assured by reason of its superior pro-ductivity rate is equally spurious. Indeed, such a notion is quickly dispelled by an examination of the growing income inequality in the US since the 1970s. In other words, since labor productivity is a function of unit labor cost, it has been increasing primarily by the reduction in the share of GDP that accrues to middle and low income Americans. Put another way, there is a positive correlation be-tween the increase in labor productivity and the increase in income inequality in the US since the 1970s. Hence, it is not that the US productivity is vastly supe-rior to that of other countries'; rather, such productivity is achieved at the ex-pense of the majority of Americans whose contribution to GDP manifests in a declining share of it (see Table 6.1 and Figure 6.1).

NOTES

1. "Bush defends free-market system," *BBC NEWS*, http://news.bbc.co.uk/go/pr/fr/2/hi/business/7728048.stm
2. "Q&A," *C-SPAN*, July 1, 2007
3. Olemacher, S. "Social Security to start cashing in Uncle Sam's IOUs, *Associated*

Press, https://news.yahoo.com/s/ap/us_social_security_ious, March 15, 2010
4. "Dornbusch offers advise on role of countries' exchange rate policies" in *IMF Sur vey, Vol 29, No.15,* July 15, 2000, p. 250
5. "US Economic Outlook," House Financial Services Committee, *C-SPAN,* February 16, 2007
6. Rook, D., "Asian nations want more muscle to flex at the IMF," *Associated Foreign Press,* Tokyo, September 10, 2008' "emerging economies want new role," http://news.bbc.co.uk/go/pr/fr/-/2/hi/business/7718277.stm
7. Laessing, U., and   Somerville, G., "Geithner to reassure Gulf allies on dollar asets," *Reuters,* July 13, 2009
8. "Bush defends free-market system," *BBC NEWS,* http://news.bbc.co.uk/go/pr/fr/2/hi/business/7728048.stm
9. Crutsinger, M., "Foreign demand for US assets down in May," *Associated Press,* July 16, 2009
10. Laessing, U., and   Somerville, G., "Geithner to reassure Gulf allies on dollar asets," *Reuters,* July 13, 2009
11. "Putin attacks 'very dangerous' US," *BBC World Service,* February 10, 2007
12. Beale, J., "US fights Latin America's suspicions," *BBC News,* https://news.bbc.co.uk, March 8, 2007
13. Gearan, A., & Flaherty, A., "Obama wants $708 billion for wars next year, *"Assoc ated Press"* January 13, 2010
14. "News Hour," *PBS,* August 27, 1999
15. Interview with Owen Benet-Jones, BBC World Service, May 4, 2008
16. Walker, D., "60 Minutes," *CBS,* March 4, 2007.
17. Crutsinger, M. "2009 federal budget deficit surges to $1.42 trillion," *Associated Press,* October 17, 2009 to $1.42 trillion," *Associated Press,* October 17, 2009
18. "US launches campaign for more foreign investment," https://news.yahoo.com/s/afp/20070510//bs
19. "US Economic Outlook," House Financial Services Committee, *C-SPAN,* February 16, 2007

Chapter Three

Free-market Capitalism in Terminal Crisis

Based on the preceding chapters, it is clear that the US has reached a limit to which it can leverage its goodwill with the world. It is equally clear that its major trading partners will eventually force it to seek reductions not only in government expenditure but also in private consumption, even at the expense of some exporting countries. Indeed, as noted in the preceding chapter, China anticipates the latter and has taken steps to reorient its economy away from the traded goods sector to the non-traded goods sector. This should make expenditure-switching less traumatic for the US and, in the process, provides it the opportunity to regain some competitiveness in the global market place, assuming it is ready to accept responsibility for its saving-investment and trade imbalances. That said, and despite the rhetoric and self-serving perspectives of ideologues, free-market capitalism is in terminal crisis.

Coup de Grâce

"Government owning a stake in any private institution is objectionable to most Americans, me included." Be that as it may, these have now become famous last words of the US Treasury Secretary, Henry Paulson, as he announced plans to purchase shares in the nine largest American banks on October 14, 2008. Moreover, on November 12, 2008, he testified to Congress that the original purpose for the US$700.0 billion request changed from buying toxic assets held by banks and other financial institutions to buying shares in banks.

By these actions, free-market capitalism premised on financial innovation—unregulated credit default swaps (CDS) or derivatives on derivatives—and heralded by the former Chairman of the FED, Alan Greenspan, as portending the end of economic downturns, was dealt the final blow, the *Coup de Grâce*. Hence, notwithstanding ex-post rationalizations by the Bush administration, the FED, chaired by Ben Bernanke, and their apologists, the metaphorical bell tolled for free-market capitalism—market triumphalism—on October 14, 2008; for those countries that have had to endure ridicule for holding firm to a manufacturing-based economic model and to resisting the lure of financial gimmickry concocted by America's intellectual capitalist class, it was not soon enough.

The spate and extent of government intervention, culminating in the purchase of shares in commercial banks, as observed by former Republican Speaker of the House and a free-market ideologue, Newt Gingrich, evidence an economic system that is premised on "capitalism going up and socialism going down." Clearly, Gingrich disagreed with any bailout by the government and voiced his preference for enterprise-failure as the disciplinary mechanism irrespective of the economic and social costs in the short run; such is his belief in free-market principles.

The purchase of shares in the nine largest US banks by the government—to the extent that US$125.0 billion would allow at the time—was, to many observers, the last available short-term tool available to the government in its attempt to unclog the credit market and thus stem the decline into economic disruption not experienced since the Great Depression of the 1930s. Interestingly, Henry Paulson's announcement with respect to the purchase of shares in affected private-sector companies followed on the heels of the meeting of the Group of Seven industrialized countries (G-7) called to devise a common policy-approach to the crisis. More significantly, it followed in the wake of the British government's offer to make cash available to British banks in exchange for equity on a voluntary basis.[1] At the same time, the Europeans, having had the lessons of recent history from which to draw, seemingly were also not unduly concerned over the notion of government intervention in times of economic downturns and appeared to have prevailed at the G-7 Summit. Evidently, the appropriateness of this approach has not been lost on the US Treasury Secretary.

The Argument for Intervention

As later reveled in testimony to Congress, the Bush administration's decision to take equity interests in US commercial banks was not exactly at the request of the banks, notwithstanding semantics. Rather, that the nine banks—which account for 50 percent of all financial transactions— "indicated their willingness"[2] to participate in the government's plan to rescue capitalism was the result of arm-twisting by the Treasury and FED. Be that as it may, they were joined by other banks, including subsidiaries of foreign banks, who took advantage of the unique opportunity to take part in the remaining US$125.0 billion dedicated to the bailout program. Also, it is noteworthy that this decision to dedicate US$250.0 billion to bank-rescue, by way of direct purchase of shares or interest-free loans to them, was an attempt at greater transparency than in past attempts at bailout which were oblique in approach as discussed below.

As rationalized to Congress, "this is a program in which we want healthy institutions to use the capital [US$125.0 billion] and we encouraged the institutions to participate."[3] The idea, according to Interim Assistant Treasury Secretary for Financial Stability, Neel Kashkari, was to infuse capital into the banking system as quickly as possible so as to attract private capital to the nine major banks or, at a minimum, to prevent further tightening up of the credit market; and, in this explanation, Kashkari was essentially echoing the FED Chairman's earlier testimony to the House Budget Committee. Not mentioned by Kashkari, was that, as later revealed in declassified documents released by New York State Attorney General, Andrew Cuomo, Bank of America was "leaned on" to purchase Merrill Lynch by both Secretary Paulson and FED chairman Ben Bernanke. According to testimony by the Chairman of Bank of America, Kenneth Lewis, both Bernanke and Paulson threatened him with dismissal if he did not keep the extent of Merrill Lynch's losses under wraps. In support of Kenneth Lewis's contention, government documents obtained by *Judicial Watch* in May 2009 confirmed that nine of the major banks were told that opting out of the program "would leave you vulnerable and exposed;" hence, they indicated their willingness.

In addition to the explanations offered by Treasury officials, specifically to avoid the label of nationalization, many within the administration, including President Bush, were quick to point out that the government's investment in the nine major banks was at the preferred-stock level, and that the banks would be allowed to repurchase all the shares at a future date. Be that as it may, the US government's action is no less ownership in private-sector enterprises in an era of extensive deregulation, privatization, and free-market rhetoric, than the British government's takeover of troubled British Banks; it is just a matter of semantics. Hence, when taken in conjunction with earlier interventions that preceded this investment decision, such intervention must, for all practical and theoretical purposes, be seen as an abandonment of the idea that the market is inviolable. In this latter connection, it is noteworthy that the former Chairman of the FED, Alan Greenspan, acknowledged fundamental errors in thinking that the market, and hence deregulation of the financial sector over the last three decades, was the elixir to eternal dominance.[4]

In addition to purchase of shares in troubled banks, the proposed use of the remainder of the bailout package—relabeled economic rescue package which has since been relabeled Troubled Assets Relief Program (TARP)—of US$700 billion approved by the US Congress in October 2008, when stripped of its open-market-operations and other pretensions of free-market characteristics, is indeed no less socialist now than were the economic measures of the 1930s in response to the Great Depression. More than that, the infusion of US$180 billion into AIG, justified on the basis of "too big to fail," was, in effect, to rescue capitalism as we know it.

To be sure, the free-market system as constructed since the 1980s and extolled by ideologues up to 2008, has simply failed. Consider this acknowledgment by President Bush:

> We believe that this decisive government action is needed to preserve America's financial system and sustain America's overall economy. These measures will require significant taxpayers' dollars on the line. . . . Further stress on our financial markets would cause massive job losses, devastate retirement accounts, further erode housing values, and dry up new loans for homes, cars, and college tuition.

If that is not an acknowledgement of market failure, what is? Clearly, the government's actions, as discussed above, could be considered preemptive in nature—an acknowledged defining characteristic of the Bush administration—having had the benefit of the lessons of the Great Depression from which to draw. Indeed, this observation was not lost on Chairman Bernanke who invoked such lessons in explaining the unprecedented intervention by the FED that included: bailout of AIG; participation in the non-banking sector of the financial market by its support of money-market funds; its purchase of Commercial Paper directly from companies; and, of course, the US$700.0 billion economic rescue package, which it supported fully. Clearly, ideology gave way to pragmatism.

Beyond Keynesian Economics in 2008

While Keynesian economics argues for government intervention in times of high unemployment or underemployment of resources (Keynes, 1964), bailout of Wall Street in 2008 took government intervention to levels that went to the foundation of free-market capitalism. It was, to be sure, not a normal response occasioned by a cyclical recession but rather a rescue of the American economy from the excesses of "greed, dishonesty, a willingness to exploit others [and] vanity" forewarned by Adam Smith in 1776 (Griswold, 1999:16–17). Moreover, it was, as remarked by the former Speaker of the House, Newt Gingrich, capitalism going up and socialism going down. Additionally, as lamented by Alan Greenspan, the edifice of risk management, which, as it turns out, stressed liberalization of financial services premised on the transfer of risks to foreigners, and pursued with his unequivocal support since the mid 1980s, has been falsely-premised, culminating in the worst financial and economic crises since the Great Depression.

The events of 2008 and 2009 have clearly demonstrated the fallacy of certainty, which has been labeled by Immanuel Wallerstein (1999: 2) as a "blinding and crippling" premise of modernity. Indeed, the collapse of the edifice of risk management that was premised on certainty and promoted by Alan Greenspan *sine quo non* end of fiscal deficits, and thus ensuring America's supremacy in the twenty-first century, left the American economy without a solid foundation at the end of 2008; and with fewer friends than before, such was the abandonment of trust and integrity for the "fine print" as the basis for international transactions.

This certainty in America's intellectual capitalism manifested in the national news media's homage to Wall Street as never before; the Sunday morning talk shows were equally effervescent in their analyses; they could not have too much of intellectual capitalism however contrived or indeed short lived. New buzz words and phrases in praise of free-market capitalism abound. Even the Bush administration and the Republican-led Congress joined the chorus, exalting the power of the market and trumpeting the virtues of deregulation. But, as the then President George Bush unwittingly observed, "Wall Street got drunk; it got drunk and now it's got a hangover."[5]

The hangover to which President Bush referred has proven to be nothing less than a financial and economic tsunami of unimaginable proportions. The proverbial "domino effect" was not the feared conversion of Southeast Asia to Communism as envisaged by various US administrations in the 1950s and 1960s; rather, it was the collapse of America's financial and industrial icons in 2008 and 2009 on a scale not seen since the Great Depression of the 1930s.

Financial Innovation or Financial Gimmick?

According to its proponents, intellectual capitalism was the uniquely American economic model that distinguished the American economy from all others. It was the mother of all models that promised untold riches attendant deregulation. Even Alan Greenspan declared budget surpluses a humbug to growth, supporting tax breaks to fuel intellectual capitalism in the process. However, whilst this new model of risk management was being extolled as evidencing American innovative prowess, its disguised function was simply to access wealth from a largely trusting and unsuspecting world; it was the ultimate instrument in service to greed; it was devoid of any moral value. Hence, given that innovation has some lasting benefits attached to it while gimmick survives until its perverse attributes are discovered, what was first represented as financial innovation was in effect financial gimmick.

As soon discovered, the quest by hedge funds—comprising the *crème de la crème* of American intellectual capitalism—for greater wealth and power outpaced the American housing market's ability to support their falsely-based models. As a knock-on effect, the over-pricing of existing CDO and CDS, the latter an insurance-based product that covers for risky sub-prime mortgage investments, could not be supported and was revealed for what it was: financial gimmickry, with overtones of fraud.[6] To be sure, the global financial system that was established on the basis of integrity and trust was rudely disabused of such long-held values by those who found it easy to deceive; the new model fostered, in the words of Nobel Laureate and US President, Barack Obama, "an economy that rewarded recklessness rather than responsibility." As a consequence, the capitalist world-economy as currently constructed, and America's standing as its moral leader, has been called into question sooner rather than later.

Even if both survived the current crisis, as they are expected to do in the short-term, they are likely to emerge weaker not stronger than before. This is

because the American economy, as argued above, has moved far from equilibrium and, as discussed in some detail in *Territoriality and the Westernization
Imperative* (Chang, 2008), has been struggling to maintain its standing relative
to others, especially against the emerging economies of Brazil, Russia, India,
China (BRIC); and since the European economies are closely linked to the US
economy, the effect on the capitalist world-economy would be perceptibly damaging. Furthermore, a sociopolitical and economic system that is founded on the
"relentless maximization of self-interest" (Sen, 2002:4) betrays a value-system
anchored in the extremes of rationality, reductionism, and existentialism, and is
short-term in horizon. As such, the play-out of such extremes, as argued in
Chapter Five, manifests in the relentless pursuit of self-fulfillment, abandonment
of societal and business norms, and excesses in the utilization of resources, as
well as the means to accessing them. Moreover, the freedom to pursue wealth
and power recklessly as hegemony conflicts with values that are foundational to
building a lasting democratic society no less than it does with the values of traditional cultures. The collapse of the US domestic sub-prime mortgage market in
mid 2007 must, therefore, be seen as marking the beginning of the demise of an
economic model premised on treating with risk as standard deviation, and the
consequential realignment of the major world economies, with the US struggling
to find its place.

In rationalizing their perceptions of market triumphalism, many have since
argued that hindsight is 20/20. However, the collapse was the inevitable and, to
many observers, predictable outcome of an ill-conceived model predicated on an
ever-increasing demand for homes at higher and higher prices and on the ability
of sub-prime mortgagees to service their loans beyond the initial tease period or,
as many were doing, flipping their purchases; it was, therefore, just a matter of
time before the inevitable panic ensued.

Panic, as observed by Immanuel Wallerstein (1999:50), occurs when "large
groups of people are making money not primarily out of the profits from production but out of financial manipulations." When analyzed dispassionately, the
precipitous drop in home prices and the increase in home foreclosure in 2008
and 2009 would be seen as arising more from the action of speculators who
found themselves unable to dispose of their investment within the tease period
rather than from true homeowners abandoning their homes. Furthermore, many
homeowners took advantage of the increase in the value of their homes not only
to recover their initial investment but also to access the equity windfall, fully
prepared to walk away from their homes in the event of a collapse in the housing
market.

That there was a panic in the financial markets in 2008 is undeniably the result of financial manipulations reaching an abrupt end; the failure of models that
were "fail-safe" coupled with the overleveraging of underlying securities were
the primary causes. Therefore, the collapse of the US housing market and its
reverberation to the broader domestic and international financial markets calls
into question the intellectual edifice of risk management in America. What is
particularly damaging was that such a framework was not only facilitated by no

regulation or lax regulation, but also found support in compliant if not complicit rating agencies whose integrity and competency have never been called into question before now. Hence, as noted above, the transfer of risk to others by way of CDO and CDS in a framework of obscurity and deceit was a blatant assault on societal norms and, more egregiously, on the long-established code of conduct governing international transactions.

In addition to lax regulatory oversight and dubious investment ratings, it is further contended that the construction and application of such a framework were aided by the FED chaired by Alan Greenspan. Clearly, Greenspan's commitment to reductionism and to the existential ethos was exploited to its fullest, notwithstanding that it conflicted with established notions of trust and integrity upon which international financial transactions turned. Indeed, based on the evidence, it was a framework impelled by the quest for an America-centric world order after the collapse of Communism in 1989, and was designed to access global savings, especially from the emerging economies and oil-rich countries, as a complement to the design for control of the world's second largest oil reserves (see Chang 2008).

Hence, notwithstanding that the collapse of the financial system occurred in 2008, it would be disingenuous to suggest that no one in the corridors of power knew of the efforts to restructure international financial markets in support of perpetuating America's hegemony in the twenty-first century. To be sure, there is a trail that goes back to the Baker Plan and to the Washington Consensus of 1989, both of which informed IMF and World Bank's lending polices that essentially mandated liberalization of developing countries economies and financial systems in keeping with the ideology of free-market economics; the urgency and relentlessness with which economic and political liberalization were pursued in developing countries in the 1980s and 1990s have been well documented from various perspectives (Chang 2006).

While privatization was pursued at break-neck speed in developing countries and in the former Soviet Republics and Eastern Europe, actions were taken in the US to rollback regulations, including numerous attempts to repeal the Glass-Stegall Act, 1933; by restricting the activities of the commercial banks to less risky investments, Glass-Stegall was seen as a constraint to capitalizing on the opportunities opened by the privatization process; it was finally repealed in 1999. Coordinating these efforts to dismantle the barriers to a liberalized financial market was, as noted above, the FED led by Alan Greenspan. Chairman Greenspan served as the bridge between successive US administrations and thus ensured continuity of purpose and focus.

Early Indications

On July 30, 2008, Mr. Bush signed into law the Housing Rescue Bill as passed and presented to him by the US Congress. Tellingly absent on this signing occasion was the fanfare that attends signing of Bills at the White House which presidents hold out as part of their legacies; on this occasion it was ominous: it was a Bill designed to assist homeowners avoid foreclosure on their homes which, in his words, "smacks of socialism" and which he had vowed to veto. Hence, by the very definition ascribed to it, it was a Bill that, in conjunction with the stimulus package[7] of two months earlier, effectively signaled the beginning of the end of the new economic model or market triumphalism—given the earlier celebratory predilection of its proponents—which defined the American economic experience since the 1980s.

In terms of cost to taxpayers, it was estimated that the new plan will cost hundreds of billions of dollars—at least US$700.0 billion—thereby adding to the US$600.0 billion already spent in 2008 in stimulus and rescue packages. Of the latter, the most significant was the rescue of AIG by the FED just three days earlier. Despite the cost, the consequences of inaction were too great a risk for any government, irrespective of how ideologically tied it is to free-market capitalism. Hence, the president's announcement was met with celebration by those who had planned on just such a bailout: the moral hazard effect.

As expected, the perceived catastrophic consequences of not rubber-stamping the administration's rescue plan for Wall Street have been echoed by the Treasury Secretary and the FED Chairman in meetings with Congressional leaders. According to FED Chairman, Ben Bernanke, the survival of the American economy was at stake. What Ben Bernanke failed to acknowledge, however, was that the dire conditions painted by him were made urgent at this point in time now that the fortunes of the intellectual capitalist class were at risk; but the American people and the world have been there before; many are reminded of the catastrophic consequences of failure to act in the case of Iraq in 2003: the entire Bush White House and its apologists were selling the idea that Saddam Hussein possessed weapons of mass destruction (WMD) and thus posed a real and present danger to the world; that failure to act at that particular point in time and in the manner proposed by the US and UK would be catastrophic: the "mushroom cloud" threat echoed by Bush, Cheney, and Rice on national television.

Clearly cognizant of this credibility gap, and, as if to redeem itself, the government seized Washington Mutual (WaMu), the nations largest savings and loans bank, on September 26, 2008; it later sold WaMu to J P Morgan Chase, making it the largest bank failure in US history. But the question remains: how realistic was the threat to ordinary Americans who, just months earlier, were told by Secretary Paulson that they should, in effect, bear the consequences of their bad home-mortgage financing decisions? Moreover, both the administration and the FED were exalting the US economy just weeks prior to the unraveling of the financial sector.

The above notwithstanding, the risks to the financial system and to the broader economy were, of course, real. The loss of 37 percent (over US$8.0 trillion) of market value in the Dow Jones industrial average, and the almost total halt of credit to the broader economy took their toll. Notwithstanding that the consequences were greater than had anticipated, it is here suggested that such risks were intended to be systemic, indeed, central, if obscured, to the new economic model. It is further contended that the likelihood of consequences were kept out of policy debates on deregulation as suggested by *ex-post* rationalization for supporting the bailout plan; that is, to rationalize consequences *ex-post* requires that they be present *ex-ante*; in other words, moral hazard was integral to the new economic model.

That moral hazard should have been presented to the Bush administration as a variant of the *Prisoner's Dilemma*, with three possible alternatives—bailout with ex-ante support of the American people (that is, come clean in the first place); unilateral bailout with ex-post rationalization; or do nothing, knowing full well that whatever the choice, there would be consequences for the economy in 2008—was in large measure a consequence of regulatory capture by the intellectual capitalist class. Indeed, like the prisoner, who in reality has no choice—hence the notion of a prisoner's dilemma—the choices presented to the government and the FED were to achieve a preconceived outcome, namely, bailout.

The Bush team and the FED were clearly challenged by the evolving consequences from such regulatory capture and telegraphed their collective predicament in policy-inconsistencies in their effort to stay true to the ideology of free-market economics; ergo the government's refusal to rescue Lehman Brothers even though the precedent was set in the rescue of Bear Sterns. Such was the state of confusion that allowing Lehman Brothers to fail not only resulted in the largest corporate bankruptcy in US history but also precipitated the crisis in confidence not seen since the October 29, 1929 stock-market crash.

Nationalization by any other Name

In terms of Game theory, letting Lehman Brothers fail evidenced an attempt by the administration to take a "do-nothing" policy-approach if only to validate its earlier claims that the rescue of Bear Sterns was not a bailout, and that the American economy was fundamentally strong and could withstand such failures. To this latter political end, Secretary Paulson went further and denied any possibility of a government bailout for AIG. Despite these denials, however, the bailout of AIG was deemed absolutely essential almost within twenty four hours of such denials. Indeed, one of the biggest rescue package—US$85.0 billion for 80 percent of the company and management control—was announced by the FED the very next day, thus adding to the mixed messages from both the administration and the FED.

Clearly, the "do-nothing" approach as one of the three choices presented to the Bush administration and FED, had given way to unilateral bailout with ex-post rationalization as the ultimate policy-option; it was strictly a Treasury/FED decision since the first option of coming clean to the American people was a non-starter in American politics. According to the Bush White House, AIG was too big to fail and, therefore, it was fully supportive of the FED action. Moreover, presaging the unprecedented decision to rescue the entire financial system—now that unilateral bailout with ex-post rationalization as the policy-option of choice was made clear by the rescue of AIG—was George Bush's acknowledgement a day before that: "America's economy is facing unprecedented challenges. We're responding with unprecedented measures. . . . We're at risk of grinding to a halt."[8]

Prior to these fiscal measures that mirrored Keynesian economic policy-prescriptions in response to the Great Depression of the 1930s, on September 7, 2008, after much hand-wringing—hidden from public view, of course—and spin over the future of Freddie Mac and Fannie Mae, Secretary Paulson announced that the US Treasury had decided to place these entities under 'conservatorship' (a euphemism for nationalization) of the US government if only because, according to Paulson:

> Fannie Mae and Freddie Mac are so large and interwoven in our financial system that a failure of either of them would create great turmoil in financial markets and around the globe. . . . These necessary steps will help strengthen the US housing market and promote stability in our financial markets.[9]

Recall that, before the all-encompassing rescue package announced by George Bush, and the de facto nationalization of AIG, Freddie Mac, and Fannie Mae, there was the bailout of Bearn Sterns. According to the Chairman of the FED, Ben Bernanke:

> Allowing Bear Stearns to fail so abruptly at a time when the financial markets were already under considerable stress would likely have had extremely adverse implications for the financial system and for the broader economy.

In addition to AIG who provided the insurance cover, Bear Sterns, Freddie Mac, and Fannie Mae, and a slew of investment banking firms, including Lehman Brothers—one of the oldest in US history—rode the wave of novel financial instruments and, in consequence, became candidates from which the government could pick winners and losers: either for the bankruptcy courts, as happened to Lehman, who clearly drew the short straw[10] or for government acquisition or bailout. Other enterprises that became charter members of the beneficiary club of the FED and the US Treasury were Goldman Sachs, Morgan Stanley, Wachovia Bank, Merrill Lynch, Bank of America, Citi Group, American Express, and several lesser known banks. While many of those listed did indeed possess toxic assets, many others saw opportunity to access cheap funding for their operations. As such, investment banks and financial services companies were quickly converted to bank holding companies. Both Morgan Stanley and Goldman Sachs, the last of the independent investment banking firms, opted to become bank holding companies, abandoning their investment-banking persona and thereby making themselves eligible to access whatever the government was doling out to the sector. For all practical purposes, then, the demise of investment banking operations as existed in America came to a crashing end on September 22, 2008.

For Lehman Brothers, however, it was a matter of bad timing. One might even find credence in the proposition that Lehman was the sacrificial lamb, being at the wrong place at the wrong time; allowing it to fail just days before the rescue of AIG was an imperative of the Bush administration in its desperate bid to keep the myth of free-market capitalism alive.

Lehman and AIG, to be sure, presented the Bush administration with decisions that have not confronted any administration since the Great Depression. As observed by Alan Greenspan:

> This is a once-in- a-half-century, probably once-in-a-century type of event.
> There's no question that this is in the process of outstripping anything I've seen,
> and it still is not resolved and it still has a way to go. And indeed, it will continue to be a corrosive force until the price of homes in the United States stabilizes.[11]

Clearly, the justification for taking control of AIG, Freddie Mac, and Fannie Mae is not dissimilar to that offered by Ben Bernanke with respect to the bailout of Bear Sterns: they were too big to fail. All three enterprises are indeed large and interwoven into the fabric of the US financial system; all three were instrumental in propagating the new economic model; and their failure would be catastrophic for the US financial system and those who have aligned themselves to it. Indeed, this is the nature of moral hazard[12] which, despite disclaimers to the contrary, is an integral aspect of the new economic model that manifested in a highly sophisticated model of risk management.

With respect to the moral hazard implications of such a model, consider this observation by Alan Greenspan:

> When Bear Stearns was bailed out, it drew a line under that level of firm, implying that anything that was larger than that firm was capable of getting federal assistance.

But, before Bear Sterns, there was Long Term Capital Management Corporation (LTCM)—a hedge fund and one of the first manifestation of America's intellectual capitalism—that was rescued in 1998 by the FED while Greenspan was chairman.

Hence, in the case of the financial institutions that comprise hedge funds, and indeed AIG, government intervention was a silent expectation not only by the US financial markets but also by the European financial markets. But, as further recognized by Alan Greenspan: "If you generalize that [bailout], it is very clear that that is an unsustainable situation in the financial markets. The government cannot set a floor below these firms." Would that such a revelation were *ex-ante*, given the now well-worn path to the new credit window at the FED and the reverberations of the meltdown around the globe.

Unfortunately for Lehman Brothers, to stop a "domino effect," the government decided to not rescue it as discussed above. In this action, to the consternation of Wall Street, it sent a signal, albeit short lived as it turned out, to the financial markets and to the global financial system that firms will be allowed to fail. As a result, Merrill Lynch, yet another victim of the "derivative on derivatives" investment market, readily accepted a US$50.0 billion takeover bid from Bank of America.

The knock-on effects of the US government's decision on Lehman, and its reversal in policy on AIG were almost instantaneous, if somewhat sea-sawed, on European governments—as clearly were the actions taken with respect to Bear Sterns, Freddie Mac, and Fannie Mae—whose financial systems are now too integrated with the US financial system to not be affected. Indeed, as recognized by Henry Paulson, it was not just the survival of the US financial system that was at stake but rather the entire Western financial system upon which global financial practices turns. Hence, the decision of several European central banks and the Bank of Japan to "pump billions of currency into markets" in reaction was propitious. Together, almost US$1.0 trillion were pumped into the financial markets and affected economies in short order by concerned governments and central banks. Needless to say, then, financial markets around the world responded favorably to the rescue package announced by President Bush on September 20, 2008; it was the inevitable option: bailout with ex post rationalization.

The above said, it has to be perceived, as it has, that the US had at long last moved from a state of denial to one of accepting responsibility for the crisis, despite those who still insist that it is wrong for the US to apologize to the world.[13] The predicament faced by the world financial system, after all, was an American creation and thus an American responsibility. Indeed, contrary to the rhetoric, most of the world economies were not so much affected by the US subprime mortgage crisis as they were likely to be by the collapse of the US economy. It is thus a curiosity and indeed disconcerting to many that the US Treasury Secretary should seek to take the moral high ground in this crisis by admonishing the rest of the world to follow the US lead and to institute similar measures, even before his proposals at the time were not yet approved by the Congress. In this connection it is instructive that, months earlier, the leader of a Chinese trade mission to the US, responding to pressure from his US counterpart to further liberalize the Chinese economy, acknowledged that while they are interested in drawing lessons from the US macroeconomic management experience, they were particularly interested in drawing lessons from how the US manages a financial crisis that they at the time perceived was evolving in the US.

The Japanese were equally blunt in their response to criticisms for not doing more to alleviate the crisis. They reminded their critics that Japan, having learned a valuable lesson from the decade-long recession and slow growth experienced in the 1990s, had returned to a culture of saving, with about US$13.0 trillion in national savings at the end of 2008. But perhaps more damaging were the reactions from Germany's Chancellor, Angela Merkel, who laid the blame for the crisis firmly at the door steps of the US and UK—and thus expectation for solutions—for pursuing lax regulation of the sector. The German Chancellor was joined by French President, Nikolas Sarkozy, who refused to contribute to the bailout of Wall Street. Indeed, both Germany and France took comfort from the fact that their adherence to tight regulation of their respective financial sectors has been vindicated by the unfolding of events in the US and UK. In addition, the Kuwaitis made it clear that they were not in the business of bailing out foreign banks.

Rationalizing the Consequences of Overleveraging

Against the backdrop of a pervading existential ethos that posed a cultural risk to the American experience (see Chapter Five), the shortcomings of capitalism aggressively pursued in the late 1980s and up to 2008 are confusingly rationalized by its proponents; they have resorted to spurious arguments premised on false-equivalencies and blame to support their claims for a swift recovery from the present crisis; their refrain is that the US economy will not just recover, as it has done before, but will rebound to an even higher level than before. As their arguments go, America is the greatest nation on earth; the fundamentals of the economy have never been stronger; and, for added measure, America's economic woes are the result of unfair trade practices of its Asian trading partners primarily, and, of course, "greedy investors in Shanghai and Dubai," to quote one candidate in the 2008 presidential nomination process.

   With respect to perceived unfair trading practices, the prevailing wisdom of redress is to talk up the US dollar while effectively allowing it to depreciate. Classical economic theory tells us that such a policy changes the consumption pattern of Americans—less imports, more domestically-produced goods—and thus is likely to change the trade dynamic between the US and its trading partners, especially China. This strategy worked in the late 1980s and early 1990s in the case of a persistent trade imbalance with Japan, and, according to proponents, there is no compelling reason to suggest that it should not work in this case with China: the model is grounded in classical economic doctrine; it is fail safe or so it is believed. Be that as it may, the US has never been in such a weakened position as it now finds itself. Moreover, the evidence suggests that the ills of Detroit, Michigan in general, can be generalized to the rest of America since 2007, that is, recovery is unlikely to be to the level of employment and prosperity prior to the onset of the recession as some production processes migrate to lower-cost producing countries. Moreover, the capitalist world economy as currently constructed, of which the US is *de facto* leader, has been weakened to the point of causing a rethink of its underlying premises notwithstanding noises; the call for a system premised on "moral capitalism" by the leader of the British Conservative Party, David Cameron, is telling.

The Greatest Nation on Earth

There are several ways to look at greatness. The most typical is in terms of a country's military might in the absence of any significant depth in historical achievements. History has proven that this form of greatness is not sustainable in the long term; many an empire has collapsed from the resultant paranoia and economic burden attendant thereto. Others see greatness in terms of survival in the face of overwhelming adversity and even in defeat; the "Long March" of the defeated Chinese Communist Party led by Mao Zedong in 1934–5 was founded in the belief that greatness is being able to get up every time you are knocked down. Yet others see greatness in terms of lasting contributions to making the world a better place for all peoples. This latter group is made up of those who have achieved peace in their hearts and speaks to the ancient Chinese Proverb: "When there is peace in the human heart, there is peace in the world." The once marauding Vikings now lead this group.

With respect to the claim of being the greatest nation on earth, no one questions the military might of the US or its economic achievements. No one also questions its enormous contributions to science and technology. However, whatever goodwill that had been bestowed upon the US by the world community in recognition of its contributions to the betterment of the world, has been largely squandered by the Bush administration pursuant the Bush doctrine of preemption; the invasion and occupation of Iraq in March 2003 and the alienation of most of the Muslim world with crusading-rhetoric have, to be sure, given pause to the notion of a unipolar world. While the Bush rhetoric ("The war we fight today is more than a military conflict. It is the decisive ideological conflict of the twenty-first century"[14]) resonated with neoconservatives and Christian fundamentalists in America and elsewhere, it was received chillingly even by those whose past histories reflect aspects of early Christian Crusades. Lest it be misunderstood, the war President Bush was referring to was not the war against the terrorists in Afghanistan, considered to be a just war and supported as such, but rather the war in Iraq, hence his pronouncement that "failure in Iraq would be disastrous for the United States."[15]

Freedom and Democracy or Access to Resources?

Looking past the religious and other pretentions of goodness of US-led interventions in other countries, of course, is the economics of interventions. Notwithstanding the Bush administration's attempt to focus public attention to the drummed-up nuclear threat posed by Saddam Hussein, many, including the former FED chairman, Alan Greenspan, saw, albeit ex-post, the war in Iraq as being all about oil.

As noted in Chapter Two, the American economy has strayed so far from equilibrium and, as such, external resources, most notably oil, were considered by the Vulcans as needed to come under America's control if the US were to stay on top of the heap in the face of competition from the BRIC—Brazil, Russia, India and China—countries. The new economy premised on financial liberalization had to be supported in more fundamental ways; cheap immigrant labor was not enough. Hence, as perceived by the Bush team, it was a propitious time in history to capitalize upon the opportunity presented by the unfortunate events of 9/11. In this perception, George Bush had a staunch supporter and ally in the then British Prime Minister, Tony Blair, who, as happened, was also driven by religiosity and visions of greatness. The less-compliant NATO members were ridiculed or denigrated—"Old Europe"—while others outside the alliance were defined in terms of "either you are with us, or you are with the enemy."

Despite attempts to situate the invasion of Iraq in the rhetoric of freedom and democracy, the Anglo-American-led military assault on Iraq served only to confirm that condign power continues to be the hallmark of hegemony in the twenty-first century, even among friends and allies. With such an approach to the use of power, the sole superpower standing at the turn of the century became a concern not only of foes but also to some of its friends and supporters standing outside of the "Coalition of the willing." Clearly, many within established alliances with the US—castigated as "Old Europe"—balked at the notion of proselytizing freedom and democracy, the rallying cry of the Bush administration, by way of the sword. Russia rejected it out of hand. The American response was, according to the then National Security Advisor, Condoleezza Rice, to "ignore Germany, forgive Russia, and punish France."

In addition to the loss of significant international goodwill and trust, the financial costs of prosecuting the wars in Iraq and Afghanistan have taken their toll on the American economy and raised questions about the continuing financial viability of the US government. The well-articulated and publicized war-dividend that was expected from the invasion of Iraq was not forthcoming; and what was conceived as a benefit swiftly turned into a cost. The US saw its national debt increased in consequence of the wars with annual fiscal budget deficit taking the place once occupied by budget surplus at the end of the twentieth century. As estimated by Blimes and Stiglitz, the cost of the Iraq war is not US$50.0 billion that was told to Congress by the then Deputy Secretary of Defense, Paul Wolfowitz; rather, it is closer to US$2.5 trillion according to Blimes and Stglitz.

Many would recall the demise of the Soviet Union was brought about not only by political and economic isolation but also by pushing the Soviet economy to bankruptcy during the 1980s. It is therefore not accidental that President Barak Obama on taking over the Presidency in 2009 should acknowledge obliquely the changing geopolitical and geo-economic dynamic. The consequences of the collapse of the America financial system in 2008 and the worst American recession since the Great Depression of the 1930s are difficult to deny. It is also not accidental that British Prime Minister, Gordon Brown should declare "The

Washington Consensus is dead" in consequence of the unparallel financial crisis since WWII.

To announce to the world that America is ready to take its place not as the leader but rather as one of the leaders of the world signals—to the dismay of neoconservatives— the end of a unipolar world and the return to multilateralism. Perhaps more importantly, it signaled moving from an ideology of dominance to one of leadership, traversing the geopolitical *pons asinorum*, if you will. This is not to say that an American-centric world order did not exist; it existed from 1994 to 2008, and during that period exposed the risk to the world posed by a nation still in the making with enormous military and nuclear capabilities.

Denying Reality

Long before the collapse, the pundits were celebrating the new economy. Recall that Alan Greenspan saw it in terms of portending the end of economic downturns; the Sunday morning talk shows could not have too much of it. Many of these experts are now faced with rationalizing the consequences of the collapse; many continue to tread on the slippery slope of justifying free-market economics while collapse is threatened by endless debates. It matters not that: the US stock market lost 50 percent of its record-high valuation reached in October 2007 in consequence of overleveraging; the reverberation from the meltdown has been global primarily from peddling "toxic assets" to those "greedy overseas investors;" global demand for goods and services has contracted to levels unequalled in a post-WWII global economy; trillions of dollars borrowed mainly from those greedy overseas investors have had to be pumped into the US economy to keep it from collapsing; and that there is still no definitive quantification of the fallout from the creation of trillions of dollars of CDO and CDS.

Not atypical of this effort to justify capitalism is Fareed Zakaria's contribution to the June 22, 2009 issue of *Newsweek*.[15] While the world wrestles with devising an equitable—long in coming, to be sure—and sustainable alternative to capitalism run amok, he writes in "Greed is Good": "perhaps the measures taken by states around the world, chiefly the U.S. government, have restored normalcy." In this pronouncement, he clearly confuses a market economy with capitalism; they are not one and the same; as discussed in Chapter Six, capitalism is premised on the relentless maximization of self-interest, whereas market economies have been around long before the capitalist world system came into being and individualism entered the consciousness of the West; moreover, the measures taken by most other governments were designed not to rescue capitalism as we know it, but as fire walls.

To reinforce his premises, Zakaria further argues that the number of times the economy rebounded stronger than before over the past 20 years has proven the likes of John Kenneth Galbraith and Nobel Laureate Paul Krugman wrong, and suggests that: "A few years from now, strange as it may sound, we might all find that we are hungry for more capitalism, not less." To this latter observation, I would not disagree; the punishment for greed is indeed a hunger for more.

In addition, Zakaria offers up the Mexican and East Asian countries' quick recovery from their respective currency crises in the 1990s—which he posits "were far more painful in those countries than the current downturn has been in America"—as evidencing the "power of market-oriented reform." It matters not that these economies were thriving market economies at the time; that, in the case of Mexico, it was excesses in portfolio investment flows (foot-loose capitalism) from across the border (Chunan, et al, 1996; Helleiner, 1997); and that, with respect to East Asia, as observed by Nobel Laureate, James Tobin, "the overzealous reach of our practitioners of global finance might bear some responsibility for the crisis" (1998: 20).

With respect to Tobin's perspective, between 1989 and 1997, total portfolio investment flows to developing countries, to be sure, increased by more than 1,150 percent, of which equity flows, consisting mainly of country-denominated mutual funds, accounting for 900 percent (Todaro, 2000: 588). Clearly, then, for Fareed Zakaria and others of like mind, confidence in capitalism must be restored to its former level, ergo, "the simple truth is that with all its flaws, capitalism remains the most productive economic engine we have yet invented."

Looking past endemic denial of one sort or another, and spurious arguments that seemingly resonate with a particular mindset, evidence of business-cycle thinking is reflected in the cautious optimism of the stock market, with any signs of an upward movement in any one of the more important economic indicators, however slight, as evidence—"green shoots" at one point in time—of the awaited up-turn. But, as George Soros—an investor who took advantage of the opportunities presented from a flawed global financial system—observes, "People want to pretend the crisis never happened. . . . They want to go back to business as usual."[16] Be that as it may, as the readiness of investors and traders to head for the exit at any sign of wilting suggests, the predicted recovery is anything but certain in terms of scope and time. While, therefore, the US economy has in the past recovered in keeping with expectations, giving validation to business-cycle theory, past performances are not necessarily indicative of the future.

It is not to deny the resiliency, industry, and ingenuity of the American people, or their ability to overcome adversity either. Far from it! The US, as a country still largely dependent on a continuing stream of motivated immigrants, has a unique formula to bolster its productivity, and thus its output—albeit at a decreasing rate—by keeping the idea of an American dream alive. Moreover, all humans, even the privileged, at some point in their lives must draw on their inner strength appropriate to the challenges they face from within and without; it is instinctive; it is what makes for the recent shift in attitude towards less consumption and more savings: from negative savings in 2005—the hay days of conspicuous consumption—to 6.9 percent (annualized) savings in May 2009.

Rather, my concerns on this occasion turn on two contradictory forces at play. First, in spite of its feel-good rhetoric and rationalization, the US is a country deeply divided along the lines of wealth and power which, not surprisingly, also coincides with other well-known fault lines; and, second, the self-serving dogma of the elite, whose past policy preferences have been at the expense of majority Americans, does not portend a sustainable economy which requires less capitalism and more egalitarianism, as discussed more fully in Chapter Six. In other words, America needs to realize that the growth experienced for most of the last twenty five years has been from exploiting the vulnerabilities of the un-informed and the trusting; it took the Anglo-American economic model beyond the boundaries of moral responsibility and sustainability, a fundamental shift not lost on President Obama, as revealed in his 2009 Budget discussion on his return from the 2009 G-20 Summit.

For the less enamored, therefore, amidst the spin by laissez-faire ideologues and the cautious optimism of Wall Street, are some deep-seated concerns that are shared by the Obama administration. For example, if one listened carefully to President Obama's refrains, one could not help but detect an underlying con-cern for the future: Where is the end to this downward spiral? What adjustments must we make, at what cost, and in what shape will we emerge from this crisis relative to where we were before, relative to the rest of the world? More impor-tantly, when the consequences of the greatest financial deception on the world are fully determined, would America—or its institutions—be ever trusted again by those who have for decades believed in its moral authority and relied on its professed integrity?

Voicing these concerns in candor has opened the president to criticisms by those who would rather he be less accepting of responsibility for the crisis inter-nationally, and be more upbeat domestically. According to his critics, "we" must never be seen as either contrite or weak lest either serves to embolden those who are "jealous" of our achievements or of "who we are"; but, such notions serve only to validate Charles Horton Cooley's "looking-glass self."[17] It is thus in-structive that *Caveat emptor* (let the buyer beware) has been invoked by Alan Greenspan whose attempt at self-absolution was that "they [foreign investors] didn't read the fine print" when they decided to invest in CDO and CDS; "they failed to adequately assess the risk attached to the securities they purchased." It matters not that, as President Obama acknowledged, Standard & Poor's, Moody's, and Fitch, the accepted authority on American institutional integrity, unconditionally attached their highest rating to these investment instruments. In addition, the FED, led by Greenspan, facilitated the creation of such instruments by keeping interest rates low and is thus equally culpable. With respect to the latter, in the heady days of home-buying, the FED chairman openly encouraged mortgage lenders to explore alternatives to the traditional 30 year fixed-rate mortgage model; such exhortations from Alan Greenspan, arguably, resulted in the creation of sub-prime mortgage instruments as one such alternative.

Not unexpected, the laissez-faire ideologues must necessarily rationalize the consequences of ill-advised policies and economic models to be able to now insist that the Obama administration be more circumspect with intervention and wait for the theoretical business cycle to take the turn to the upside, in the hope that all that is wrong will be righted. They continue to argue that there is no compelling reason to think that this crisis is anything more than the downturn, albeit steeper than expected, after a protracted recovery and peak from the last business cycle; and, that the casualties of the downturn is par for the course based on free-market principles. It is what the respected business schools have long come to embrace and have taught; it is what informed US economic growth and prosperity, especially since the 1980s. For the sake of ideology, therefore, they readily rationalize the collapse of Bear Sterns, AIG, Lehman Brothers, General Motors, Fannie Mae, Freddie Mac, Chrysler, and a myriad of household names in the financial and retail sectors—from afar, to be sure—and, of course, the consequential social disruption attendant loss of employment, income, and savings by millions of ordinary Americans.

Conclusion

As I see it, the danger on this particular occasion clearly lies in the misidentification of causality, and thus misdiagnosis, as evidenced by the spurious argument advanced by Fareed Zakaria: "If, in the years ahead, the *American consumer remains reluctant to spend . . . then private-sector activity will become the only path to create jobs* [emphasis added]." Moreover, it is equally spurious to hold out the economic progress in China and India as vindication of capitalism as Zakaria contends; to do so, is akin to holding out collective-bargaining, laws enacting and protecting workers rights and the economic progress of the working class, derived in consequence of such laws, as vindication of Marxism-Leninism. On closer examination, Zakaria and others of similar persuasion would find that while both China and India have grown their economies from feeding the voracious appetites of the West, particularly the US, they do so on terms that benefited their respective peoples directly rather than from the periphery of past economic models, and certainly not from capitalism as an ideological pursuit; and that neither country has adopted any of the ten recommendations of the Washington Consensus; that time might well come, but free-market capitalism has yet to prove itself to the ancients.

It is noteworthy that the Chinese economy, despite its reversion to market economic principles, is still very much a state-directed economy. In that role, it allows the Chinese government to be definitive and decisive in its approach to the current crisis while, in the citadel of capitalism, the wrangling over both content and form of the stimulus and bailout packages, and fundamental reforms, calls to mind Jonathan Swift's Lilliputians.

While our twenty-first century Lilliputians debate reforms, based on the evidence it would be very wrong to treat with the present crisis as if it were just another trough in the business cycle or to equate this crisis with the Mexican and East Asian financial crises. To do so is to beg the question; more than that, it would be falling prey to false equivalencies designed to distract from the underlying causes of the collapse of free-market capitalism. Supporting this observation, as discussed in Chapter Two, is the unprecedented government intervention—not unplanned for as a last resort in the game-theoretic models of the intellectual capitalist class—that marked the end of the arrogance of certainty and market triumphalism premised on human rationality—discussed in Chapter Five—at least in the short run. Why only in the short run? Because there is a theory out there that says the mistakes we have made in our thinking today will be forgotten in 16 years, allowing for a new kind of arrogance to emerge.

Clearly, that massive government intervention became necessary was primarily because of the reengineering of the Anglo-American economic model premised on false logic, an incentive system skewed to perversity, and sham, during the late 1980s to mid 2000s as discussed in Chapter Two. As shown, free-market capitalism was hung by its own petard; exploitation of the vulnerabilities of others by means of overleveraging and aggressive marketing of complex financial instruments to foreigners has clearly boomeranged. More importantly, the consequences of such interventions are yet to be fully understood and explained to the public, and explanation does not come in rhetoric. What does not need explaining, however, is that government intervention brought to an end the experiment with capitalism as we know it, or at the very least, market triumphalism. Because of this, we need to treat with past recessions and recoveries not as prologue but as sources from which to identify deviations in the 2008–9 collapse. To this end, we need to recognize that while the recession in the 1980s was engineered by the FED headed by Paul Volker as a means to reducing high inflation and thus could have been reversed at any time, the 2007–08 recession was the result of capitalism run amok, with consequences far beyond what had been previously experienced in post-WWII America.

As suggested above, then, the present crisis is different in fundamental ways from economic downturns of the past in terms of causality. Also, the only real similarity between this crisis and the Mexican and East Asian financial crises is that the latter were engineered by the intellectual capitalist class mainly operating from New York and London, with tentacles in emerging economies. Moreover, this was not a downturn in the economic business cycle sense. Rather, it was the collapse of one of the main pillars of the capitalist world-economy that has been premised increasingly on false logic and greed, the consequences of which have been hidden from public view so as to prevent the complete collapse of capitalism not unlike that of communism in the late 1980s and early 1990s.

The difference between then and now is that, whereas the Soviet Union, the perpetrator and thus bastion of communism, was left without a base, the US, as the bastion of the capitalist world-economy, found support in the self-interests of other Organization for Economic Cooperation and Development (OECD) countries, and in a relatively strongly-positioned Asia, specifically China and India, in 2009. Moreover, unlike the demise of communism, the collapse of free-market capitalism in 2008 was self-inflicted.

In terms of response, clearly the unprecedented government interventions around the world saved the day, not for free-market capitalism, but rather for another form of market-based economic system still to be determined. Indeed, the large scale intervention by the US was unavoidable because, as explained by the current FED chairman, Ben Bernanke, it was necessary to avoid making the mistakes of the 1930s, that is, of not supporting the banking system. Moreover, the risks are greater on this occasion.

Intervention notwithstanding, while some of the answers to the current problem are found in fiscal and monetary intervention of a third kind, they do not address the fundamental problems. Thus, we need to look elsewhere for longer term answers to our dilemmas, which the less ideologically-driven have come to regard as systemic.

Placed in the context of the reality of the excesses of capitalism as evidenced by the data, then, capitalism premised on "freedom" or indeed on "free market" is a contradiction in terms. As observed by Wallerstein (1999: 63), the free market "is the mortal enemy of capital accumulation." Hence, the existence of the state is to protect the capitalist against the free market, ergo the 14,000 lobbyists in Washington, D.C. Failing which, "the capitalist would be reduced to the income of the hypothetical proletarian of the nineteenth century, living off what might be called 'the iron law of profits in a free market,' just enough barely to survive." To be sure, there would be no sustainable opportunity for "economic profits" in a free-market environment as competition would ensure that only "normal profits" are earned.

NOTES

1. "Bailout fears hit banking shares," *BBC*, http://news.bbc.co.uk/2/hi/business/7834296.stm
2. Bernanke, B, "Economic Stimulus Strategies," House Budget Committee, *C-SPAN*, October 20, 2008
3. Kashkari, N., "Government Response to Credit Markets," Senate Bank and Houing Committee Hearing, *C-SPAN*, October 23, 2008
4. "Financial Market Regulators" House Oversight Committee, *C-SPAN*, October 23, 2008
5. "Countdown with Keith Olberman', *MSNBC*, July 23, 2008
6. Gordon, M., "SEC accuses Goldman Sachs of defrauding investors," *Associated Press*, http://finance.yahoo.com/news/SEC-accuses-Goldman-Sachs-of-apf20142808.html/print?x=0
7. The stimulus package injected US$158 billion into the economy in the second qua ter of 2008 by way of outright tax rebates; a first in recent history, and certainly reminiscent of 1930s Keynesian economics.
8. Reichmann, D., *Bush says government role essential to ease crisis* http://news.yahoo.com/s/ap/20080919/ap_on_go_pr_wh/bush_mark
9. C-SPAN, September 7, 2008
10. Patrick M. Fitzgibbons. *Lehman shares drop as Wall Street questions survival'* http://news.yahoo.com/s/nm/20080911/bs_nm/lehman_dc
11. Greenspan: *Tough decisions await in Lehman case* http://news.yahoo.com/s/ap/greenspan
12. Moral hazard occurs when the unintended consequences of financial risks under-

taken by private-sector financial institutions are perceived as tacitly underwritten by the Federal government or the FED.

13. Johnson, G., "Romney accuses Obama of wrongly apologizing for the US," http://news.yahoo.com/s/ap/20100302/ap_on_el_pr/us_romney_book_tour, March 2, 2010

14. Bush, G. Televised address to the nation on September 11, 2006.

15. Zakaria, F., "Greed is Good (to a point)," *Newsweek*, June 22, 2009.

16. Giannone, J.A., and Ablan, J., "Soros predicts 'stop-go' economy and higher rates," *Reuters,* June 30, 2009

17. A phrase coined by Cooley to characterize the image people have of themselves based on how they believe others perceive them.

Chapter Four

The 1990s: American Triumphalism on Steroids

Since the collapse of communism in 1989, changes to the global political and economic systems were on a fast track, directed by the US as the unchallenged superpower. This was especially so at the turn of the century and up to the unraveling of free-market capitalism beginning in mid 2007. As witnessed throughout most of the first decade of the twenty-first century, political and economic dicta emanated from Washington with an air of authority and triumphalism. From a geopolitical perspective, therefore, US hegemony became visibly aggressive premised on its perceived moral authority—a variant of Manifest Destiny—while the formulation of a new economic model engineered by Nobel Laureates sought to convert the rest of the world to financial-market liberalization and to a culture of consumerism.

America's perceived moral authority found expression in language games, playing upon the binary distinction between good and evil, especially under the George W. Bush administration; ergo "Axis of Evil" to label Iraq, Iran, and North Korea, as targets for derision, and much more. Axis of Evil provided "freedom and democracy" with its opposite and, as a part of the American vocabulary, empowered the right wing news media and the religious right to reinforce their message of hate, notwithstanding that few grasped the full implications of their involvement. Indeed, such is the extent to which contemporary public discourse is anchored in America's self-righteousness that the Reverend Pat Robertson found it acceptable to pronounce the January 2010 Haitian earthquake as resulting from "a pact with the devil 200 years ago." Despite their appeal to a certain mindset, these comments go beyond the pale and say more about America than they do about other countries and their peoples.

Beyond its shallow appeal, demonization of Iraq, Iran, and North Korea, was clearly an attempt at propagation and legitimization of a pan–American self-righteousness that sought to recruit grassroots support for the Bush administration's agenda. It played upon the vulnerability of the lower-income groups, especially new immigrants desperately seeking to identify with the American culture in their quest for the American dream. In very many ways, it mirrored nineteenth-century pan–European racism that sought to imbue the working class with a national identity premised on a perceived racial superiority vis-à-vis non-Europeans (see Wallerstein, 1999). The difference, of course, is that while the Europeans were unpretentiously colonizing Africa and Asia in the twentieth century, American imperial ambitions were shrouded in the mantra of freedom and democracy in the 1990s and into the twenty-first century.

But, while such labels resonated with a particular mindset, as did Adolf Hitler's denigration of the Jewish people with anti-Semites, it was received by the wider world as betraying a deep-seated phobia anchored in a belief that, to love who you are you must hate what you are not. Thus, the idea "either you are with us or you are with the enemy" was met with this response from Singapore's prime minister: "Good relations between America and the major countries are critical because the Southeast Asian countries want to be friends with both [the US and China], and do not want to have to choose sides with either."[1] While Singapore's prime minister was referring specifically to US-China relationship, a BBC poll conducted in January 2007 showed that 75 percent of respondents disapproved of America's foreign policy. According to the BBC:

> The poll underscores conclusions drawn from several other surveys. . . . that anti-Americanism is on the rise, and the more the US flexes its hard power, the more it deploys troops abroad or talks tough diplomatically, the more it seems to weaken its ability to influence the world.[2]

More recently, former governor of Massachusetts, Mitt Romney, rather than seek to understand the several reasons for the almost global distrust of America, found it appropriate to decry President Obama's attempt at reconciliation with the wider world. According to Romney:

> There are anti-American fires burning all across the globe; President Obama's words are like kindling to them. . . . In a world composed of nations that are filled with rage and hate for the United States, our president should proudly defend her rather than continually apologize for her.[3]

Clearly, Mitt Romney still believes in the notion of a Manifest Destiny; that the US has a Devine right to depose governments and destroy cultures around the world; and, as observed by Thucydides some 2400 years ago: "right must give way to might; the strong will do what they can and the weak what they must." But, as John Rawls (1999: 128) reminds us, interstate relationships are governed, not by any theory of justice found at the domestic level, but rather by other considerations such as coexistence, interdependence, and non-intervention that are designed to uphold sovereignty of states rather than individualism. Hence, no external state can bring "freedom and democracy" to the peoples of other states without violating their sovereignty.

Concurrent with the exercise of America's assumed moral authority, the new economic model, supported by a Republican-controlled Congress and an indulgent FED chaired by Alan Greenspan, found expression in free-market capitalism—financial-capitalism premised on financial derivatives in contrast to the manufacturing-driven economic model of "old Europe" and others—within a largely deregulated or non-regulated domestic financial sector. But, what was billed as innovation, soon proved to be nothing less than gimmicks designed not to build wealth but rather to transfer wealth from the unsuspecting in keeping with the notion that "greed is good."

As we have seen in the preceding chapters, the new economy consisted primarily of marketing CDS and CDO and other incompressible financial instruments masqueraded as "AAA–rated" investments. These were targeted at an increasing global pool of free-market neophytes with deep pockets in an environment of minimal transparency and accountability. In this role, the new economic model, as contrived, functioned as the primary means to accessing global savings to fuel the unrelenting desire for capital accumulation by the intellectual capitalist class: The financial services sector became the growth sector of the US economy since the mid 1990s. At the same time, however, it also fueled greater income inequality in a society that was and still is beset by divisions of one kind or another and, curiously, at a time when grassroots support was being recruited in support of an overly-ambitious foreign policy.

From a global perspective, then, both US foreign policy—premised on the distinction between good and evil, or us and them—and the new economic model—premised on aggressive capitalism—had as their fundamental requirements triumph over oppositional political and socio-economic systems. To this end, between 2001 and 2008, systems perceived as oppositional to the neoconservative agenda were identified for elimination by the Bush team; it would have continued as policy had Mitt Romney been elected President in 2008, as is clearly implied his pronouncements quoted above. To the world at large, schooled as it were in the belief of coexistence in a pluralist world order, however, such policies evidenced hegemony not as leadership but as dominance. Hence, examined below from a geopolitical and geo-economics perspective is the reification of such ideas by a largely triumphant America in the 1990s as a means to giving added context to the collapse of free-market capitalism.

The Geopolitical Dimension

In terms of the geopolitical, then, at the extreme was a strategy premised on the idea of a unipolar world dominated by the US as its sole superpower, with the United Nations Security Council comprising the US as the only member, as advocated by Ambassador John Bolton. Such strategy was constructed by a loosely-formed shadow planning group of conservative Republicans comprising Donald Rumsfeld, Richard Cheney, Condoleezza Rice, and Paul Wolfowitz as principals—the so-called Vulcans—during the Clinton presidency (1993-2000).

When this group was brought together as part of the George W. Bush administration in 2001, it came with a predetermined strategy and road map for ensuring US's hegemony in the twenty-first century, which, as ridiculous as it must appear to dispassionate analyses, was the exercise of America's unequalled military power preemptively, as first choice; diplomacy, according to Bolton, was too slow a process; stability was an unacceptable condition for this group, intoxicated as it were by superpower status and by the dream of greatness.

The goal of this strategy, attributed to the then Secretary of Defense Donald Rumsfeld, was two-fold: first, to demonstrate what US policy is all about and second, to dissuade America's up and coming competitors from engaging in "asymmetrical challenges" to the US (Suskind, 2004). Such a goal had been articulated earlier by Paul Wolfowitz in a leaked Pentagon memorandum when he was Assistant Secretary of Defense in the G.H.W. Bush administration in the early 1990s. As told by G. J. Ikenberry (2004), the goal as outlined in the memorandum was for a "fundamental commitment to maintaining a unipolar world in which the United States has no competitor." Hence, as contended in Chang, (2008), the play-out of US foreign policy after 9/11 speaks to the actualization of this grand strategy of which bringing the Middle East to heel was only the first step. For the Vulcans, bringing the Middle East under Western control was the easy first step, slam dunk if you will, given the weakened status of the Arab states on the one hand, and the growing ambitions, assertiveness, and military strength of Israel, America's trusted ally and wedge in the Middle East, on the other hand.

Those who crossed the defining line between friend and foe—good and evil—as determined by an increasingly-assertive US administration in the 1990s and since, were brought to heel condignly, to wit Somalia and Sudan in the mid-1990s, albeit cautiously so, and Iraq in 1991 and again in 2003. The invasion of Iraq in 2003 was designed to deter any potential challenge to US supremacy, as evidenced by "Shock and Awe" pursuant the doctrine of preemption as policy. Equally telling, was the Bush administration's willingness to support Israel in its preplanned attack on Lebanon in the summer of 2006 in the hope of destroying opposition to the process of universalizing "freedom and democracy" in the Middle East and to paving the way for Israel's control of region (Chang, 2008). In this regard, many would recall President Bush's reluctance to allow British Prime Minister, Tony Blair, to mediate an immediate ceasefire to the conflict, and to Secretary Rice's rationalization of Lebanese civilian casualties as "the birth pangs of a new Middle East," so confident were they in Israel's ability to "get the job done," to quote President Bush.

The Specter of Manifest Destiny

While the play out of the doctrine of preemption—opportunely revived by the Bush administration as a US foreign-policy response in knee-jerk reaction to the terrorists attack on 9/11—shocked the world to the extent that the invasion of

Iraq was claimed as a task given to George Bush in his commune with a "higher father" (Woodward, 2006), and by his administration's unqualified support for Israel's attacks on Gaza and on Lebanon in 2006, the idea of preemptive strikes is not new to the American experience; neither are the religious underpinnings of them. Both have been inculcated into the American belief-system—psyche, if you will—over the centuries as a Devine right—"a right to defend"—and served to define America's relationship with others ever since, as reflected in the pro-nouncements of American politicians. But, as played out time after time, it is a notion anchored not in wisdom or in Divinity as professed, but rather in what has morphed into self-righteousness—Manifest Destiny—largely derived from an ingrained desire for conquest, despite the consequences that attend conquest, to wit insecurity and mistrust of difference, however primitive. Hence, whereas it was a sense of freedom of expression that initially drove the first Pilgrims to seek out a new homeland, and found a new society on the values brought with them, Manifest Destiny underscored conversion and conquest of difference in the land of "savages" and beyond by those who are themselves different from the first Pilgrims.

It is ironic that despite opposition to the very idea of a Manifest Destiny from within, many well-meaning Americans, who themselves or their grandpar-ents have been victims of such a doctrine in its myriad manifestations, should find themselves in the role of perpetrators; and in denial of their background. But, while this attitude might be regarded as a betrayal to those who still seek official acknowledgment of past wrongdoings perpetrated in the name of a Manifest Destiny, it speaks curiously to the need to belong, to identify with a larger collective; more curiously, it speaks to the power of indoctrination; per-haps more importantly, it speaks to the lengthy process of incorporation that comes only with maturity and in the fullness of time.

Meanwhile, integration premised on pluralism in America—recognizing and supporting separate identities of disparate ethnic and racial groups and ra-tionalized in politically-correct jargon—is embraced as evidencing greatness, notwithstanding its detraction from reality. To this latter point, consider, for example, this statement by Cardinal Francis George of Chicago in response to the invitation to President Obama to deliver the 2009 commencement address at University of Notre Dame: "It is clear that Notre Dame didn't understand what it means to be Catholic when they issued this invitation." The implication, of course, is that President Obama not only is not catholic but is allegedly Muslim if only by upbringing; his father, as everyone was reminded by the Republican campaign during the 2008 Presidential election, was a Muslim from Kenya. For a country that is struggling for a real and sustainable identity, therefore, the Car-dinal's pronouncement is just another manifestation of the challenges faced by America.

In terms of America's struggle at nation-building, then, I rather suspect that Chinese Premier, Cho en Lai's, comments on the French Revolution—"it is too early to say"—could easily have been directed with equal measure at the American experiment with nation-building. Clearly, transcending the several divides that plague America is still a very, very, long way off.

The Chinese Premier was clearly using the Chinese experience of over 2,000 years as a reference point. In the fullness of time, of course, people do become "Han Chinese" as in the case of China, French in the case of France, Swedish in the case of Sweden, German in the case of Germany, or whatever identification chosen by those comprising such societies because, in the final analysis, people are truly not individuals but rather components of a collective: They function and thrive best as a homogeneous society with a common all-inclusive purpose.

Therefore, whether peoples from disparate tribal groups, thrust together in artificially-created political structures, can function as a cohesive whole within such unnatural structures and be able to achieve maximum efficiency and effectiveness, depends crucially on how genuinely and quickly they can become incorporated as a society. History tells us—more recently, the Rwandan and Bosnian conflicts in the 1990s—successful incorporation depends crucially upon how disposed dominant groups are to taming their tribal instincts to dominate. To this end, respect and care for others, full acceptance on equal terms, and the wisdom to be patient and buy the requisite time for incorporation are primary; more than that, they are determinants of a society's longevity. These comprise the criteria that have been proven in by the ancients who continue to exist in the modern world. By these criteria, and as history instructs, bravado is often an indication of insecurity and immaturity, both for an individual as well as a country. Moreover, cohesion bought with economic benefits survives only as long as those benefits continue to flow; it thus requires increasing access to resources beyond national boundaries, as evidenced by the invasion of Iraq in 2003.

The US today is still being regarded by its leaders as an example of multiculturalism, with the emphasis on pluralism; the 2010 Census reinforces this devotion to separateness. However, it needs to move beyond rationalizing its failure to eradicate disparate racial and ethnic identities that continue to feed the idea of a hierarchical racial and religious structure and actively seek a society of one. Denigrating one another in racial and ethnic terms—coded or otherwise—in the twenty-first century is indicative of a long, long road to haul. To embrace the notion that there is no such thing as society as Margaret Thatcher pronounced in *Vanity Fair* in 1987 is to be on the wrong side of history. Hence, with respect to forging a new society, it is indeed too early to say, especially when the *modus operandi* of free-market capitalism is individualism and self-fulfillment.

With respect to the Bush doctrine of preemption, as noted above it is not new; its self-righteous underpinnings can be traced to the early European settlers' interaction with the indigenous peoples of North America. As part of their expansion in the New World, settlers, mainly English, fleeing religious persecution in their native homeland in the sixteenth century, found it propitious to launch preemptive attacks first, on the Pequot people of Massachusetts whom they believed held unfriendly intentions toward them, and thereafter, buoyed by their successes, on other vulnerable native tribes. To justify their actions, then as now, preemptive attacks were rationalized by their perpetrators as a right to defend. Similarly, much to the consternation of Josef Stalin, Hitler launched a preemptive attack on the Soviet Union in June 1941, despite having signed a non-aggression pact with Stalin, primarily because he saw it as a defensive strategy.

The perceived right to defend on those early occasions, as in almost every other occasion since, was against being expelled from lands the settlers believed were endowed to them by a beneficent God. With such underpinnings, the right to defend morphed into preemptive strikes and has become contemporary foreign policy of the US and others seeking geographic and economic expansion. But, like the doctrine of *Estoppel*, as defined by the British Law Lord, Lord Denning, the "right to defend" must be used as a shield and not as a sword; indeed, it is an absurdity to premise foreign policy on the belief that the greatest and most powerful nation on earth needs to defend its freedom from the rest of that world that is comprised of lesser mortals.

The Economics of Preemptive Strike

Reinforcing the notion of preemptive strike were the resultant economic benefits to be had. To be sure, the output—an abundance of cleared fertile, even tilled, land—that comes from preemptive strikes against Native American villages was at minimum costs to the settlers; that is, less and less inputs in terms of time and resources were required to subdue native peoples as diseases brought over by the settlers took their toll and divestment strategies were refined and enforced by superior weaponry. This calculus is still clearly discernible in US interaction with the wider world as the testimonies to Congress by Paul Wolfowitz and others seeking to justify the decision to invade Iraq in 2003 evidenced. It is this calculus that elicits an attitude that says we were right to invade Iraq even if the whole world disagreed with us, as announced by Richard Pearle, the former Pentagon official in the Bush administration. Interestingly, having failed to bring Iraqi oil production and reserves under direct US control, Pearle was discovered in 2008 seeking oil contracts in Mosul, the hard way.

Underlying intervention in other peoples' lives, as noted earlier, is the belief in a Manifest Destiny. However, this belief in a Manifest Destiny propelled the process of conquest westward beyond the Mississippi river and, from a historical perspective, evidenced the rapid development of an Anglo-American sub-system within the modern world-system at the expense of others. Indeed, motivated by the spoils of preemptive strikes, the persecuted became persecutors, proselytizing their new-found religion and way of life by way of a self-determined right to defend.

In modern geopolitical language, then, preemption translates to a right to establish and protect strategic interests around the world, not unlike those of empires past. However, it is a practice that has no boundaries—no equilibrium—and does not contemplate failure, and, therefore, no exit strategy. In this, it is limitless both in ambition and resource-requirement; and, in this, strangely enough, its demand for ever-increasing inputs for decreasing outputs will eventually result in negative returns and irrationality which rebounds to the detriment of its purveyors in the long run. When this point is reached, collapse is inevitable, as evidenced by the collapse of past empires (see Diamond, 2005). At the very least, preemption as doctrine has no virtue; it promotes paranoia and fortress nations which eventually collapse under the weight of their own paranoia.

The above said, preemptive strikes in the short term come as one's ideological preference only when one is strong, to borrow the phraseology from Jagdish Bhagwati (1988). It is thus instructive that Israel launched a preemptive attack on its Arab neighbors in 1967, not entirely because of the massing of troops by Egypt and Syria on their borders but because it believed in the overwhelming superiority of its military; and that the sea was full and the current serving. Similarly, Israel's attack on Lebanon in 2006 was premised on its superior military strength against Hezbollah. In contrast, in the case of the strained relationship between India and Pakistan over Kashmir, Pakistan merely matched India's massing of over 80 percent of its ground forces and armored divisions along their mutual borders as a stand-off with India; both India and Pakistan possess nuclear weapons.

Such is the power of mutual destruction that neither India nor Pakistan wanted to attack the other. It is further instructive that the US adapted its previously hard-line approach to North Korea's belligerency to reflect the latter's possession of nuclear weapons despite calls for a preemptive strike against the communist state. Clearly, the vulnerability of American forces in the region to North Korea's missiles demanded a readjustment in strategy. The Bush administration engaged in political rhetoric over Russia's incursion into Georgia in response to the latter's military incursion into South Ossetia in 2008 simply because military action against Russia was *non sequitur* despite calls from those who sought such a confrontation.

Landmark Geopolitical Events

There were several landmark geopolitical events that have been etched into history to mark the 1990s as a period of great changes. Some of them are examined in context of an increasing US influence either directly or indirectly during this period.

First, the demise of Soviet and Russia hegemony was made complete in 1994 by the *coup d'état* that propelled the politically-malleable Boris Yeltsin into power. Yeltsin was what the West had hoped Mikhail Gorbachev would be. However, Gorbachev had proven to be a stronger than expected proponent of Marxist-Leninist ideology that underwrote Russia's hegemony and, as such, was impatiently decried as a ditherer by British Prime Minister, Margaret Thatcher (Thatcher, 1995). Hence, Boris Yeltsin was a welcomed if silent outcome of the coup. Indeed, from a Western perspective, it was clearly a matter of the king is dead, long live the king.

To be sure, the removal of Mikhail Gorbachev allowed for quickening the pace of integration of former Eastern and Central European satellites into the West, and for isolating further the remaining communist satellites in far-off lands—Cuba, Cambodia, and North Korea, for example—at will. At the same time, the removal of the infamous Berlin Wall that divided east from west is increasingly being cast more in terms of the triumph of good over evil and thus a validation of America's moral authority. It matters not that the wall was torn down, not by Mikhail Gorbachev as admonished by Ronald Reagan, but by Germans from both sides, albeit with tacit approval of the East German military, seeking unification on the one hand and economic well-being and political expression on the other hand.

Political reforms that had their roots in *"Glasnost and Demokratizacya"*—conceived and implemented by Gorbachev (1987) in the latter half of the 1980s—were fast-tracked under American ownership and active participation by American democracy experts. Additionally, with Gorbachev removed from power, Russia became a target for the universalizing process of democracy and capitalism under US sponsorship and supervision. Hence, as pronounced by most Western observers, communism was dead; the "evil empire" was no more. Russia's fortunes were now dependent entirely upon the goodwill of the Western powers, specifically, the US. As concluded by one political observer, Francis Fukuyama, it was the end of history. Of course, official US policy under George W. Bush sought to portray Russia as a diminished power, no longer to be taken seriously, to be forgiven, as pronounced by Condoleezza Rice in the run-up to the invasion of Iraq in 2003.

The process of universalizing democracy in Eastern and Central Europe, needless to say, fostered the triumphalist mantra of "freedom and democracy," with the American system held out as the ultimate in political governance; it was a return to Europe in the wake of WWII. Amidst the euphoria, however, few sought to equate the clamor for freedom and democracy by the newly independent countries of Eastern and Central Europe to Africa's clamor for independence from colonial rule in the 1960s or India's quest for independence from centuries of British dominance in 1948 or, for that matter, the birth of the state of Israel in 1948 for the Jewish people after centuries as a Diaspora. They all represent the desire of people to identify with a particular collective that is reflective of their tribal roots. Indeed, there is resurgence in the clamor for tribal identity in Britain, strangely enough by the conquering English no less.

The second, and perhaps more important event in terms of its human dimensions, was the end of white rule in South Africa. On May 10, 1994, Apartheid in South Africa was replaced by a government of national unity under the auspices of the African National Congress (ANC) led by the now-revered Nelson Mandela. Prior to 1994, Mandela and other ANC leaders had been considered inferior human beings and terrorists (in today's vernacular) and were, in consequence, imprisoned for over 27 years while the consequences of social and economic degradation attendant racial and political suppression struggled to penetrate the consciousness of the more powerful states, and to find expression in human rights terms.

That black rule became a reality in South Africa in the early 1990s could be attributed, arguably, to the lessening demand on Western attention to a moribund Soviet Union in the throes of total disintegration since the late 1980s. Having pushed for and supported independence from perceived oppressive regimes, it would have been unconscionable to advocate freedom and democracy in Eastern and Central Europe whilst continuing to ignore the injustices perpetrated by a suppressive regime premised on Apartheid in a predominantly black country by a minority white settler-group. Also, that the transition to black rule was relatively peaceful and marked not by retribution as many had feared but rather by a commitment to a process of truth and reconciliation was in no small measure a credit to ANC leadership, and to the groundswell of public outcry and support from many US corporations and activist organizations around the world.

Third, George Herbert Walker Bush restored America's confidence in its military (lost in the Vietnam War) in roundly defeating Saddam Hussein in the 1991 Gulf War. It was the first show of America's military might since the Vietnam War, and was celebrated accordingly. For Iran, having spent most of the 1980s in a proxy war with Iraq, it was a welcome event to see the US turned on its friend; it validated Lord Palmerston's belief that, in terms of national interests, there are no eternal allies or perpetual enemies.

Fourth, and equally significant to the collapse of the Soviet Union, was German unification which had been delicately progressed so as not to alarm its immediate neighbors and Britain, who were still suspicious of German ambitions. At the same time, the end to the conflict in Northern Ireland was in sight, again, under US leadership. In Asia, North Korea had agreed with the US to suspend its nuclear program for food aid and light water reactors. Last but not least, were the strengthening ties between Washington and London under Margaret Thatcher, a process that gained momentum between President George W. Bush and British Prime Minister Tony Blair after 9/11.

From a geopolitical perspective, then, despite some set-backs, a new world order had been firmly established under US leadership in the 1990s, and was unabashedly displayed accordingly. At that time, China was still considered a communist state and did not warrant attention, according to Gerald Segal (1999) and others. The US was the sole superpower; it ruled the world, giving rise to the notion that "there has got to be some advantage of being a superpower" in a post 9/11 world.

The Geo-economics Dimension

On the economic front, market liberalization—globalization, if you will—as envisioned by the Washington Consensus was also being progressed gratifyingly in keeping with plans, aided, of course, by the IMF and the World Bank whose enhanced structural adjustment funding programs (ESAF) ensured investment opportunities for Western capitalists in emerging markets. According to IMF data, private capital flows to developing countries and Eastern Europe increased from an annual average of US$11.6 billion for the period 1983-88, to US$114.3 billion for the period 1989-93, and to US$166.4 billion in 1995 (Helleiner, 1997: 4). Indeed, privatization programs were pushed through by these institutions in almost all but the poorest of the poor countries, facilitating foreign private investment, especially in the emerging markets of Eastern Europe and Russia (Chang, 2006:10).

Arising from the privatization push, foreign direct investment (FDI) as a percentage of privatization sales was greatest in Eastern Europe and Central Asia, and in Latin America when compared with East Asia and sub-Sahara Africa (Chang, 2006: 9; Sader, 1993): The East Asian countries presented very little opportunity to foreigners, preferring their own internal sources, whilst the African countries were considered less attractive in light of their relatively low income per capita, thus rendering investment in capital-intensive industries less attractive (World Development Report, 1997; Stewart & Basu, 1995).

Privatization in Hungary, the Czech Republic, and Poland were accomplished primarily with private capital flows, mainly from the US and gave impetus to the American domestic financial sector. Between 1988 and 1992, privatization accounted for 73.41 percent of the total FDI flows to the Czech Republic, 86.24 percent to Hungary, and 64.84 percent of FDI to Poland. With respect to the Russian experience with privatization, according to Martin Feldstein, "it was one of the 20th century's most remarkable achievements."[4]

The rush for a stake in these emerging markets by Western capitalist was met with trepidation from the local inhabitants. Corruption was rife in all quarters, and included those foreign investors who saw opportunity in naivety.[5] Meanwhile, privatization in sub-Sahara Africa was all but a whisper during this period, having been pushed through in the 1980s under the auspices of the IMF and World Bank in keeping with a change in policy to development aid and in the belief that the Debt Crisis of the mid 1980s was a sham (Chang, 2006: 16). With respect to the latter, many developing countries' governments were of the view that Washington was seeking to impose democracy by holding development assistance hostage to political and economic reforms by adopting a "take it or leave it" approach (Killick, 1995).

Meanwhile, the Asian economic model that underscores Japanese industrial prowess and Southeast Asian economic development and growth during the 1960s and 1970s became susceptible to external manipulation in the 1990s. As such, by early 1990s, the perceived economic threat posed by Japan to US economic dominance was successfully contained partly by targeted revaluation of the Yen, and partly by the resort to unilateral trade sanctions as provided for in Super 301 of the Trade and Tariff Act, 1974. The four Asian Tigers—Hong Kong, Singapore, Taiwan, and South Korea were contained through anti-dumping tariffs, countervailing duties, and successive versions of the Multi-

Fiber Agreement (MFA). These trade-restricting instruments governed the exports of certain products, including textile and clothing, from Asia to the US and Europe for most of the last quarter of the twentieth century. During this period, perceived "market disruption" in the US and Europe from Asian exports was a justifiable cause for sanctions. Indeed, in the case of textile and clothing, as provided for in Para 4, of the MFA III, "decline in the rate of growth of per capita consumption in textiles and clothing is an element which may be relevant to the recurrence or exacerbation of a situation of market disruption."

During the 1990s, the intellectual capitalist class, concentrated mainly in New York and facilitated by an indulgent FED, headed by Alan Greenspan, and by an ideologically-driven Republican US Congress, was well on its way to reaping the benefits from what Chairman Greenspan dubbed a new edifice of risk management. As evidenced by the more than doubling of transaction on the various specialist financial and commodities markets, this new edifice of risk management included aggressive short selling of stocks, commodities, and currencies. However, while such a practice was hailed as financial innovation, on closer examination it was inherently predatory; hedge funds within the big banks and investment houses with access to unlimited financial resources were able to indulge in short-selling at will, thereby forcing holders of targeted securities, currencies, and commodities in margin accounts to sell to satisfy margin calls as a first step to creating self-fulfilling prophesies of sorts.

In addition to the above, the growth of the Washington lobby—from about 400 in the 1970s to over 14,000 in the 1990s—ensured that members of Congress remained reminded of their dependency on corporate America and other special interest groups for campaign contributions. Hence, perceived regulatory constraints to economic growth were systematically removed, partly by deregulation and partly by weak or non-regulation of the financial sector; the "ENRON loophole" that permitted unregulated trading of energy derivatives and the Gramm-Leach-Bliley Act, 1999 that repealed the Glass-Stegall Act 1933, speak to this observation.

The new economic model, premised on hedging, that, in the minds of their architects minimized financial risks to levels that make such risks almost nonexistent, received a boost in confidence from the Asian financial crisis of 1997–8. For those who witnessed the rise of East Asia since the mid 1960s, the crisis evidenced, in the words of most American economic observers and commentators, the triumph of the American system of financial capitalism over the Asian economic model; it was an event that was long in coming for the ideologically-driven. Long in coming because, as shown in Figure 4.1, the average annual GDP growth rates for Japan, South Korea, and East Asia as a whole, were more than double that of the combined OECD countries, and over three times the average GDP growth rate of the US economy during the period 1965 to 1989.

The rapid industrialization of Japan and South Korea was achieved within the uniquely Asian model of market-augmentation in which the state directed productive resources to achieve growth rates comparable to or greater than those achieved by the more technologically-advanced Western economies. Marketaugmenting mechanisms included targeting subsidies and "getting relative prices wrong" in targeted export sectors, and were the economic strategy of choice (Amsden 1989). As further observed by Amsden (1989: 154), there were strong positive externalities arising from South Korea's ability to raise capital from its export of light manufacture. This allowed it to resist the push for wholesale privatization.

Despite state intervention, including the use of multiple exchange rates, South Korea's model was hailed by the World Bank as an outward-oriented economic model and was thus recommended to other developing countries. The general perception in the West was that such a model was not sustainable and that it will fall flat on its face in short order, hence the complacency with which it was viewed. Be that as it may, as discussed in Chapter Seven, the development strategy that emphasized exports and recommended by the World Bank was applied with equal success in China and accounted for its extraordinary economic growth rates for most of the last two decades.

Figure 4.1

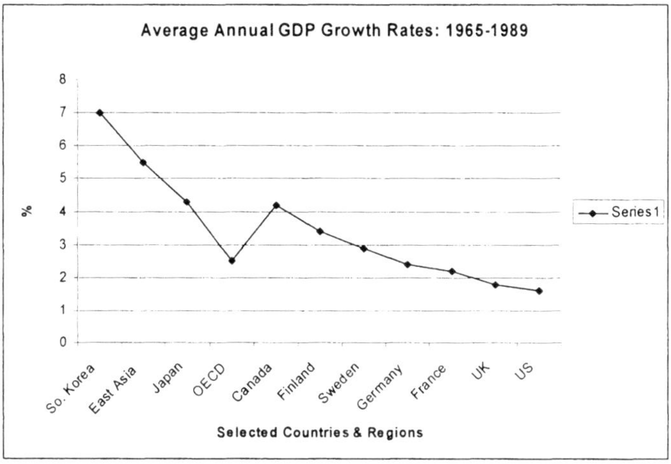

Average Annual GDP Growth Rates: 1965-1989

Selected Countries & Regions

Source: (Adapted from Chang, C., *Privatisation and Development*, 2006: 33)

The American economy received a further boost from the emergence of the "Dotcom" industry during the 1990s. America's leadership in information technology provided the impetus for further innovation in technology and thus growth. The result was the creation of several hundred millionaires every year, many in their early twenties. The increase in personal wealth for the upper 10 percent of income earners in the US was reflected in an increase in aggregate demand and formed the basis for asset bubbles that climaxed in 2007 with the collapse of the housing market.

Last but not least was the bipartisan agreement to operate with a balance budget and to reduce the budget deficit created by Ronald Reagan. Hence, in addition to consistent economic growth, both the Clinton administration and the

Congress led by the then Speaker of the House, Newt Gingrich, worked towards reducing the budget deficit: "Pay as you go" was endorsed as policy and America was well on its way to a budget surplus by 2000. America, to be sure, was invincible at the turn of the century, and the world simply followed the leader into the twenty-first century.

NOTES

1. "Singapore PM warns US over China," *BBC NEWS*, https://news.bbc.co.uk/, May 5, 2007
2. "Listen more is world's message to the US," *BBC World News*, https://news.bbc. co.uk, June 3, 2007
3. Johnson. G., "Romney accuses Obama of wrongly apologizing for America," *AP* http://news.yahoo.com/s/ap/20100302/ap_on_el_pr/us_romney_book_tour; March 02, 2010
4. Feldstein, M., "Russia's Rebirth," *The Wall Street Journal*, September 8, 1997
5. Reed, J., "Foreigners Transform Hungary's Banks," *The Wall Street Journal*, September 24, 18997, A18; See also, Robbins, C., and Liesman, S., "How an Aid Program Vital to New Economy of Russia Collapsed," *The Wall Street* Journal, August 13, 1997; See also *The Wall Street Journal*, September 16, 1997, A16

Chapter Five

The Confluence of Rationality, Reductionism and Existentialism

As discussed in Chapter Three, the conventional wisdom is to look for answers to our current economic problems in established economic ideology. However, a dispassionate critique of our value-system and approaches that have been fashioned in adherence to particular ideas of economics or political philosophy is more likely to lead to sustainable solutions. I say this on two premises. The first is, as observed by John Maynard Keynes (1964; 383), "the ideas of economists and political philosophers, both when they are right and when they are wrong, are more powerful than is commonly understood." I believe we have never been more influenced to the short-term perspective of self-fulfillment and wealth accumulation than in recent decades. The second premise is that, a sociopolitical and economic system that is constructed on ideas of instant wealth and power, betrays a value-system anchored in the extremes of rationality, reductionism and existentialism, and is short-term in horizon.

The play-out of such extremes manifests in the relentless pursuit of self-fulfillment, and abandonment of societal and business norms; it also manifests in excesses in the utilization of resources and the means to accessing them. Furthermore, to regard individualism and wealth accumulation *a priori* greatness conflicts with values that are foundational to building a lasting democratic society no less than it does with the values of traditional cultures premised on holism. Hence, as observed by Derek Bok (1996:4), "in 1960, the vast majority of Americans believed that the nation was progressing nicely and would be even more successful in the future than it had been in the past, by 1991, 64 percent of the public believed that the country was 'headed in the wrong direction'" despite its total embrace of individualism and its enormous accumulation of wealth.

With respect to the first premise, there is no denying that American intellectuals have done an incredible job of influencing thought for most of the twentieth century; the number of Nobel prizes they have taken home over the period stands in evidence. Furthermore, many of the ideas that emanated from this group have been to the betterment of humanity and speak to a long-term horizon and thus to holism. Without the ideas of those dedicated to making the world a better place, advances in medicine, the sciences, and technology would not have been possible.

In recent years, however, many intellectuals—including Nobel Laureates—in the social sciences, especially politics and economics, have managed to convince themselves and the West that rationality, reductionism and existentialism are mutually-reinforcing ideas, and are the elixir to unlimited capital accumulation and continuance of US hegemony. Hence, evidencing the maximization ethos of capitalism, economic and financial transactions, such as options and hostile takeovers that were once considered sleazy by the gentlemen of Wall Street, according to Steven M. Sears of *Barron's*,[1] proved "too lucrative to ignore ... besides, firms are no longer respectable."

The enormous wealth accumulated by the US over the last 50 years, the resort to aggressive unilateralism in international relations, and the new economic model premised on overleveraging—discussed in some detail in Chapters Two and Three—speak to the convergence of ideas that informed game-theoretic models which governed US political and economic policies and approaches in the latter half of the twentieth century. However, based on the evidence, many of these ideas have been almost entirely short-term in perspective, and, thus, unsustainable. Consider, for example, the scramble by highly respected Wall Street firms for TARP funds. It was not because JP Morgan Chase & CO., American Express Co., and Goldman Sachs & Co. were in dire financial straits that prompted them to change their corporate identity to bank holding companies; rather, it was because they wanted to access the TARP funds as a means to enhancing their profitability in the short term.[2]

With respect to the second premise, the growing excesses in selfishness, wealth accumulation, and conspicuous consumerism have caused greed and excessive accumulation of wealth to be added to the list of deadly sins issued by Pope Benedict XVI. Their groundings are thus examined in the trinity of rationality, reductionism, and existentialism in this chapter, not from a theoretical perspective necessarily—there are erudite expositions too numerous to mention—but rather, more from an empirical, if subjective, point of view which, frankly, are more relevant to understanding our current dilemmas, and somewhat safer for lesser mortals. Furthermore, besides being a haven from which to evaluate, it is inspired by Charles Dickens's admonishment: "We must teach these boys and girls the facts and nothing but the facts." If, therefore, what follows is regarded as empiricism, so be it.

While the purpose of this manuscript is to treat with the facts, we need to be cognizant of the ever-present philosophical influence of Friedrich Nietzsche's contention that "there are no facts, only interpretations." We should also be aware that Nietzsche's pronouncement has contributed to endless debates, to indecisiveness, and to obscuration as a matter of course; ergo, "the world over borrowed," not the US, even though the US is now the greatest debtor nation in the world and must continue to "over borrow" to fund its budget deficit.

Nietzsche's perspective further allows us to rationalize ineptitude, and to this end, provides a haven for the articulate incompetent.

It should be noted also that this discussion on rationality and the reductionist ethos is not intended to dispute their importance to the central themes of economics, philosophy, and the social sciences; human rationality and the reductionist ethos are central to the claim of economics as a science. Without the assumption of "rational behavior," the concept of equilibrium, for example, would be without foundation. Likewise, without the reductionist approach we would not be able to speak of "specialization" and "efficiency" in their various disaggregated forms and contexts.

At the same time, however, it should be recognized that greater inequality among sub-sets—both within national boundaries and among members comprising the capitalist world-economy—is the likely outcome, as aggressive capitalism, informed by the liberalization and maximization ethos of this trinity, becomes the primary driver for economic growth and development on a going forward basis. One would therefore find inequality both within the individual capitalist economy, such as the US, as well as within the capitalist world-economy—the G-7, and OECD, for example—given that the latter arguably manifests a hierarchical structure premised on relative capital accumulation. This contention is discussed more fully in Chapter Six.

The above presumed hierarchical structure makes for interesting international relations even among those comprising the capitalist world-economy. It does, for example, explain the willingness of a dominant member to seek to increase its capital accumulation at the expense of other members—the rationality effect—and to treat with them as enemies—the existential effect—even though they are friends and allies vis-à-vis other state actor(s) outside the group: the bickering between the US and the European Union (EU) over trade barriers is a case in point. Equally telling is the ready cooperation between the US and the UK on matters of mutual interest vis-à-vis any other member or group of members within the capitalist world-economy, especially the "Euro-zone" members. Clearly, convergence of interest is the determinant of cooperation among rival members in any formal socioeconomic and political structure; again, lending credence to the nineteenth century British Statesman, Lord Palmerston's, candid pronouncement on national interests as eternal and perpetual.

Rationality

The idea of human rationality that, "all persons will act in their own self-interest if allowed to perceive it correctly" (Wallerstein, 1999) or as freedom "rightly understood,"[3] has its roots in the Enlightenment to the extent reason is considered Western. As such, it is essentially a European sociopolitical phenomenon and the foundation of the reductionist ethos and, of course, existentialism that has come to complete the philosophical matrix of the modern world system. I say essentially European mainly because these ideas were introduced as principles of governance to other cultures largely by way of colonization; certainly not because human reason is uniquely European.

As a result of this societal transformation anchored in the Enlightenment, Western society—broadly defined to include former European colonies—turns on human rationality, in contrast with other societies not affected by the Enlightenment and which, therefore, continue to be guided mainly by traditional values and religion. A few such cultures continue to exist either because of their size or because of the depth of their underlying culture or both, and, in the light of the discussion above, are viewed as oppositional to the capitalist world-economy even though they exhibit the trappings of modernity.

China, of course, is one such society. The size of China and the depth of its culture have in the past allowed it to absorb other invading cultures over time (Seo, and Takewana 2006: 224; Kesselman, et al., 1996:372-3). Thus China in its present socioeconomic and political configuration is perceived as outside the framework of the capitalist world-economy and oppositional to the Westernization imperative. Indeed, as argued in Chapter Seven, China is perceived as portending a geo-economic alternative arrangement in cooperation with other major emerging economies—Brazil, Russia, and India—to that offered by the dominant leaders of the capitalist world-economy vis-à-vis other developing countries. This perception has been largely validated by the constructive role played by China in the wake of the 2007–08 collapse of the Western financial system and attendant wide-spread recession.

India is also a challenge to the existing modern world-system, even though as a former British colony, it is closer to the West than China. However, because of this historical relationship with the West, India is susceptible to its influence and, although this is not a given, to final absorption by it, despite Anouar Abdel-Malek's (1981) conception of the composition of civilization. On the other hand, India, like China, has a value-system that is deep in tradition as it is nurturing of those traditions, and has survived invading cultures over the centuries. But, unlike China, as the once British "Jewel in the Crown," India is intimately familiar with the workings of the Western mind and could break to either side of the ideological divide. Be that as it may, if one accepts Abdel-Malek's (1981: 43; 179; 185) notion that there are only two civilizations—Indo-Aryan and Chinese, and that the latter includes all of Asia and the Asian-Islamic zone—then India, being on the other side of the Abdel-Malek's "time-dimension" of the Indo-Aryan civilization, is likely to resist being absorbed by the West. It therefore remains to be seen if India will perceive its role as integral to a revitalized and assertive Asia or become the de facto jewel in the crown of the capitalist world-economy by reason of its historical association. Clearly, India's brooding over the Obama administration's self-interested embrace of China and Pakistan bears watching; but so also is India's assertive stance on economic issues, such as, for example, raising interest rates by one-quarter of one percent in March 2010 at a time when the West would prefer that it did not do so.

As argued above, human rationality is one of the most influential ideas coming out of the Enlightenment; and to the extent that self-interest is widespread and permeates not just political, economic, and social systems in the West but almost everything that is accepted cross-culturally, it is likely to survive as an integral aspect of whatever system results from the "terminal crisis" of the modern world-system.

Rationality as Freedom "rightly understood"

The idea of rationality as freedom "rightly understood" is similarly subject to interpretation, even in Western society. It is "rightly understood" in terms of form, time, and place differently from one society to the next and from one time period to the next. To be sure, the notion, having been coined in the late nineteenth century when empire was the rage, is rooted in the belief of a hierarchal social structure of man; hence, at one point in history, "the king can do no wrong" was written into the laws of England as doctrine; even now, no one is free to touch the British sovereign without his or her permission, even though the British people have enjoyed considerable freedom since the signing of Magna Carta, in 1215.

Freedom rightly understood in Australia permits White Australians to call their prime minister "mate" while native Australians have been denied the freedom to preserve their cultural identity.

In America, many Americans have had their freedoms violated[4] in the "land of the free" in the interest of national security or, more frequently, in consequence of racial and other forms of profiling, and homelessness.[5] Indeed, it took the Voting Rights Act, 1965, to guarantee the right of Black Americans to vote. Prior to that, it took the Civil Rights Act, 1964, to guarantee equal rights for all Americans. Even then, voter-intimidation is an empirical reality and there are incidents where legal judgments from the bench have been made on the basis of "no human involvement" (NHI) after four decades of ostensible civil rights.

But Black Americans are not the only race discriminated against. By a policy of forced relocation in the 1950s, hundreds of thousands of Native Americans were deprived of their right to preserve their cultural identity. Similarly, the transportation of thousands of orphans from the UK to Australian up to the mid 1960s is yet another example of egregious violation of fundamental rights at a time when developing countries were criticized for their human right violations.

In many non-Western and so-called primitive societies, individualism is not *sine quo non* higher quality of life or indeed survival; it does not exist in the language of many such societies, just as greed is not a part of their vocabulary. Hence, in many such societies, freedom is rightly understood only when it speaks to the interest of the group. For example, freedom from hunger is often a policy objective in many non-Western societies which have been labeled undemocratic or authoritarian. In this regard, China has long elevated the feeding and clothing of its people above the outward display of wealth. This is not to say that greed does not exist in China; rather, it is dealt with harshly when it surfaces, and often to the chagrin of those who thrive on it.

Clearly, the idea of freedom is as subjective as it is dynamic, and is not unique to Western societies. Even in the citadel of "freedom and democracy" there is a difference between theoretical freedom and substantive freedom as evidenced by the examples cited above. Moreover, "liberty" or freedom to pursue one's self-interest—a defining characteristic of a capitalist society—is contrary to the notion of equality, a defining characteristic of democracy broadly understood. Hence, by definition, capitalism and democracy are contradictory ideas, as discussed more fully in Chapter Six.

Education in Self-interest as Key

Clearly, capitalism is derived from a market economic system, which is not uniquely Western. However, aggressive capitalism, as practiced in the West, thrives on its perverse ability to control access to existing markets and the creation of new markets, and to extract from others maximally in a framework of no regulation or minimum regulation; its appetite, as noted above, is insatiable. Thus, for aggressive capitalism to thrive, the world must be converted to the ideology of consumerism premised on a perception of self-fulfillment, or greed. To this end, the intellectual capitalist class must be unleashed upon the world, as indeed it was since the mid 1980s, to keep the US in hegemonic relationship with other international actors—even within the framework of the capitalist world-economy—if only, as perceived by Samuel Huntington (1996: 312), "to maintain Western technological and military superiority over other civilization."

The idea of self-interest—individualism—gave birth to a myriad of philosophies and socioeconomic theories that served to inform our present-day belief system for good or evil. Hence, while some of these philosophies and theories speak to modernity, and have guided, and continue to guide, our everyday interaction with one another for the betterment of all, many of them, as suggested by the evidence, gave birth to perversity in the pursuit of wealth accumulation and power in the last quarter of the twentieth century.

Without the underlying concept of self-interest, there is no game theory—the *Prisoner's Dilemma*—or the "Nash equilibrium" or "rational expectation" or indeed freedom of choice. Indeed, they all turn on the idea that if humans can be made to believe that their existence is best determined by their own perception of self—helped, of course, by the self-interested perspectives of others—and are rationed the tools to pursue what they are allowed to perceive as their respective self-interests, then mechanisms that would allow the capitalist class to control transformation of the masses from one level of existence to the next can be constructed to govern behavior at different levels of existence. It is no less an extension of the condition-response experiment conducted by Ivan Pavlov; only in this case, it is at the human level. This is very evident in our approaches to government transfer payments, to production incentive systems, to trade agreements and, of course, to foreign policy, to wit the idea of "carrots and sticks" in the case of the latter; with respect to this latter notion of carrots and sticks, it is ludicrous for the dominant state to take the position of not rewarding bad behavior as if it were ordained by some higher power.

Therefore, how an individual correctly perceives self-interest in turn depends crucially upon the definition of "correctly" and the approaches constructed to support that definition and generalized by way of education. Under these conditions, education can thus be defined as the formal inculcation of ideas or processes to achieve a preconceived end which will be pursued so long as the idea or process is perceived or is made to be perceived as beneficial to the individual. It does not have to be actually beneficial, just perceived as such, as Bernard Madoff's recent Ponzi scheme aptly demonstrates.

In addition to the tenuous construct of self-interest, examination of the empirical reality reveals inherent contradictions in the notion of human rationality. What might be perceived correctly in terms of self-fulfillment under one set of rules may also be deemed incorrectly perceived under a different set of rules within the same time and space. Hence, as Samuel Huntington (1996) argues, a clash of civilizations is likely to result when, for example, modernity and the Westernization imperative are regarded as one and the same—which they are not—by the dominant state seeking to impose its value-system upon its weaker neighbors. Clearly, the critical facilitator or constraint to human rationality in all cases is embodied in the phrase "if allowed to perceive it correctly." And therein is the rub. It is all about trading one perception for another and effectively one master for another, even in so-called free societies.

Consider, for example, the idea of personal bankruptcy. The social stigma and loss of certain civil rights attached to personal bankruptcy can be traced to nineteenth-century England as memorialized in Charles Dickens's *Little Dorrit*. In nineteenth-century England, a bankrupt and his family had to suffer the indignity and loss of social standing from being sent to live in a Debtor's prison.

In present day America, a bankrupt has the stigma of being labeled as an untrustworthy person, to whom credit, and increasingly employment, is denied for a period of time. This worked as a disciplinary mechanism for as long as Americans were constrained by ethics and morality. Indeed, for most Americans, the very idea of being labeled a bankrupt was a deterrent until it became public knowledge that members of the elite have included personal bankruptcy as an aspect of their personal financial-planning model. As a result, ordinary Americans swiftly come to realize that their self-interest is also served from exercising their constitutional right of equal access to and protection under the law; the result is an increasing number of Americans now regard bankruptcy as the legal route to a fresh start.

The response by the capitalist class to an increase in personal bankruptcy filings by ordinary Americans was swift, with fundamental changes to the law that would make it more difficult for them to avoid paying their debts. Clearly, the self-interests of the enterprise and political classes merged to curb this perceived disruption to the capitalist system. Why? Because the long-established

mutually-reinforcing interests of both groups must be defended at all costs; the
system simply cannot permit a consumer-class that accounts for over 70 percent
of GDP avoids its debt obligations. Hence, in a country of laws and not of men,
such legal rights, while rooted in principles of equality, which democracy pro-
fesses, are, in reality, anathemas to capitalism. Capitalism would not survive if
debt-avoidance were endemic; politicians as the guardians of the capitalist system and dependent as they are on corporate donors for political contributions
would have to look elsewhere for campaign contributions.

Clearly, an education system devoted to promoting self-interest must necessarily conflict with one that promotes holism; it necessarily assumes that the
sum of all individual self-interests is greater than the whole if only to rationalize
the casualty of self-interest, which is income equality. More importantly, self-
interest is by definition oppositional to group loyalty as is implicit in the *Prisoner's Dilemma*, a construct of game theory; as such, it renders the notions of
trust, integrity, and loyalty obsolete as discussed above.

It further follows that since, like a leach, a self-interested person has loyalty
to none but himself, such a person is a lethal weapon in the hands of manipula-
tors. Indeed, infused with certain perverse ideas, such a person operates to the
detriment of others or to society as a whole, a Manchurian candidate next door,
if you will. Moreover, to ensure that self-interest is perceived "correctly," those
charged with defining "correctly" usually have a beneficial interest in structur-
ing and targeting education or processes.

This perverse aspect of self-interest is not new or necessarily unique to the
American experience. In ancient China, Confucius had to remind the governor
of Shea that there is integrity in a father covering up for his son, and a son for
his father. Interestingly, in the 1950s, some 2,500 years after Confucius, as Lisa
See tells it in *Shanghai Girls*, the American immigration authorities promised
US citizenship to those Chinese immigrants who would first confess to being
illegal—even if they were not—and second, identify family members or friends
as communists or communists sympathizers. The premise, of course, is that the
desire to become a US citizen is intrinsically greater than loyalty to family and
friends.

In the extreme, as in recent foreign policy applications, the pursuit of national self-interest receives cover in political rhetoric and in the demonizing of
difference or "Other" as discussed above. It survives by recruiting others of like
mind or by converting others by way of condign or compensatory power (Chang
2008); however, it falls on false-equivalencies when generalized beyond its cultural and philosophical underpinnings as evidenced by President Bush's be-
mused characterization of Iraqis resistance to foreign occupation: "the enemy
loves death more than life."

The idea of suicide-bombers in place of tanks clearly conflicts with the
Western notion of human rationality, of self-interest, upon which models of
modern warfare have been premised. Such is the nature of self-interest that it
required devising a counterinsurgency strategy to include cooperating with pre-
viously-labeled enemies as a means to defeating the unplanned-for-insurgency.

This strategy required subscribing to the idea that the enemy of my enemy is my friend, at least until my perception of my interest changes. Recall, Saddam Hussein was a good friend of the US in the conflict with Iran, as was the Mujahedeen in Afghanistan against archrival, the Soviet Union; both became enemies in short order as America's perception of self-interest changed.

To be sure, the American approach to foreign policy as evidenced by the Afghanistan and Iraq experiences seemingly draws upon this observation by the nineteenth century British Statesman, Lord Palmerston:

> It is a narrow policy to suppose that this country or that is to be marked out as the eternal ally or the perpetual enemy of England. We have no eternal allies and we have no perpetual enemies. Our interests are eternal and perpetual, and those interests it is our duty to follow.

Incidentally, it also explains the seemingly contradictory relationships the US now has with China and Pakistan; the national interests of the US dictates that both China and Pakistan be considered in friendlier terms.

This devotion to self-interest has been promoted as a fundamental pillar of the American culture, and thus experience, as discussed in Chapter Three. Many of those in the corridors of power are there largely because they excel in the discipline of fostering self-interest; in the field of economics, they are a credit to John Nash's genius, and to Ayn Rand and her avowed disciple Alan Greenspan; they are highly effective in acting out their indoctrination to the best of their abilities; but, they are no less slaves to the trinity of rationalism, reductionism, and existentialism as proponents of other cultures are to their primitive beliefs.

This reverence for self-interest often befuddles those whose backwardness provides a basis for resistance to the universalizing fervor of the US, and who are equally misunderstood by the rationally-enlightened; ergo, the notion of a clash of culture, or more pointedly a *Clash of Civilization* in the vernacular of Samuel Huntington (1996), or Arnold Toynbee (1948). This is especially so when, as noted above, modernity and Westernization are regarded as synonymous, requiring the marginalization if not destruction of oppositional cultures, as addressed by Arnold Toynbee (1948) and Leslie Sklair (1995).

Where the pursuit of self-interest coincides with communal interest, it has redounded accidentally, as recognized in Adam Smith's characterization of the invisible hand of the market, to the benefit of community as, for example, most pursuits in the fields of science and medicine, and may be considered Pareto-efficient, that is, socially welfare-enhancing, albeit unintended. To this latter point, it is instructive that almost 1850 years before Adam Smith's publication of *The Wealth of Nations* in 1776, the Chinese historian Szema Chien, in his essay *On Wealth and Commerce* should observe:

> The farmers produce them, the wholesalers bring them from the country, the artisans worked on them, and the merchants trade them. All this takes place without the intervention of government or of philosophers. Therefore prices seek their level, cheap goods going to where they are expensive and higher prices are brought down. . . . All things are produced by the people themselves without being asked and are transported to where they are wanted. Is it not true that these operations happen naturally in accord with their own principle? (Lin, 1960: 208).

Outside the realm of happenstance, the pursuit of self-interest as a necessary characteristic of Western capitalism, as the invisible hand seems to suggest, is a social construct premised on human rationality informed by greed. Therefore, to impute, "reasoned understanding of close connections between conduct and consequences" (Sen 2004: 50) to "our first perceptions," which Adam Smith (1790: 319) contends "cannot be the object of reason but of immediate sense and feeling," is to suggest that successful hunts by the wild dogs of Africa, for example, reflect reasoned understanding of causality; and that "reasoned understanding of close connections between conduct and consequences" likely would impel them to share their kill among members of the pack if only to ensure successful future hunts and, to be sure, survival of the specie.

Reductionism

The reductionist looks at or approaches things—objects, issues, or processes—from the perspective of their respective individual components, in contrast with holism, which views such things from the perspective the whole, that is, the whole determines the nature and characteristic of the individual components. Thus, the reductionist would perceive America as the greatest country in the history of the modern world whilst holism would suggest that it is the world that has accorded America greatness.

The holistic approach contains a lesson still to be learned; greatness is an accommodation by others, and it is fluid. In other words, the developer of the most powerful engine sees only the power of it—the reductionist perspective—which is meaningless unless there are other parts that together comprise not just a vehicle but one that can accommodate such power fully—the holistic perspective. Moreover, a redesigned and reengineered chassis would likely require a different technology or less powerful engine, relegating the once most powerful engine to a lesser status. Perhaps, more importantly, such an engine would be useless in an environment that is accommodating only of bicycles.

The above said, there is no denying the enormous contribution of reductionist philosophy to the efficient use of resources and to human development. By the process of sub-division, endless opportunities for specialization are created which in turn increase skills, knowledge, and output both in terms of quantity and quality. Thus applied, reductionism has been the main driver of economic growth and prosperity in the West in the twentieth century. This is no more evident than in the sciences and medicine, as it is in manufacture around the world.

Reducing a process or a function to its lowest possible denomination allows for greater control and minimization of wastage and, of course, risk. In terms of the latter, reductionism provided the theoretical basis for a risk management regime premised on hedging—insurance and options—and has given impetus to the financial service industry in the last quarter of the twentieth century, especially after the mid 1980s. The existence of specialized markets is also a consequence of applied reductionism.

Rational Actor or "Rational Fool"?

The downside to reductionism is that it conditions people to view objects, processes, and issues from ever-narrowing perspectives which make them vulnerable to myopia and thus manipulation. Hence, we mainly perceive trees in a forest not from the perspective of an ecosystem but as rather as lumber to be harvested pursuant self-interest: from the very basic—shelter and fire wood as needed by inhabitants of the forest—to wealth accumulation by the capitalist class, the latter more destructive than the former.

Similarly, most people are kept on a "need to know" basis primarily for the purpose of control; few are therefore able to perceive or comprehend issues of national or global importance in holistic terms; most approach them from narrowly defined perspectives, seeking refuge in the now familiar haven of "outside my pay grade" or, indeed, self-interest.

Clearly, reductionism as described above necessarily suppresses holism; people's choices are limited to those falling within their pay grade, so to speak, and by their inability—by reason of being denied the tools to make informed choices—to differentiate dispassionately between various distinct alternatives. Consider, for example, the invasion of Iraq in 2003; support for it has been garnered on the basis of fear and intimidation, denying the freedom of thought to the majority sub-set of Americans: "We cannot wait for the final proof. It could come in the form of a mushroom cloud;"[6] and "either you are with us or you are with the enemy." By these pronouncements of the controllers of thought, Americans were transformed to the status of "rational fools," their freedom of thought repressed by an administration bent on invading another country in pursuit of capital accumulation and power (Chang, 2008). More egregiously, it was, as testified to by the British Ambassador to the United Nations, Sir Jeremy Greenstock, to a British government inquiry into the Iraqi war in 2009, largely contrived by a Bush administration "hell bent."[7]

Consider next, former Secretary of the Treasury, Henry Paulson's, request to Congress for US$750.0 billion bail-out funds. In suggesting that the Congress approves his proposal for US$750.0 billion to rescue the financial system (discussed in Chapter Two) without any oversight, legal recourse, or accounting for how and where the money is spent, he effectively treated the American tax-payers as "rational fools." Many observers saw this proposal as seeking to bene-fit the intellectual capitalist class at the expense of tax-payers, and as reim-bursement for taking risk necessary to keep the US on top of the heap in the capitalist world-economy. Indeed, earlier reports that the Bush administration overpaid the banks and deceived the American people with respect to the sol-vency of them have been confirmed in the report issued by the Inspector General appointed to look into the matter.

Consider further, the efforts of banks and credit card companies to enhance their revenue streams. "Free checking" came into being not because banks wanted to offer their customers a free service for opening a bank account with them. Rather, it was offered, according to its innovator, Shailesh Mehta, *a priori* enhancement to bank revenue, and, as such, a trap for those who are less able—less disciplined, if you will—to manage their financial transactions on a daily basis. Banks, according to Mehta, benefit not only from the increase in the use of bank checking accounts but also from the overdraft fees they can legally charge for each transaction that is in excess of the customer's bank balance. As Mehta characterized it:

> As long as I'm in compliance with what the government says, it's none of any-body's business to tell me what to do. That's the kind of mind-set with which some people work. . . . You make the stupid laws, I'll comply, and I'll make money. . . . Tell me the rules, and then I'll outsmart you all.[8]

Overdraft fees have been a significant source of revenues for the 16 largest banks since the invention of the debit card. According to a July 2009 Consumer Federation of America survey, many banks now process debit-card purchases, even though the amount of the purchase is more than the balance in the cus-tomer's bank account. To be sure, debit card transactions are outside the scope of 2009 legislation passed ostensibly to protect consumers against predatory lending by banks and credit card companies. Indeed, banks are still able to charge between $25.00 and $35.00 for every debit-card transaction in excess of the customer's bank balance,[9] notwithstanding its predatory characteristics.

In terms of our relationships with others, then, we increasingly engage in subdividing humans in levels that allow us to control their behavior to our ad-vantage. In the extreme, such sub-division provides the basis to hate what we are not, and to marginalize or dehumanize others who are perceived as threatening to the capitalist world-economy, both within and without. To this end, the ten-dency is for the dominant sub-set to recruit others to its cause as noted above. Indeed, Immanuel Wallerstein's (1999: 22) perception of a "pan-European ra-cism—the White man's burden, the civilizing mission, the Yellow Peril, a new anti-Semitism—that served to incrustate the European lower strata" continues as an all too familiar tool of the powerful in a Western-dominated world, even in the twenty-first century. In this latter regard, it is telling of human emotional fragility that subjects of earlier civilizing missions—Manifest Destiny, if you will—are now absorbed mind, body, and soul in the civilizing mission perpetrated by their masters in pursuit of the means to wealth accumulation in foreign lands. In this connection, such behavior speaks not to individual or societal achievements but rather to the extent to which the majority sub-set is conveniently reduced to the status of "rational fools," unable—not by choice but rather by intimidation and psychological manipulation—to truly differentiate their self-interest from that of their handlers.

The above described approach is no less true in our everyday activities, such as competitive sports and in the workplace, than it is in wars with other cultures; it is just a matter of degree. Hence, the other person or team is always cast in derogatory terms on or off the field, or in or out of the workplace. As a result, Black Americans and other minorities are still not accepted on equal terms in America and, as the sub-prime mortgage crisis revealed, are subjected to exploitation in keeping with the prevailing reductionist ethos. Indeed, that the government continues to classify Americans according to ethnicity and race speaks to the need to monitor the effectiveness of the Civil Rights Act, 1964, and other policies aimed at redressing inequality in the US even after four decades of monitoring.

More callously, at an international level innocent civilians are killed by unmanned armed drones in far away lands because they have been reduced to a level that allows for the remote drone operator to regard them as lesser beings, and to go home and have dinner with his or her family after a kill; their otherness permits them to be classified as either enemies or potential enemies. This observation finds support in the contrasting approach to seeking out and killing or capturing "IRA terrorists" in Northern Ireland; the Irish Catholics, even though they were suspected of harboring IRA fighters or were themselves potential IRA fighters, were still regarded as human beings; they spoke the same language, ate the same food, drank from the same well; indeed, they were cut from the same cloth as the Protestant Irish—kith and kin—and that made for greater respect in their treatment. On the other hand, seventy years ago, the reductionist ethos allowed for European Jews to be relegated to a status that led to six million innocent human beings murdered in cold blood.

Rationalism and reductionism are thus interconnected and mutually reinforcing in the modern world. As such, abstracting from the cruelty in the extremes of human rationality cited above, everyone in the West is affected by either or both; and most people indulge to varying degrees in both. To be sure, both rationalism and reductionism provide the framework of our modern Western political and economic systems and thought processes: "I think, therefore I am" evidences both rationalism and reductionism; combined, they form the basis by which subjective ideas of self-interest are pursued both as a shield and as a sword.

By advocating freedom and democracy through the idea of human rationality, individualism as a human right is further generalized by those who seek to pursue their self-interest through others. In this pursuit, rationalism and reductionism inform subjective ideas about human rights, and manifest most powerfully in notions of self-fulfillment and choice primarily because there is more to be gained from their advocacy, especially in politics and economics. Hence, the greater the perceived benefit to be derived from promoting individualism as a human right to the wider world, the greater the intensity of the advocacy, even to the point of subversion. Be that as it may, despite these obvious perverse applications of the concepts, self-determination and choice underscore the mandate of the United Nations Commission for Human Rights (UNCHR) and, as such, reach deep into the fabric of other cultures; good intentions, to be sure, but it calls to mind one of Aesop's fables of a black child that was placed in a tub and scrubbed until he died, because he was thought to be dirty. For many cultures, then, the exercise of America's "moral authority" is as uninformed and misguided as the belief that if you are not white, you are dirty.

Human rationality has given rise to approaching the study of economic transactions in terms of "rational behavior" of economic actors, with consumer choice determined on the basis of relative satisfaction between alternatives, which also includes spending or not spending. The empirical reality in the twenty-first century is that consumers, American consumers primarily, have never been more irrational in their behavior than presently. The first stimulus package of US$158.0 billion in March 2008 was proposed and signed into law entirely on the basis of the propensity of Americans to spend and the need for them, according to President George W. Bush, to "go out and spend." So ingrained is the idea of consumer-spending in US economic experience that the Treasury Secretary, Henry Paulson, boldly projected the creation of 600,000 jobs from such spending.[10]

Clearly, people as consumers, like the trees in a forest, are seen in terms of their individual contribution to the relentless accumulation of wealth by the intellectual capitalist class. To this end, the choices they make are essentially conditioned-responses to external stimuli—fear, shame, and the all-powerful greed—practiced as ideas for wealth transfer up the ladder in keeping with the reductionist ethos. Consider, for example, the marketing of the drug Fosamax by the pharmaceutical company Merck. According to an in-depth report by Alix Spiegel of *National Public Radio* (NPR) the less-than-expected sales of Fosamax as a treatment for osteoporosis was boosted by promoting the condition labeled "osteopina"—a naturally-occurring bone condition associated with growing old—as a precursor to osteoporosis, and the company's efforts to expand sales of Fosamax on the basis that osteopina requires medical treatment, more precisely the use of Fosamax.[11]

Equally telling is the observation by Harvard University's Michael Sandel that, if one paid attention to the advertisements on American television, one would come away with the idea that the crisis facing the country today is not the economic recession but erectile dysfunction.[12] More disquieting but just as telling, is the television commercial promoting *IKEA's* pre July 4, 2009 sale in which a female customer is shown shouting to her husband to "Start the car! Start the car!" as she runs away from the store. Why? Because she is portrayed to believe that the cashier made a mistake in registering the sale and that she should get away as quickly as possible before the mistake is discovered. It speaks to the extent to which social norms have been debased in the pursuit of self-interest.

Existentialism

In addition to rationality and reductionism which have their roots in the Enlightenment as discussed above, there is the influence of existentialism that gained significance in the mid 1960s. In fact, existentialism is taking rationalism and reductionism to their extremes in service to self and thus capitalism, with mind-altering ideas of selfishness, and the abandonment of social norms that have guided societies throughout the ages. Interestingly, the existential ethos gained momentum at a time recognized by Immanuel Wallerstein as marking a world-wide revolution in the modern world-system.

As I see it, then, our contemporary dilemmas reside in the changes to our perceptions of self—as evidenced by our self-serving interaction with one another—as evolved since the 1960s and, as noted above, in an incentive system for wealth creation that is predicated on human rationality and, as we have witnessed in the last decade, increasingly on the perversity anchored in the existential ethos. More significantly, the economic prosperity enjoyed by Americans in the 1950s and 1960s—derived primarily from the absence of international competition and from the rebuilding of Europe in the late 1940s and 1950s—fostered a new American-centric perception that focused on individual rights and liberties at home—for Blacks, it was equal but separate—and, of course, a revival of notions of Manifest Destiny vis-à-vis other cultures.

This new perception of self provided the impetus for Sartre's existential ideas to thrive and to permeate thought; ergo Ayn Rand. As a result, the general tendency is to engage in spurious ideas of freedom to reengineer oneself, to alter the environment, and to convert other cultures to our subjective image of an ideal society by way of condign power; proselytizing freedom and democracy in convenient self-serving fashion as part of the American foreign policy experience while rationalizing the inherent contradictions in the simultaneous embrace of capitalism, which, as discussed above, is synonymous with selfishness and greed. Hence, in addition to some exogenous factors beyond our control—such as the oil shocks of the 1970s—most of the changes to our perceptions after the 1960s can be attributed to the abiding conflict inherent in pursuing a sociopolitical and socioeconomic system premised on the impossible combination of capitalism and democracy that increasingly manifests in self-absorption and at the expense of holism, and, more egregiously, income inequality.

Self-absorption in the 1960s gave birth to intellectual capitalism which thrives on its perceived fail-safe model of risk management, constructed not as a mathematical certainty but rather in the certainty of bailout by the government as a prisoner to the capitalist ethos. Moreover, this new class of capitalist as represented by hedge funds, either as stand alone or as wealth-creating enhancements to commercial banks and insurance companies, were allowed to operate outside the regulatory framework with a nod and a wink from regulators and legislators; regulatory capture was complete with the passage of the Gramm-Leach-Bliley Act, 1999, that finally removed the vestiges of over 60 years of regulatory oversight provided by the Glass-Steagall Act, 1933.

As to the assertion that moral hazard is not accidental to the unregulated new economic model but rather crucial to it as argued in Chapter Two, consider the testimony of the current Secretary of the Treasury and former governor of the New York Federal Reserve Bank, Timothy Geithner, to the Senate Banking Committee on June 18, 2009. According to Secretary Geithner, his plans for designating the largest financial institutions as "Tier One Financial Holding Companies" allow for limiting their risk-taking and for their break-up should they pose a threat to financial stability if they failed; also, his plans taken together, would "help mitigate the *inherent moral hazard* risks in any system that comes from emergence *of large institutions* [emphasis added]." By implication, then, "too big to fail" was not accidental but rather a consequence of unregulated capitalism promoted by the FED and Congress, with those practicing the new-found freedom to become large institutions deliberately incorporating moral hazard as strategy in their quest for greater wealth accumulation. Indeed, the rescue of LTCM by the New York Federal Reserve Bank in 1999 lend credence to the notion of "too big to fail" as strategy.

The Empirical Reality

As a result of a slow and lengthy process of conditioning in the twentieth century, evidence of changes to our thinking and value-system abounds in varying forms in almost all aspects of our social, economic, and political interaction in the twenty-first century. While some of these changes have been gradual and are considered normal to societal development and, therefore, are not the subject of this critique, most have resulted from conscious efforts to manage thinking and behavior toward a particular outcome, in this case, self-fulfillment however irrational, in furtherance of the endless accumulation of capital.

In terms of the latter, many such changes are anchored in postmodernist ideas inculcated as knowledge at prestigious tertiary educational institutions and reinforced by a growing number of "think-tanks" and "talk shows" as the anointed guardians of intellectual capitalism. However, stripped of their intellectual garb, most of these guardians derive significance from the shallow pursuit of self-interest both within and without, while others have been motivated by a false sense of freedom surreptitiously infused into public consciousness by those who stand to benefit; almost all indulge in redefining issues or reframing questions so as to provide scripted answers or, in the case of the sophisticated, tease out answers that validate their narrowly conceived perspectives.

With respect to the infiltration of existential ideas in our educational system, consider the theoretical construct of the "Pareto-liberty conflict" offered by Amartya Sen (2004: 387). The example of the "work-choice case" of two competing individuals as illustrating choice is telling to the extent that preference is perceived not exclusively in productive terms but rather more in destructive terms as suggested by these two sentences:

> But, spoiled as they are by the *competitive society* in which they live, each *prefers* that the other be jobless. . . . Indeed, each is green-eyed enough to *get more fulfillment* out of the joblessness of the other than from his own job [emphasis added].

What is significant in Amartya Sen's example of the Pareto-liberty conflict is that it is not a representation of his personal perspective but rather an observation of human rationality that evolved since the 1960s and found its way into the literature as acceptable social choice theory.

Clearly, as illustrated by Sen, winning, "as the only thing," has been superseded by the existential notion that greater fulfillment can be had from ensuring the failure of one's competitor. It thus demonstrates the extent to which perversity has permeated the reasoning process in the West, particularly in the US, in the last quarter of the twentieth century. By extrapolation, postmodernist sense of fulfillment comes not just from winning but more from ensuring that one's competitor fails. Hence, the idea that you get more fulfillments from the misfortunes of your competitor promotes the notion that you can construct a model and measure success on how well you were able to orchestrate the demise of a person, family, community, or country. For many, such a model is preferred to engaging in a head to head competition, which is often more costly in terms of time and resources; it is what the perverse aspect of market efficiency as generalized since the 1980s is all about; it is the basis of the new economic model premised on aggressive capitalism; it is what covert subversive activities at all levels, internal and external, are predicated upon.

Substantive Existentialism

America's early enthrallment with individualism blossomed into a national pursuit couched in terms of "freedom of choice" and "virtue in selfishness" since the late1960s. The ideas of existentialism perpetrated in the US by Ayn Rand during this period became increasingly influential on behavior with respect to self, to family, and to community, and gave birth to the "Me generation." More than that, such ideas marked the bifurcation between old and new: the counter-culture revolution of the 1960s. Whether or not Ayn Rand would have endorsed the extremes to which her ideas have morphed in the twenty-first century is open to debate; I very much doubt that she would have; she probably would have subjected her ideas to closer scrutiny. Be that as it may, the empirical reality is that traditional values are now cast as anathema to the pursuit of self-fulfillment, to be destroyed in the remaking of the world to an existential ethos. In this reality, such destruction evidences the dark side to human rationality.

Clearly, the dark side to human rationality is the inevitable expansion—not extrapolation—of Ayn Rand's argument in support of selfishness which, I contend, she did not think through fully: As interpreted by extremists, it is not only okay—virtuous, according to Rand—to not jeopardize your own life in attempting to rescue a drowning person if you cannot swim but also equally acceptable that you should not throw a life-line to the drowning person if that person is your arch-competitor whose demise provides you with greater fulfillment. While there are still many who would consider such an idea immoral, in the larger scheme of things, morality is a constraint to wealth accumulation; and America is committed to wealth accumulation, body, mind, and soul, even as it tenuously if not pretentiously clings to a value-system informed by the morality of its Founding Fathers.

In support of the above contentions, consider first, the Tonya Harding-Nancy Kerrigan incident in 1994, in which Harding conspired to injure Kerrigan in the final round of the Women's US figure-skating championship. Based on the "work-choice case" example quoted above, it is not unreasonable to suppose that Tonya Harding's choice was motivated not necessarily by her desire to win the championship but rather because there was greater fulfillment to be had from ensuring that her rival, Nancy Kerrigan, not win.

There is, of course, no denying that Tonya Harding wanted to win, driven as she was by the prospects of untold riches that attend winning the figure-skating championship. But since there was no guarantee of winning—falling on the ice or missing a triple-toe loop were ever-present risks—she took the path of least resistance because fulfillment from Kerrigan not winning was guaranteed and calculated to be the least-cost option. Whether she actually did or did not engage in such thought-processes is immaterial; what matters is that this perverse aspect of human rationality has entered our personal and business decision-making processes and has become integral to game-theoretic modeling, destroying the foundation of integrity and trust as a consequence. Hence, Tonya Harding should not be judged by society as harshly as her crime suggests. Rather, it is the perverse value-system within which she was brought up that should be questioned: Harding merely acted out what existentialism, the prevailing American philosophy, is all about.

Much in keeping with the Harding-Kerrigan incident of 16 years ago is the incident between George Hincapie of team Columbia HTC and, according to Hincapie, his former team-mate Lance Armstrong of team Astana, and team Garmin Slipstream at stage 14 of the 2009 *Le Tour de France*. Hincapie was the presumptive yellow jersey for most of the race but, with ten kilometers to go he was chased down by the Peloton led by his ex-team mates in Garmin Slipstream and by Astana who did not want him to win the yellow jersey. It matters not that no one on either the Garmin team or on the Astana team had any chance of getting close to winning the yellow jersey on that day—the yellow jersey was in the Peloton—unless something happened to the holder; they just gained greater fulfillment from preventing Hincapie from winning the yellow jersey as a member of a different team. Also, given that both Lance Armstrong and his team director were at the time expected to head up a Radio Shack team at the 2010 *Tour de France*, it would not help the sponsorship if an American other than Lance Armstrong were to wear the yellow jersey. Moreover, George Hincapie was Armstrong's *domestic* in the hay days of the seven time winner of the *Le Tour de France*.

Contrast the above incident with the results of stage 17 of the Tour. The Schleck brothers, Andy and Frank, lived up to expectation and made the last stage in the Alps a memorable one for the yellow jersey, Alberto Contador, who staved off brilliant attacks by the Schleck brothers. In honor to Frank Schleck, who was credited for doing most of the work up the mountains, and whose valiant efforts the yellow jersey clearly wanted to honor, Alberto Contador proposed to Andy Schleck that they should not challenge Frank for the stage win. It is noteworthy that the Schlecks are from Luxemburg and Alberto Contador is from Spain.

Consider next, the relationship most Americans now have with their parents or grandparents since the counter-culture revolution; most no longer consider it an obligation to take care of the aged parent or grandparent at home. Home care has become inconvenient to two-income households and to those who found caring for the aged distracting to their pursuit of self-fulfillment. As such, the aged are hived off to nursing homes and assisted living facilities that thrive on promoting such external care. Thus, a new service industry grew out of this "need" for external care for the elderly, as did providing for such care by way of long-term care insurance; both helped provide impetus to US economic growth.

Similarly, television has become the babysitter and mentor to latch-key children whose parents must work at two or more jobs just to avoid the scorn heaped upon them by advertisers whose function is to either make them feel guilty, shameful, or inadequate if they do not acquire and display the trappings of the American dream. At the same time, children become captive to enhanced-marketing business models and, again, serve to reinforce the notion of market triumphalism and wealth accumulation through the promotion of consumerism.

Still at the level of the individual, consider further, the act of donating blood to a blood bank. Whereas before it was an altruistic act by one human being towards another to give blood, it has now been reduced to the level of a tradable commodity to which a price is attached in the brave new world of modern capitalism. Blood banks are not just another market; they are another source of wealth accumulation for the intellectual capitalist class, and a source of income for the economically-disadvantaged.

Self-interest and Politics

It is not only at the level of the individual that the dark side to human rationality is revealed. Consider the response by former Republican Speaker of the House,

Newt Gingrich, to President Obama's nomination of Judge Sonia Sotomayor for the US Supreme Court. In labeling Judge Sotomayor a "racist," Newt Gingrich arguably gets greater fulfillment from resorting to this destructive option than from suggesting an alternative candidate; it matters not that her alleged racist comments were made in 2001, and at a time when Newt Gingrich could have objected to her appointment as Appeals Court Judge. Hence, the question: Why now in 2009? Clearly, it is not because the honorable and distinguished Judge deserves such a label; rather, it is because her nomination and later confirmation as Justice Sotomayor at this particular point in time in US history represents the triumph of "Other" over the established existential order. Newt Gingrich's attack on Judge Sotomayor evidences a realization that, in terms of the appropriateness and survival of existential ideology, it is a question of time and space: the former limited and counting down; the latter rapidly contracting.

It is instructive that Newt Gingrich's is not alone in his attack on Judge (now Justice) Sotomayor. In denying Judge Sotomayor his vote at the confirmation hearing, Senate Republican leader, Mitch McConnell, cites the judge's eight year old comment as the basis for his decision, and accuses her of making the nominating process "racist" by such a comment, albeit eight years after.

Consider further, the Presidential campaigns at the turn of the twenty-first century and since. Few would disagree with the observation that the preferred mode of political campaign has changed from emphasizing the positives of the candidates to one premised on character assassination of the opposing candidate. Again, as the "swift-boating" of Senator John Kerry in 2004, and the attempt in 2008 to create a link between "Obama" and "Osama" evidenced, the objective was not to win but rather, to ensure that neither Senator Kerry nor Senator Obama wins; in the case of Senator Obama, it was taken to the point of making the most egregious accusation ever in a political campaign: "He associates with terrorists . . . . "What do we do with him?" Clearly, deliberately seeking to destroy the opponent's—in this case, a black American—personal and professional credibility, was the Republican political campaign preference constructed in a framework that was premised on existential ideology narrowly defined in the extreme. It is what has come to define politics in America in the twenty-first century, even among "friends."

In the brave new world of twenty-first century American politics, then, fulfillment thus comes increasingly from destroying one's opponent than from highlighting one's own achievements; such is the warping effect of the existential ethos. In this connection, Newt Gingrich's pronouncement at a Republican Party fund raiser in June 2009 that President Obama's plans to rescue the economy "has already failed" is telling. Equally telling is the accusation by House Minority Leader, John Boehner, that President Obama has a "radical agenda . . . to bury our children and the middle class under a mountain of debt," while actor John Voigt labeled the president a "false prophet" for his valiant attempt to restore America's integrity and respect around the world. These negative pronouncements are motivated not out of concern for the majority of Americans but rather by self-interest and are designed to destroy the Obama presidency at the expense of truth and the economic wellbeing of the US and its growing minority; they evidence the destructive forces of an ideology that has no place in a pluralist society or world. They further evidence the extent to which the US has become a haven for ambitions long considered dangerous for evil; and, in this, mark the beginning of implosion. To this latter point, it is noteworthy that the superpower that was Rome in 100AD benefitted ordinary Romans; the superpower that was America after 1994 benefitted a sub-set—the intellectual capitalist class—as evidenced by the growing income inequality gap between the lowest 20 percent and the highest 20 percent of American households (Table 6.1).

If Newt Gingrich and other members of the Republican Party were the purveyors of existential ideology in the US in the twenty-first century, former British Prime Minister, Margaret Thatcher, must be regarded as the primary force behind the destruction of a value-system that had been essentially premised on social cohesion in Britain prior to the 1980s. In proclaiming the demise of society vis-à-vis individualism in Britain in 1987, the traditional social order premised on family and community that existed for generations was sacrificed for wealth accumulation by a sub-set of Britons in keeping with notions of free-market capitalism. Indeed, according to the then Financial Secretary of the Treasury, John Moore (1986), it was the way to grow the British economy, to stimulate the competitive juices, even among kith and kin, and, of course, to ensure Mrs. Thatcher an extended stay at Number 10 Downing Street.

Mrs. Thatcher, it should be noted, was not alone in this thinking. Across the Atlantic, similar changes to the American socioeconomic system were being contemplated by an American President that long entertained a dislike for communal efforts. Thatcherism and Reaganomics were essentially one and the same; both trumpeted the efficiency of free-market economics and capitalism; both sought to destroy the support base of their respective political oppositions. In terms of the latter, trade unionism suffered its biggest blow under Margaret Thatcher in Britain and under Ronald Reagan in the US. At the same time both countries began to push through privatization of state-run or state-controlled enterprises, not only within their own countries but also around the world through their surrogates the IMF and World Bank: In Britain, the mantra was bringing market discipline to bear on state-owned enterprise whilst in the US, it was reducing the size of big government; both were anchored in self-interest and individualism, ergo Prime Minister Margaret Thatcher's pronouncement on the nonexistence of society.

With privatization firmly entrenched as policy in Britain, many of the state-owned and controlled enterprises were sold off at below market valuation as a way of creating a "new enterprise class" of voters favorable to the British Conservative Party ideology and to Mrs. Thatcher as its leader. In the US, deregulating state-regulated monopolies and the introduction of competition premised on the efficiency of the market found equal support from those who stood to benefit from the process. As such, between 1984 and 2000, the telecommunications, road transportation, energy, and financial services sectors were *de facto* deregulated, not entirely by specific Acts of Congress but rather, by the increasing laxity in enforcing existing regulation; both regulators and lawmakers turned a blind eye to transgressions, especially in the financial services sector, the fastest growing sector of the US economy.

Self-interest and International Relations

Situating international relations in a framework of existentialism instead of one premised on international law and organizations, leads necessarily to paranoia and international conflicts. In such a framework, a country is compelled to be ahead of the game and must seek to contain another's economic, military, and other development (see Huntington 1996: 312); it is for this reason that the US sees itself as being under constant attack from others; the fear of others developing the capability of defending themselves induces paranoia at a national level.

This existentially-derived imperative to contain other state actors necessarily results in the destruction of international unity commonly thought to be necessary for the formation of peaceful communities, and international standards premised on law and justice by which to adjudicate between competing interests. Indeed, as observed by John Rawls (1971: 128), interstate relationships are governed by the need to uphold the notion of sovereignty rather than individual rights and freedom. Hence, no external state can bring freedom and democracy to the peoples of other states without violating their sovereignty.

More significantly, in imposing on others a value-system rooted in existential ideology, those labeled "Other" are automatically presumed to have ill-intentions unless they can prove they harbor no ill-will; they must prove a negative or be dealt with condignly, and, as discussed in Chapter Three, preemptively. These are not my rules; rather, they are the empirical reality of America's self-ordained right of preemption in international relations in the twenty-first century after 9/11 (see Suskind, 2006: 76; Ikenberry, 2004: 321); they also portend military conflicts in the twenty-first century as sovereign states exercise their right to defend.

In terms of international economics relations, self-interest predominates to the exclusion of notions of fairness and international agreements. This is especially true in periods of economic downturns when every country finds itself in a condition of rising unemployment. Consider, for example, the imposition of "new punitive tariffs on all car and light truck tires coming into the United States from China."[13] According to a ruling by the US International Trade Commission, "a rising tide of Chinese tires into the U.S. hurts American producers" and, therefore, entitles the US to unilaterally impose tariffs to protect American workers. This argument is not dissimilar to that of the U.S. Congress House Committee on Energy and Commerce (1985: 85) in the run up to imposing stiffer restrictions via MFA IV on the importation of textile and clothing from China:

Apparel produced in countries with abysmally low living standards and virtually
no workers rights threatens living standards in this country and destroys badly
needed employment opportunities for our low-skilled workers.

In a similar vein to the US argument for the imposition of tariffs on tires from
China, the EU's Competition Commissioner, Neelie Kroes, felt obliged to warn
Germany that "State support should not be subject to noncommercial conditions
such as the location of investments and restructuring measures," with respect to
General Motor's proposed sale of Opel GMBH.[14]

Consider next, the basis for complaints filed by the US and EU in June
2009 against the Chinese government's imposition of an export tax on raw materials it considers harmful to the environment. According to the complaints, such
export tax amounts to an unreasonable restraint of trade, asserting a presumed-
right to access China's natural resources for their respective home industries
under WTO rules. What is curious about this complaint by the US is that its own
economic stimulus package announced by the government and passed by the US
Congress two months earlier contains a "buy American" clause that, by any and
all standards, contravenes the spirit and letter of WTO rules. It is therefore possible that China's imposition of an export tax on certain raw materials was in
retaliation and a direct challenge to the US "buy American" policy: it certainly
forces the WTO to address both issues in tandem. In other words, WTO's decision on one of the issues cannot be made in isolation of the other.

Yet another example of self-interest and perceived hegemony is the US reaction to the Chinese government's requirement for personal computers sold in
China to be equipped with filters—Green Dam—against pornographic materials
accessible on Western search engines such as Google. Not unexpectedly, and for
reasons not entirely economic, this filtering requirement premised on protecting
Chinese children and culture from the perceived debasing influences of "lewd
and vulgar content" easily accessible on Western search engines has been criticized by the US Secretary of Commerce, Gary Locke, whose office has called
for its revocation.[15] According to US Trade Representative, Ron Kirk: "Mandat-
ing technically flawed Green Dam software and denying manufacturers and *consumers* freedom to select filtering software is an unnecessary and unjustified
means to achieve that objective, and poses a serious barrier to trade" [emphasis
added].

There is no denying the honesty of Ron Kirk's belief in the freedom of
manufacturers and consumers to select filtering software in the US. But, as we
are so often reminded by the Chinese and others, when we seek to impose our
value-system onto them, it is usually in pursuit of our self-interest, not theirs. It
is our arrogance, or more likely, greed that seemingly blinds us to this as a possibility. Moreover, many traditional societies regard the American value-system
as shallow and still evolving as evidenced by an *Associated Press* report that the
US Congress is considering a Bill that would impose broad new rules on Web
sites and advertisers. According to the report: "too many people [Americans]
have no idea that Internet marketers are tracking their online habits and then

mining that data to serve up targeted pitches – a practice known as behavioral advertising;"[16] it is what the Chinese clearly do not want and are not quite ready for at this point in their reemergence.

In the same vein, Alan Greenspan's responses to questions on the current worldwide financial crisis quoted earlier speak to the extent to which existential ideology has permeated American business culture and governance at the highest level and, therefore, international economic relations. Countries doing business with the US are now required to read the fine print; evidence of yet another aspect of aggressive capitalism; you ignore the fine print at your peril, as Iceland and others doing business with American financial institutions have found out.

An earlier indication of Greenspan's thinking was had from his expressed position on and thus policy-approach as chairman of the FED to the 1997—8 Asian financial crisis. According to the then FED chairman, the Asian financial crisis was essentially limited to those economies that had over-extended themselves and was simply a matter of the financial market operating as the disciplinary mechanism in restoring balance, insisting that the hedge funds be allowed to follow through on their strategies even though to do so would harm others (the affected economies) in the process. As played out, the concern of the FED was in fact for the US money-center banks and hedge funds that were involved in currency speculation and were overleveraged in consequence.

At the same time, however, in addition to the official US position on the crisis, the Asian financial crisis was greeted as the triumph of Western capitalism over the Asian economic model by those who found fulfillment in orchestrating the near collapse of it. As played out, the fly in the ointment was the willingness of the Hong Kong government to intervene in the markets to the full extent of its foreign currency reserves which stood at about US$96 billion; and, given that sacrifice is not part of the existentialist equation, such intervention was regarded as interfering with the workings of the market; it elicited the ire of the FED chairman in consequence.

Greenspan's willingness to have certain other foreign economies collapse to prove a theoretical construct speaks volumes to his belief in and commitment to existential ideology, and to the shaping of US economic policy narrowly in the direction of self-interest during his eighteen-year reign as chairman of the FED. To this end, he mesmerized the US Congress with his iconic incoherence—if you understand what I am saying then I am not saying it right, he once remarked—while Wall Street and private equity fund managers could not have too much of it. As chairman of the FED, he was the proverbial fairy godmother of intellectual capitalism; and in these roles he was embolden to pronounce on the triumph of the American economic model as hedge funds and Anglo-American investment bankers extended their reach beyond national boundaries to a largely unsuspecting and financially-unsophisticated world; a world that still embraced the notion of trust and integrity.

Consider next, the notion of cap and trade with respect to carbon emissions reduction. The moral responsibility of every human being to reduce his or her carbon footprint has been negated by the idea of "Cap and Trade." Commoditizing the rights of every country to a certain level of carbon emission provides a loophole for the rich countries to evade their moral responsibility to reduce carbon emissions. This they can do by buying emission-rights from poorer less-developed countries on the spurious argument that the revenues generated benefit the poorer countries. But given the self-serving attributes of capitalism, giving cognizance to Virgil's refrain, *timeo Danaos et donna ferentes* (I fear the Greeks even when bearing gifts) would not go amiss. In accepting such payments, developing countries may well find that cap and trade serves to reinforce the development gap between rich and poor countries, and to keeping the center-periphery relationship in tact, as did the EU's ACP sugar protocol of 1974.

The center-periphery relationship has also served to provide an out to the moral responsibility of developed countries to accept refugees from other countries. As reminded by Harvard University's Michael Sandel, in his *2009 Reith Lectures*, many rich countries have found it beneficial to out-source their moral responsibility to accept a given number of refugees from poorer countries by the commoditization process. By such means, they discharge their responsibility by simply paying other countries—the economic-dependent—to accept refugees and or immigrants from a third country on their behalf. Again, the argument advanced in support of this arrangement is that the receiving countries benefit from the payment for taking in the refugees and from the talent many refugees bring with them. Be that as it may, it is no different from paying another country to accept toxic waste: a commercial practice that is just a step up from "donating" unwanted obsolete electronic equipment, the disposal of which would be excessively costly to the donor country.

Rationalizing Self-interest

In the light of this unbridled commitment to self-interest, how does one rationalize acts that offend nature, humanity, ethics, and even the perverted-self who must eventually come to grips with the idea of a *Dante's Inferno*? One answer, of course, is through process of human reason. Redemption comes not from God or from buying exemptions from the Church but from self-absolution through human reason. It becomes acceptable to explain away the invasion and occupation of Iraq as "liberation," and the killing of innocent civilians as "collateral damage" or as "the birth pangs of a new Middle East." In international economics, buying carbon-emissions rights on the market designed to avoid the moral responsibility of carbon-emission reduction is explained away as "benefitting the poorer countries," as discussed above. In domestic political affairs, denigration is rationalized as "tough campaign." But rationalization does not always offer redemption, not when there is the ubiquitous social conscience that soon or late compels public repentance.

In economic affairs, America's voracious appetite for the world's savings is couched in term of "the world over borrowed." Rationalized thus, it provides political cover for those engaged in the practice of external borrowing. But it also masks social and economic atrophy not unlike empires past, and, therefore, will not escape the annals of history for the concern is not about the official national debt that stood at $14 trillion at the end of 2009 but rather about the hidden debt burden of over US$54.0 trillion, or about 400 percent of GDP.

As argued above, existentialism as inculcated into the fabric of American culture has given rise to unprecedented greed, manifesting in the pursuit of instant gratification; it has given rise to avoiding responsibility perceived as encumbering to self-fulfillment, and to redefining the inconvenient questions. It has further give rise to relabeling, and to the abandonment of *mores*. But, as discussed above, there are consequences, many of them severe enough to threaten the very foundation of society-building. Those who are not endowed with the economic capacity or are denied help from the system often resort to a life of crime, again, in pursuit of what they are conditioned to believe as the American dream. Their failure is rationalized as deviant behavior to be punished by a system that is fundamentally intolerant of weakness.

Conclusion

As discussed above, reductionism facilitated the psychological technique of framing as a means to alter perception and thus choice. This form of psychological manipulation was perfected during the last quarter of the twentieth century and became endemic in the decision-making processes at all levels ever since. Thus, a new approach to and expression of individual freedom of choice evolved and became embedded into the American psyche in consequence; self-interest became an American pursuit, more overt and intense, especially in the 1990s and beyond.

In addition to reductionism, existentialism, like the Enlightenment, provided the final break with tradition and swiftly became an aspect of Anglo-American culture and beyond. Some observers point to the counter-culture movement as the early beginnings of self-fulfillment. More erudite observations identified the 1960s as giving birth to modernism, to cutting the shackles of Puritanism, and to classical liberalism that views individual humans as essentially autonomous. Selfishness was okay, indeed a virtue, according to Ayn Rand. Hence, individualism replaced community; self took precedence over family; the Nash equilibrium premised on Game Theory, itself a manifestation of framing, replaced Pareto–Optimality principle, the cornerstone of welfare economics; and human reasoning was elevated to the status of the sole path to truth and certainty. But, as argued above, not only did this new approach give further support to a culture of consumerism anchored in instant gratification, it also served as the basis for the relentless accumulation of capital at increasing costs in terms of fundamental values; it further underwrote the notion that "Greed is Good."

In terms of international relations, framing became the sole basis for approaches to inconvenient issues and for the removal of perceived constraints; it serves to reinforce the notion of certainty premised on unrivaled economic and military power, as evidenced by "Shock and Awe" in the case of the invasion of Iraq, and in seeking to correct trade imbalances by way of targeted revaluation, discussed in Chapter Eight. However, as the events of the first decade of the twenty-first century serve to remind us, certainty is no more a given than human reasoning is an infallible tool; only our arrogance allows us to think otherwise. Indeed, as Immanuel Wallerstein (1999, 250) sees it:

> In all these arrogances, we have betrayed first of all ourselves, and have closed off our potentials, the possible virtues we might have had, the possible imaginations we might have fostered, the possible cognitions we might have achieved.

NOTES

1. Sears, S. M., "The Fortunes of Reversal," The Striking Price, *Barron's Online*, August 3, 2009
   http://online.barrons.com/article/SB124907943942197981.html?ru=yahoo
   While many of these institutions have since repaid the government, many found it financially expedient and profitable to access such unprecedented low-cost funding. To be sure, many of them were able to declare record earnings as a result of the wide interest-rate spreads afforded by cheap government funds. To the extent that funding is fungible, a few TARP recipients were able to rescue their hedge-fund divisions by channeling some of these funds to them.
2. An 1881 conception of freedom expressed by T. Green and quoted by Sen (2002: 7)
3. Hess, P. "Report: Bush program extended beyond wiretapping," *Associated Press*, July11, 2009.
4. According to the Miami Coalition for the Homeless, Florida ranks number one as the meanest state to the homeless in the country, criminalizing homelessness in the process.
5. President Bush's televised broadcast, October 7, 2002.
6. Greenstock's statement http://www.iraqinquiry.org.uk/media/38479/sirjeremygreenstock-statement.pdf
7. "The Card Game," Frontline, *PBS.org*, http://www.pbs.org/wgbh/pages/frontline/creditcards/interviews/mehta.html. January 26, 2010
8. *Consumers report. org*, November 25, 2009
9. Aversa, J., "Paulson: Govt Will Act to Aid Economy," *Associated Press*, March, 16, 2008
10 Spiegel, A., "How a Bone Disease Grew to Fit the Prescription," All Things Considered, *NPR*, December 21, 2009
11. "Reith Lectures, 2009 – Markets and Morals," *BBC World Service*, June 9, 2009.
12. Loven, J., "US, China at odds over tire imports," *Associated Press*, http://finance.yahoo.com/news/US-China-at-odds-over-tire-apf164626163.html?x=0&sec=topStories&pos=main&asset=&ccode=, September 12, 2009
13. *Associated Press*, "EU warns against protectionism in Opel sale," http://finance.yahoo.com/news/EU-warns-against-apf-3667306394.html?x=0&sec=topStories&pos=1&asset=&ccode=, September 12, 2009
13. McDonald, J., "China accuses Google of spreading pornography," *Associated Press*,

25 June, 2009.
14. J. Tessler, "Congress weighs landmark change in Web ad privacy," *Associated Press,* http://finance.yahoo.com/news/Congress-weighs-landmark-apf-1258028143.html?x =0&sec=topStories&pos=2&asset=&ccode=, September 7, 2009

Chapter Six

The Abiding Tension between Capitalism and Equality

As argued in Chapter Five, the quest for greater wealth and self-fulfillment premised on rationalism and existential ideology dominated the US socioeconomic experience since the 1980s. As a result, I believe the growth experienced since then came at the expense of traditional social values and holism, thereby exacerbating the tension between capitalism and equality. This observation is premised on two ideas advanced by Immanuel Wallerstein (1999: 3). The first is that "an undemocratic system is one that distributes power unequally, and this means that it will distribute all other things unequally." The second is that a world system "cannot be democratic if it is not egalitarian since an inegalitarian system means that some have more material means than others and therefore inevitably will have more political power." In other words, democracy is not just about the right to vote; rather, it is a sociopolitical system that upholds equality substantively and not just in principle.

Capitalism, as we know, thrives on the relentless accumulation of wealth, and *de facto* distributes power, and thus wealth, unequally. It is therefore an inegalitarian system; and, by this definition, it is an undemocratic system. Hence, it is not accidental that there is a positive correlation between the increased role of intellectual capitalism in America and the UK, and the widening income inequality gap since 1975 (see Figures 6.1 and 6.2 below).

There is also a positive correlation between the relentless accumulation of capital and the increasing tension between democracy that, in theory, speaks to equality, and capitalism that, in both theory and practice, speaks to unequal distribution of wealth, power, and other material means. Indeed, since the passage of the Equal Pay Act, 1963—as an amendment to the Wages and Hours Act, 1938—the Civil Rights Act, 1964, and the Voting Rights Act, 1965, democracy in its broader definition of equality has been put to the test, with less than encouraging results for working-class Americans, especially Black and Hispanic Americans, as evidenced by the US Bureau of the Census data and the several indices of the United Nations (UN) quoted below.

Despite the elapse of more than thirty years since the passage of the three Acts mentioned above, minority Americans continue to lag the majority in terms of income, access to affordable healthcare, and education, as basic human needs, if only because of the existence of an asymmetric incentive system that favors capital accumulation. As observed by former President of Harvard University, Derek Bok, (1996: 90), "our practice of maximizing incentives by allowing high rewards for the successful has not managed to lift all Americans to levels of prosperity above those of citizens in other economies."

More importantly, in addition to not lifting all Americans to levels of prosperity above those of citizens in other countries, is the consequential eroding economic status of 80 percent of Americans—particularly the lowest 40 percent—relative to the highest 20 percent since 1980 (see Table 6.1). As shown in figures 6.3 and 6.4, the US has the greatest income inequality amongst the developed countries, and ranks below several smaller European countries on the UN's Human Development Index (HDI) as discussed below.

The increasing tension between capitalism and equality, or democracy broadly defined, could not have been more evident than during the 2008 Presidential campaign and since. To be sure, a line has been drawn in the sand by the Republican Party and its supporters with respect to government transfer payments to lower-income Americans, as evidenced by the new lows to which presidential campaign in America has sunk.

As well-documented in debates between Republican Senator, John McCain, and Democratic Senator, Barack Obama, any proposal made by Senator Obama to benefit the lowest 20 percent of Americans from a progressive tax system that would increase taxes on the highest five percent of Americans—the intellectual capitalist class—elicited charges of socialism by the McCain campaign and the Republican Party. Moreover, the extremes to which the Republican presidential campaign went in trying to prevent Senator Obama from winning the presidency serves to reaffirm the polarization of Americans along sociopolitical and economic ideologies: Republicans firmly committed to capitalism and thus accepting of inequality, whilst Democrats continue to press for social and economic equality and thus for income redistribution.

This polarization serves to confirm that as a result of capitalism, America has become more existential in the twenty-first century, and that equality is perceived by Republicans as anathema. Hence, conservative Americans, as represented by the Republican Party, approach democracy from a Socratic perspective, which is to reject populist values, questioning the idea of a shared value-system—the bedrock of Athenian democracy—as evidenced by Newt Gingrich's open embrace of a capitalist and imperial America, personified by the intellectual capitalist class, and reinforced in "tea parties." On the other side of the coin, is the Democratic Party's perspective that is premised on three things as equal rights: a reasonable income and safety-net for all; access to education for self and for one's children; and access to healthcare (Wallerstein, 1999:18). Despite these differences, both parties lay claim to democracy, with Republicans stressing freedom of choice whilst Democrats stressing equality; both, with very different perspectives on outcomes as reflected by the differences in policies between the Obama administration and its predecessor Bush administration.

While the Bush administration propelled individualism and capitalism to new heights between 2001 and 2008 with near-catastrophic consequences, President Obama, as the first Democratic president in the twenty-first century charged with the responsibility of picking up the pieces and of preventing a collapse of American democracy, is seeking to restore the idea of a shared value-system that was Athens'. However, as the debates over healthcare evidence, the bringing of such values to bear on policies at this point in time signals, for good or evil, the sooner emergence of a deeper divide, made inevitable in consequence of the contradiction between capitalism and equality. I say this on the basis that a free and fair market system is an oxymoron, as the discussion on capitalism above suggests, and on the empirical evidence offered below.

Income Inequality

In October 2008, the Secretary-General for Organization for Economic Co-operation and Development (OECD), Angel Gurría, observed: "Growing inequality is divisive. It polarizes societies, it divides regions within countries and it carves up the world between rich and poor."[1] The Secretary-General was clearly drawing from the data on the majority European countries in the 28-country OECD, with the UK standing out as the European country with the highest income inequality, second only to the US. In addition to increasing by seven percent over the last 20 years, income inequality in the OECD countries increased three fold among single-parent households over the same time period even though spending on family-oriented policies was three times more in 2008 than it was 20 years prior.

It is noteworthy that earlier studies have found that, whereas 20 percent of the people in the richest countries had 30 times the income of the poorest 20 percent in 1960, that multiple had increased to 74 times in 1997 (Wermuth 2003). Interestingly, the increasing inequality between rich and poor countries coincides with the changing value-system of the West, especially the US and UK; it was made more acute by the privatization imperative of the US and UK pursuant the Washington Consensus during the 1980s and 1990s (see Chang, 2006).

The indefensible increase in inequality between rich and poor countries elicited a changed approach to development funding at the World Bank in the late 1990s: from structural adjustments at all costs to treating with inequality as a moral imperative. This changed approach by the World Bank came about for three main reasons: the unrelenting criticisms of IMF/World Bank policies by developing countries' governments and activists; a substantial shift in governance—from authoritarian regimes to democracy, if only in name—since the

1980s; and because the privatization in developing countries had run its full course by mid 1990s (Chang, 2006).

From around the mid 1990s, therefore, the World Bank targeted its funding programs to empowerment of the poor, emphasizing redistribution of resources, equity, transparency, grassroots participation, and sustainability as primary elements of empowerment (Bank, 2006; Narayan, 2002; Bank, 2001/02: 77-81). Confirmation of this turnaround in Bank policy came in the form of the long-awaited acknowledgement by the then president of the World Bank, James Wolfensohn, which is, that, "reducing inequality is a question of morality."[2] Even then, inequality between rich and poor countries grew at an even greater rate in consequence of the boost generated by the relentless accumulation of capital under the George W. Bush administration. Indeed, Wolfensohn's successor, Paul Wolfowitz, sought to return the Bank to a mode that supports US economic and political agenda rather than poverty reduction in the Third World; his policies premised on the notion that there has to be some advantage to being a superpower brought him into conflict with the Bank's professional staff.

Income Inequality in the US

With respect to income inequality in the US, consider the data on income distribution between the periods 1975 to 2006 as shown in Table 6.1. According to data compiled from the US Bureau of the Census,[3] the distribution of income has become more unequal since 1975, especially between the lowest 20 percent of households and the highest 20 percent of households. As shown, the highest 20 percent of American households accounted for 50.5 percent of total income in 2006, compared with 43.2 percent in 1975 (an increase of 16.9 percent); during the same period the lowest 20 percent of American households experienced a decline from 4.4 percent to 3.4 percent—25 percent decrease—and this was in a period of economic growth. At the same time, the top five percent of households' share increased from 15.9 percent in 1975 to 22.3 percent in 2006 (an increase of 40.2 percent), evidencing the shift from a manufacturing-based economic model to one premised on financial market liberalization supported by a Republican Congress, a facilitating FED, and twenty years of Republican administration during the period 1981 to 2008.

Table 6.1
Percentage of Total US Household Income
by One-fifth segments and top 5 %

Year	Lowest 20%	Second 20%	Third 20%	Fourth 20%	Highest 20%	Highest 5%
1975	4.4	10.5	17.1	24.8	43.2	15.9
1980	4.3	10.3	16.9	24.9	43.7	15.8
1985	4	9.7	16.3	24.6	45.3	17
1990	3.9	9.6	15.9	24	46.6	18.6
1995	3.7	9.1	15.2	23.3	48.7	21
2000	3.6	8.9	14.8	23	49.8	22.1
2006	3.4	8.6	14.5	22.9	50.5	22.3

Source: Data taken from Bureau of the Census

Figure 6.1

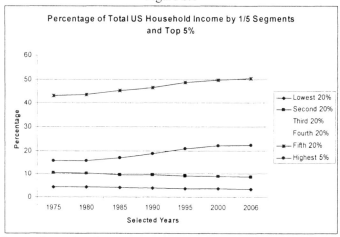

Source: Data taken from Bureau of the Census.

Perhaps more significant than the above data is that, of the 3.4 percent share of income attributed to the lowest 20 percent of American households, 75 percent of it comes from government transfer payments—unemployment benefits, social security, food stamps, other welfare programs, and the like. As such, any proposal to decrease taxes and simultaneously cut government transfer payments to this group, as pressed for by Congressional Republicans, would automatically increase the income inequality gap and poverty in America. Not surprisingly, then, in the era of Republican political dominance, both in Congress and the White House, the number of Americans living in poverty reached 37.3 million in 2007 compared with approximately 25.0 million in 1978 (an increase of 49.2 percent).[4] It is equally significant to note that between 1993 and 2000—the Clinton years—poverty decreased, albeit slightly, before increasing again during the George W. Bush administration, thereby evidencing the polarization of the American socioeconomic system along political ideology.

There are several explanations that are offered for this growing income inequality gap. Conservative economists suggest as primary the greater demand for highly-skilled workers in the information technology, financial services, and biotechnology industries; they further cite wage difference between college graduates and high schools graduates. While there is some measure of truth in these explanations, as can be discerned from Table 6.1 above, the trend nevertheless is for a decreasing share of the pie at all but the highest 20 percent of households and, more blatantly, at the highest five percent. Moreover, the Bureau of the Census data is positively correlated with the United Nations 2008 Report that shows growing income inequality in the US as measured by the GINI coefficient depicted in Figure 6.2. In addition to the above, as discussed in greater detail below, the drop-out rate for Americans entering tertiary education institutions is considerably higher than the OECD average as shown in Figure 9.1

Figure 6.2

Source: Constructed from UN Human Development Index, 2008

A more realistic explanation for the disparity in income is the growth in the financial services industry attendant deregulation in the 1980s and 1990s, and the rise to prominence of intellectual capitalism since the 1980s. Consider, for example, the bonuses paid out by the major "bank holding companies"— recipients of TARP funds—in 2008 even as the country struggles to emerge from the worst recession since the Great Depression. As reported, Citigroup—a recipient of US$45.0 billion of taxpayers' money as part of the government TARP program—paid out US$5.33 billion in bonuses in 2008, with 738 employees receiving at least US$1.0 million each, with another 124 executives receiving more than US$3.0 million each. Similarly, Bank of America, another recipient of US$45.0 billion of taxpayers' money, paid out US$3.3 billion in bonuses to 172 employees. JP Morgan-Chase & Co and Goldman Sachs & Co (both beneficiaries of the TARP program) made similar bonus payments in 2008 to 1,626 and 953 employees, respectively.[5]

The political response to what is now considered excessive bonus payments evidences shifting of responsibility from regulators and legislators onto corporate managers who, in reality, are simply complying with the mandate of a capitalist system—relentless accumulation of wealth—made abundantly clear by deregulation of the financial services sector; it is what a free market system—as opposed to a fair market system—is all about. It is, therefore, not that "they just don't get it," as charged by Senator Christopher Dodd, but rather that the consequences of an absence of foresight by legislators in approving deregulation of the financial services sector pursuant a falsely-conceived economic model came home to roost.

Another explanation for the income-inequality gap has been offered by Brink Lindsey of the CATO Institute. According to Lindsey, the disparity in income levels in the US is the result of the "inability or unwillingness of the lower income earners to take advantage of the opportunities offered by the US economy."[6] However, this is spurious argument from a societal development point of view. What Brink Lindsey fails to consider is that inequality on all levels is a direct consequence of aggressive capitalism; that the weak is inherently disadvantaged; and that the strong will always prevail in an environment that thrives on inequality. Indeed, aggressive capitalism contributes to poverty in the US primarily because of its dependency on a flow of cheap immigrant labor and on rationalizing the varying shades of discriminatory or antisocial practices inherent in a free-market system.

Lindsey also posits that the richest people in the world are the happiest people in the world. But, as observed by Samuel Johnson: "Poverty is a great enemy to human happiness; it certainly destroys liberty, and it makes some virtues impracticable and others extremely difficult."[7] Hence, where there is inequality, there is poverty and where there is poverty, human happiness is on hold. Moreover, a United Nations survey on happiness conducted in 2008 puts the Danish people, not Americans, as the happiest people in the world even though the Danish economy is much smaller than the US economy. Furthermore, Denmark, as shown in Figures 6.3 and 6.4 below, has the lowest income inequality of the European countries surveyed. Indeed, as shown in the World Development Indicators,[8] in 2000, the lowest 20 percent of the Danish people shares 8.8 percent of total income whilst the highest 20 percent shares 35.8 percent compared with 5.4 percent and 45.8 percent respectively for American households. More telling is that the highest 20 percent of income earners in the US earns more than the cumulative total of the lowest 60 percent—31.8 percent—by a sizable margin as depicted in Table 6.1.

Interestingly, the UK is shown as closely following the US, with the highest 10 percent of income earners accounting for 28.5 percent of total income in 2000 compared with 29.9 percent for the highest 10 percent in the US as shown in Figure 6.3. Furthermore, as shown in Table 6.1, the percentage for the highest 20 of income earners (44.0 percent) also exceeds the cumulative total of 33.5 percent for the lowest 60 percent of income earners. However, it should be noted that even though the UK experience closely tracks the US experience since the 1980s, the UK has had a more egalitarian approach to governance and continues to show some semblance of social justice in its socioeconomic policies, hence the call for a new economic system premised on "moral capitalism" by no less a person than the leader of the Conservative Party, David Cameron.

The difference between the two approaches to socioeconomic issues is also reflected in members of the British government taking exception to criticisms leveled at the British healthcare system by the American press and lawmakers. One such response came from British Prime Minister, Gordon Brown: "NHS [National Health Service] often makes the difference between pain and comfort, despair and hope, life and death. Thanks for always being there." Even the British Conservative Party leader, David Cameron, sought to distance himself from criticism of the British NHS in Europe and the US.[9]

In Germany, the corresponding income data are 22.1 percent for the highest 10 percent and 8.5 percent for the lowest 20 percent which puts it as having less income inequality than the UK as depicted in Figures 6.3 and 6.4 below. The German experience tracks closely with Sweden's whose numbers are 22.2 percent and 9.1 percent respectively (Figure 6.3). It is noteworthy that unlike the US, UK, and France, the proportion of total income for the highest 20 percent of income earners in Germany and Sweden does not exceed the cumulative total for the lowest 60 percent.

Figure 6.3

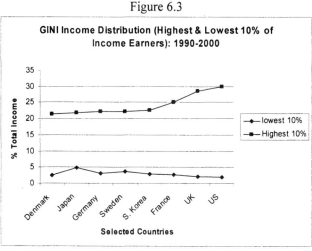

Source: Compiled from *World Development Indicators*. www.worldbank.org

Figure 6.4

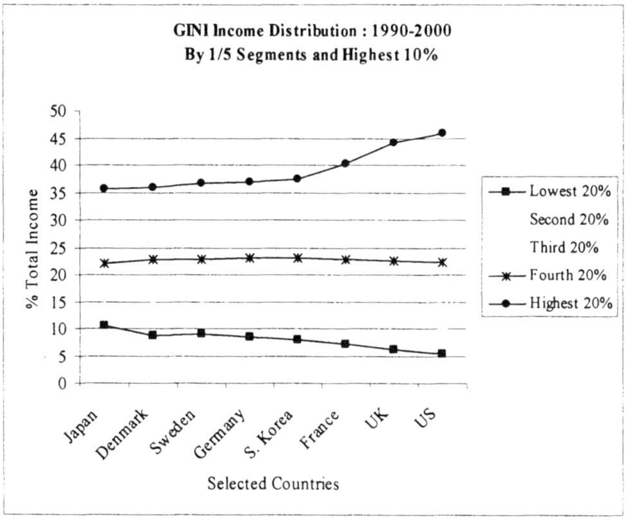

GINI Income Distribution : 1990-2000
By 1/5 Segments and Highest 10%

Source: Compiled from *World Development Indicators*. www.worldbank.org

Equally spurious, is the selective basis in the use of statistics on average household income which politicians are wont to quote as evidencing America's superiority. While the average household income in the US was amongst the highest in the world at US$ 66,570 in 2006, it masks the reality of inequality and the predatory predilection of aggressive capitalism even at the domestic level.

Based on the Bureau of Census data for 2006 quoted in Table 6.1, less than one-half (49.5 percent) of total income is shared by 80 percent of households in America. As such, the average household income for the 80 percent majority subset of Americans is considerably less than the national average of US$66,570. Indeed, with total households of 78.454 million in 2006, the average for the lower 80 percent (62.763 million households) is approximately US$41,606 or 37.8 percent less than the national average. For the upper 20 percent (15.691 million households), it is US$166,423 or approximately four times greater than the lower 80 percent. For the lowest 20 percent of households, the average drops to US$11,317 (a mere 17 percent of the national average or 6.8 percent of the highest 20 percent of households). Analyzed thus, the results speak to Derek Bok's observation, the GINI coefficient, the OECD's findings on inequality, and the speciousness of the national average household income.

Clearly, the US is not the only country in which there is unequal distribution of wealth and power. As would be expected, all countries comprising the capitalist world-economy have, to be sure, some measure of inequality. For example, as is so often raised by proponents of American capitalism, there is greater unequal distribution of wealth—in terms of ownership—in Sweden. Absent in this observation, however, is the greater need for ownership of income-producing assets in the US compared with Sweden, whose unequalled social safety-net in the West is a decidedly mitigating factor to asset-ownership; hence, the comparison in terms of asset-ownership begs the question. Moreover, such argument is an attempt to distract from the reality of income inequality in the US. For example, the OECD Report shows that, while on average, the richest 10 percent earns almost 9 times more than the poorest 10 percent in the sample countries as a group, it is over 15 times more in the US. As such, what is being stressed here is that, abstracting from the many developing countries in which the income-inequality gap between rich and poor is wider than in the US, the US has the highest level of inequality of the developed countries and, therefore, makes it more vulnerable to social disruption sometime in the future in keeping with Francis Fukuyama's (1999: 15) observation that: "A society dedicated to the constant upending of norms and rules in the name of increasing individual freedom of choice will find itself increasingly disorganized, atomized, isolated, and incapable of carrying out common goals and tasks."

The American Dream: The American Greed

The American Dream is a sponge phrase with multiple definitions and is often used interchangeably with "our way of life," yet another ambiguous phrase invoked by politicians in the absence of substance. For example, according to one perspective offered on the financial news network, CNBC, "the American dream is to be able to consume like Americans," our way of life, if you will; it is, according to the commentator, why so many foreigners want to come to America.

A less uninformed perspective is that the American dream is to be able to migrate from a status of having government transfers account for 75 percent of one's income, to becoming a member of the highest 20 percent sub-set of Americans with the ability to influence policy directly. It is the carrot that is kept dangling in the faces of new immigrants or would-be immigrants. Few, however, have been allowed entry into that elite sub-set. Hence, for the majority of new Americans and would-be Americans, the American dream, as with all dreams, is as illusive as winning the lottery; but it must be kept alive as an incentive to keep the economic wheels churning. The reality for most immigrants is that their lives are bound up either in misery or in working at two or more jobs just to be able to stay abreast with the financial costs of satisfying the habit of conspicuous consumerism acquired on the way to becoming American; more than that, despite the cost in human dignity and family values—rationalized as being the lesser of two evils for most immigrants—the American dream must be kept alive if capitalism were to be progressed at the preconceived pace.

Without low cost labor, high consumption, and foreign investments, American capitalism premised on the existential would be in terminal crisis. As it is, looking past rhetoric, the US is highly dependent on foreign investment capital flows; without such flows, unemployment will increase and would likely trigger social unrest if not total collapse of the existing sociopolitical structure. It is a conundrum that has been reinforced over time by being "Pareto-inefficient" in the pursuit economic growth at the expense of low-income earners and equality.

In the face of this dilemma, the FED Chairman, Ben Bernanke, in testifying to Congress, made the observation that "consumer spending [which accounts for 70 percent of GDP] is the mainstay of the American economy" and would have to be raised to a higher level to cover increases in the minimum wage rate approved by Congress. He further contends that entitlement programs account for 10 percent of GDP, and if maintained at its current level, tax revenues will have to be increased from 18 percent of GDP to 25 percent of GDP by 2030. Because of this, according to Bernanke, "the most direct way to address savings is to try and improve savings in the government sector,"[10] another way of suggesting a cut in government transfer payments to the poor and to educating the poor; and, effectively, another blow to bridging the income inequality gap.

Clearly, implicit in Bernanke's testimony to Congress is support for a reduction to entitlement programs, such as Medicare, social security, and other government transfers to the poor while sheltering high-income earners from an increase in taxes. But, as noted above, the lowest 20 percent of households in America receives 75 percent of its income in government transfer payments. Therefore, to reduce entitlement programs would add to the poverty statistics; it is a cost the FED Chairman either did not consider or was willing to incur in the name of capitalism.

Despite the risk of adding to the poverty statistics, like the lottery, there has to be some tangible evidence of the American dream; not only is it necessary to have standard bearers for those who must toil in the land of opportunity, it is vitally important to have such standard bearers serve as the beacon to new immigrants; their successes are celebrated and are held out as evidencing America as the land of opportunities. How else would the US be able to attract the hoards of new immigrants needed to toil at low-income jobs and to keep domestic consumption at the high rate envisaged by the FED chairman? How else would it be able to keep inflation in check and productivity rates high? How else would it be able to keep the "people" quiet, other than by sending them off to wars in foreign lands, if not by holding out the American dream? Yet, as clearly depicted in Table 6.1 and Figure 6.1 above, 60 percent of Americans are being left behind simply because the incentive system that supports relentless capital accumulation discriminates against them.

This is not to say that there are no genuine success stories of immigrants making it in America. Abstracting from the beneficiaries of Affirmative Action—itself a sad commentary on the notion of freedom and democracy—a good many immigrant-Americans have made it by dint of hard work and perseverance. Their successes are not to be belittled; neither should the achievements of those whose social programming—dehumanization in the eyes of many—over the generations was nothing less than unforgiving in human history. But being able to overcome poverty is not uniquely American, nor is it a license to decry those who have not been as fortunate, or indeed to belittle the efforts of those whose sacrifice made it possible for others to succeed. Lest we forget, the history of immigrant-Americans is largely a history of sacrifice for future generations.

To continue the myth of opportunity for all, many are wont to offer the inter-group movement among the income-classification segments shown above as an explanation; that is, lower income workers are migrating to higher paying jobs and are thus upwardly mobile. Plausible, but it does not explain the trending downwards in the share of total household income for 60 percent of the population unless, of course, we accept systemic discrimination as an aspect of capitalism. In other words, the majority of immigrant workers—the new American working class—is predominantly represented at decreasing lower income levels as depicted in Table 6.1 and, as such, adds credence to the rhetorical questions asked above. And, if systemic discrimination were an aspect of capitalism, then inequality must necessarily be a defining characteristic of capitalism. Extrapolating, the more aggressive is capitalism, the greater must be inequality within the framework of the capitalist world-economy. The data is telling.

Inequality: Good or Bad for Growth?

By any measurement, income inequality is highest in the US than in any other developed country, not because low-income earners are unwilling to take advantage of the opportunities offered by the US economy, as Brink Lindsey claims; rather, because of policy adherence to a concept that would have been better left in the context in which it was conceived. I am, of course, referring to Arthur Lewis's contention that inequality provides opportunities for investment and, therefore, good for growth (Lewis, 1955).

Clearly, Sir Arthur's notion turns on the savings-investments relationship as a tenet of theoretical economics of the time; it also turns on the idea that savings for investment comes necessarily from the higher income groups rather than from the lower-income earners whose propensity to consume is highest amongst income earners and whose consumption habits must be kept stimulated if capitalism were to be progressed as envisaged. In addition, cross-border capital flows were limited in the 1950s and, therefore, not considered a significant source of investment. Moreover, the myriad of legal restrictions imposed on foreign ownership and participation in the domestic economy in the US—banks, financial services, shipping, telecommunications, and oil refining, for example—add some theoretical substance to Lewis's contention since, in a condition of full employment—an assumption of orthodox economics—what is not consumed is saved and, therefore, available for investment; but the American economy is consumption-driven, and, therefore, savings is no longer treated as *a priori* economic growth; not when there are foreign savings to be harvested like wheat or corn.

However, given deregulation and the relaxation of restrictions on foreign participation in the US domestic economy during the last quarter of the twentieth century, Lewis's idea of an inequality-growth synergy lost currency. To be sure, with these restrictions removed, foreign investment became an important source of growth for the US economy. Additionally, given the political and economic stability of the US, foreigners became an increasing source of funding for the government budget deficits, especially under the George W. Bush administration.[11] The willingness of foreigner to finance both private-sector investments and government budget deficits not only transformed the US to being a giant vacuum cleaner of other countries' savings but also functioned as a perverse incentive for greater consumption.

Notwithstanding the above-mentioned eroding influences on Lewis's thesis over the years, the saving-investment relationship continues to provide a basic theoretical understanding of growth in a *closed* economy, which is still the dominant model for constructing economic theories. Outside of that relationship, however, it clearly has little or no significance, especially in context of the global economic system or indeed to reality. To be sure, a significant proportion of investments in US comes from foreign countries that not only have lower income per-capita but also less income inequality than the US. The US is now highly dependant on lower-income foreign countries to fund a substantial proportion of its growth as evidenced by this statement issued by the former Secretary of the Treasury, Henry Paulson: "We just want to make it very clear that we welcome foreign investment and it is vital to our economic strength going forward."[12] More than that, the US is now deeply dependent on other countries with lower per-capita income to fund its growing budget deficits.

Notwithstanding that Sir Arthur Lewis's thesis has lost currency in an era of cross-border investment flows and US dependency on investments from lower-income countries in a global economic framework, opponents to income equality continue to advance the argument of an equality-efficiency trade-off in its place. They hold firm to the notion that the incentive for both high-income and low-income earners to increase production would be taken away by any form of government redistribution, resulting in an equality-efficiency trade-off. Their argument is not dissimilar to the argument that there is a work-leisure trade-off predicated on the marginal tax rate. According to proponents of that theory, lower marginal tax rate would increase the opportunity cost of leisure in terms of work; people, they argue, would in consequence prefer work to leisure and vice versa.

But, just as the idea that higher marginal tax rates act as a disincentive to work, the equality-efficiency trade-off argument is not supported by the evidence; indeed both ideas speak to the nomothetic pretentions of economics in a largely existential socioeconomic system that has come to represent the capitalist world-economy. In reality, as we have witnessed over the last three decades, free-market capitalism seeks out ways to increase income and thus wealth accumulation even in an environment of high income taxes. Therefore, even if the marginal tax rate were 90 percent, current tax-havens and tax-loopholes provide enough of an incentive for the intellectual capitalist class to continue to create income; it is what aggressive capitalism is all about. Hence, despite the assertion by Republicans that the US has the highest marginal corporate tax rate compared with its competitors, the *effective* tax rate—which is what really matters—is considerably less than the marginal tax rate as a result of tax havens, tax breaks, and other incentives provided by a compliant Congress.

Also, when examined in the broader context of allocative-efficiency of resources—an important premise of utility maximization and profit maximization—the equality-efficiency trade-off argument is found wanting. In other words, if we accept the theory that increased demand for a product creates opportunities for economies of scale, it should follow that, by reducing income inequality, the demand for certain goods and services—albeit inferior goods—would be increased, thereby providing the incentive for large-scale production which should result in more efficient use of resources and lower prices to consumers. The Wal-Mart experience in securing supplies for its thousands of stores and the abundance of lower-priced products speak to this contention. Hence, rather than an equality-efficiency trade-off, it could be argued that there is an inequality-efficiency trade-off arising from greater equality.

In addition to the counter-argument offered above, consider the cases of Japan and South Korea from the perspective of growth. Japan remains the second largest economy in the world even though the lowest 20 percent of income earners account for 10.6 percent—almost double that of the US—of total income whilst the highest 10 percent accounts for 21.7 percent compared with 29.9 percent in the US, as shown in Figure 6.3. The data for South Korea are 7.9 percent and 22.5 percent respectively which makes it more egalitarian than the US. Nonetheless, both Japan and South Korea, indeed East Asia in general, in spite of their egalitarian leanings, experienced higher growth rates than either the US or UK. To be sure, as shown in Figure 4.1, the growth rate of East Asia was more than double that of the US and UK for the 1965–89 period. Indeed, also as shown in Figure 4.1, of the countries surveyed, the US and UK have the lowest average growth rates for the period 1965–89 even though for most of that time they pursued growth premised on inequality compared with the other countries surveyed. Thus the successes of both Japan and South Korea serve to make more spurious the argument that equality reduces the incentive for growth. Moreover, the Asian countries appear to have weathered fall-out of the 2007–08 financial crisis better than the Western countries primarily because of their greater equality.

Inequality and Human Development

The Human Development Index (HDI) is the internationally-accepted standard for measuring human development. It is an index that represents progress in terms of life expectancy, literacy, GDP per capita, and poverty reduction. Thus, access to healthcare, education, employment opportunity, and income inequality as measured by the GINI coefficient, are key components of the HDI.

Notwithstanding its position as the largest economy and the claim of being the most progressive in the world, the US, as depicted by the HDI, is behind several countries of lesser status. For example, the HDI for 2008 ranks the US at 15, below Iceland (1); Norway (2); Canada (3); Sweden (7); Japan (8); France (11); and Denmark (13).[13] The UK, in consequence of reactive-capitalism of the 1980s, is ranked 21. Two components of the HDI, the Human Poverty Index (HPI) and the Education Index (EI), are supportive of the overall ranking and are therefore discussed below in addition to healthcare issues.

Needless to say, there are those who would dispute the GINI coefficient as an accurate measurement of inequality on methodological grounds. Be that as it may, like the Consumer Price Index (CPI) as a measure of inflation, consistency in application in cross-country studies and in time series analyses makes the GINI coefficient as much an important and valuable indicator of human development as the CPI is an important determinant of real GDP.

Despite its shortcomings, the HDI is a reasonable basis for cross-country comparison since, with few exceptions, the criteria are consistent for all countries, although detractors would argue differently. Therefore, when taken in context of the discussion on income inequality above, the relative rankings of the selected countries are telling. For example, in terms of the GINI coefficient as a measurement of income inequality, for the year 2005 the US had a coefficient of 46.9 compared with a coefficient of 31.0 for the European Union (EU).

Poverty

On the Human Poverty Index (HPI) for 2007–08, the rankings are consistent with the HDI: Sweden (1); Norway (2); the Netherlands (3); Finland (4); Denmark (5); Germany (6); Canada (8); France (11); Japan (12); UK (15); and US (16). The relatively low ranking of the US is supported by the evidence that 37. 5 million Americans live in relative poverty in 2008. More telling than the absolute numbers is that 24.5 percent of Black Americans and 21.5 percent of Hispanic Americans live in poverty compared with 8.2 percent of non-Hispanic White Americans and 10.0 percent of Asian Americans.[14] These numbers are even higher than first thought as a result of a flaw in classification discovered in 2009.

Interestingly, the percentages for Black Americans and Hispanic Americans living in poverty are not far removed from those of many "Third World" countries. For example, the percentage of Black Americans living in poverty to say, India, when translated, is equivalent to 294 million Indians living in poverty; not far removed from the most quoted statistic of poverty in India, which is 300 million. Hence, 24.5 percent of Black Americans are in effect relatively no better off than 294 million inhabitants of India. More egregious, India makes no claims to being the greatest country in the world; also, its GDP per capita is a fraction of that of the US.

In contrast, the intellectual capitalist class comprising the highest 10 percent of Americans has no compunction in paying its members billions of dollars in bonuses from the taxpayer-funded TARP program, even as the country struggles to come to grips with a collapsed financial system and a recession of enormous consequences not experienced since the Great Depression. For example, Bank of America was fined US$33.0 million by the Securities and Exchange Commission (SEC) for misleading its shareholders regarding the payment of US$5.8 billion in bonuses to executives of Merrill Lynch as part of the agreement to acquire that firm.[15]

Evidently, the superior skills at extracting from others—the *raison d'être* of capitalism—by this group must be rewarded at any cost. Consider, for example the hiring of a division manager by Bank of America in the wake of the fine imposed by the SEC. Never before in the corporate history of American banks has a non-corporate officer—with no fiduciary responsibility to shareholders—offered a salary of US$15.0 million per annum, as was done by Bank of America in August 2009 whilst still operating on government TARP funds. It is interesting also that the large Wall Street banks, specifically Bank of America, Goldman Sachs, and Citigroup, have been labeled "public pariahs" as a result of their access to and use of TARP funds.[16]

Some might find it ironic, indeed a sad commentary on capitalism, that the TARP program has been largely funded out of funds borrowed from societies decried as enemies of capitalism. More ironic, is US Treasury Secretary Geithner having to reassure the Chinese government that the US will reduce its operating budget deficits, not so long after the US and UK were exacting similar assurances from Third World governments via the IMF and World Bank. It speaks to Wallerstein's (1999: 2–3) contention that the present capitalist world-system premised on capital accumulation has moved far away from equilibrium and that what we are witnessing is a transition to a historical system that is likely, although far from certain, to be "substantively rational" but at the same time "largely egalitarian and largely democratic."

Clearly, the low rankings of the US and the UK on the UN's HPI are the consequences of systemic failures. In the case of the US, its low ranking speaks to the polarization of Americans along ideology in the land of freedom and democracy; it speaks to policy initiatives that seek to reduce transfer payments to the poor and to the argument for lower taxes to facilitate the relentless accumulation of capital by an already well-enriched highest 20 percent of US households; it speaks to the refusal by many job-holders to accept furloughs even when to do so would help keep families from sliding into poverty; it speaks most blatantly to selfishness and to a pervading callousness attendant an existential socioeconomic framework discussed in Chapter Five. Only in America is it a crime in some cities to feed the poor on the streets; the argument advanced by the purveyors of such insensitivity is that the presence of panhandlers and homeless on the streets is offensive to the consuming public and, therefore, bad for business. In contrast, the Chinese government has pursued an egalitarian policy premised on the Confucian analects: "The people must have sufficient food and good dress before they can talk honor. The good customs and social amenities come from wealth and disappear when the country is poor" (Lin, 1960: 208-09).

What is particularly instructive from the debate on poverty reduction or poverty alleviation in America are the extent to which political considerations influence policy, and the reliance of both Republicans and Democrats on a decision-making model premised on game-theory, that is, having a "zone of acceptable outcomes" consistent with avoiding blame at all cost for "bad choices." For example, as observed by R. Kent Weaver (2000: 382):

> Politicians constantly sought 'good choices' (options that would make them better off on multiple dimensions and worse off on none) and that they tried to avoid 'hard choices' (better off on some or all dimensions, worse off on others) and 'bad choices' (worse off on some dimensions, better off on none).

Weaver's observation speaks to the abiding tension between equality (democracy) and capitalism even with a Democratic President.

It is interesting to note that despite its relative unequal distribution of wealth discussed above, Sweden is ranked highest in terms of equality amongst the developed countries referenced. Such ranking speaks to the contention that the fulfillment of basic human needs in some societies is more important than creating an "ownership society," even in a capitalist world-economy, and, perhaps more significantly, to the status of Sweden as a social-welfare state. Furthermore, government transfer payments have had greater impact on poverty reduction in France, Germany, Sweden, and the UK than in the US despite the amount spent by the US in absolute terms is substantially greater than the four countries (Bok, 1996: 344–5); indeed, poverty in the US after government transfers is still double that of the four countries.

In less ideologically-driven countries, poverty is mitigated by having a social safety-net of significance as evidenced by the experiences of the Scandinavian countries, the Netherlands, Canada, and Germany. In these countries, unemployment benefits are central to keeping the unemployed off the streets and to keeping healthcare costs in check; with respect to healthcare costs, by limiting the impact of unemployment-related health issues. Moreover, cross-country studies conducted by the World Bank and others show a positive correlation between social inequality and crime. It is therefore not accidental that law-enforcement divisions in cities across the US resist cuts to their budgets on the basis that crime is expected increase in times of recession.

In further contrast to the US experience is the Chilean experience of the 1990s. Reductions in business and upper-class benefits and the targeting of increased taxes on the rich in Chile resulted in a reduction in poverty, from 44 percent prior to 1990, to 22 percent in 1993; they also resulted in a significant reduction in crime (Wermuth 2003: 188–9). That Chile took this bold step at a time when the conventional wisdom and policy prescriptions from the IMF and World Bank were for privatization at the expense of domestic employment evidences a commitment to social and national cohesion by all Chileans.

Healthcare and Education

The level of healthcare has been and will continue to be an important indicator of human development in countries rich and poor. Indeed, the major donor countries and international agencies have made the provision of adequate healthcare a condition for grants and soft loans to developing countries, more specifically to those seeking relief under the Highly Indebted Poor Country (HIPC) initiative sponsored by the IMF and World Bank. With respect to the importance of education to socioeconomic development and growth, indeed to nation-building, there are lessons to be learned from the experiences of countries that are regarded as economically backward vis-à-vis the US. These experiences both with respect to healthcare and education will be explored more fully in Chapter Seven.

Conclusion

Despite attempts by some politicians and ideologues to frame the American socioeconomic experience in the best possible light, supported often by selected data and spurious arguments, the conflict between capitalism and equality cannot be wished away. Indeed, if ever there were indicators that speak unequivocally to the US being behind other countries in the socioeconomic growth and development game in the twenty-first century, they are those comprising the HDI. As shown in the several indicators cited above, the US not only ranks below the selected countries of the OECD but, more importantly, is at risk of imploding as a society in the twenty-first century in consequence of the growing inequality which cannot be explained away as easily as many have tried to do in the recent past. As history has shown, this aspect of the human experience, that is, growing inequality, is no more sustainable in the US than it is in developing countries; therefore, it is disingenuous and dangerous for ambitious politicians to deny the reality of the time by proclaiming the US as "the most progressive nation in the history of mankind," and that the Obama administration, in seeking to level the playing field for all Americans, is stifling America's "exceptionialism."

NOTES

1. "Income inequality and poverty rising in most OECD countries," www.oecd.org, October 21, 2008.
2. National Press Club Address, Washington, DC. October 29, 2003
3. Bureau of the Census, *Historical Income Tables*, www.census.gov
4. Figure 6.2. "Number in Poverty and Poverty Rate: 1959-2007," *Bureau of the Census*, www.census.gov
5. Bernard, S., "NY AG details big bonuses at bail-out banks," *Associated Press*, July

30, 2009.
6. Lindsey, B., "Book TV," *C-SPAN2*, May 30, 2007
7. Johnson letter to Boswell, 7 December, 1782. (*Boswell, life of, Vol.* 4. p. 157).
8. World Bank, *World Development Indicators*, www.worldbank.org
9. Selva, M. "Britons defend their healthcare from US criticism," *Associate Press*, http://news.yahoo.com/s/ap/20090814/ap_on_re_eu/eu_britain_us_health_care, A gust 14, 2009
10. Bernanke, B., "US Economic Outlook," House Financial Services Committee, *C -SPAN*, February 16, 2007.
11. Crutsinger, M. "Government announces plan to borrow $27.0 billion," *Associated Press*, http://news.yahoo.com/s/ap/20080730/ap_on_bi_ge/federal_borrowing
12. "US launches campaign for more foreign investment," http://news.yahoo.com/s/ afp/20070510//bs_afp/useconomytrade,
13. World Bank, *World Development Indicators*, www.worldbank.org
14. Figure 6.2. "Number in Poverty and Poverty Rate: 1959-2007," *Bureau of the Census*, www.census.gov
15. Associated Press, http://finance.yahoo.com/news/BofA-pays-33M-SEC-fine-for-apf 460238921.html?x=0&sec=topStories&pos=main&asset=&ccode=, August 3, 2009.
16. Ellis, D., "Banks line up for second round of TARP," *CNNMoney.com*, http://money.cnn.com/2009/08/06/news/companies/tarp_banks/index.htm?source=ya hoo_quote, August 6, 2009

Chapter Seven

China on the World Stage

As suggested in the introduction, the emergence of China on the world stage came sooner rather than later. The financial crisis that shook the world in 2008 acted as the catalyst; it arguably took the Chinese government out of its comfort zone, content as it were to follow if not piggyback on the leadership of the US as first envisaged by Zhang and Tang, (2005). Be that as it may, at the end of 2009, China was firmly established as a major source of funding for the US-government-led domestic economic recovery program, and as the potential vehicle for world economic recovery.[1] Indeed, China's economy is said to have recovered in 2010 as evidenced by a reported growth of 10.7 percent in the fourth quarter of 2009 and by the adoption of tighter monetary policy by its central bank in consequence.[2] Therefore, while China, in the phraseology of Gerald Segal (2004), is "a middle power" and is perceived by some as deserving no more attention than Brazil in contemporary geo-economics and geopolitical discourse, its role since 2008 has made it worthy of respect beyond that which many were willing to accord to it at the turn of the century.

Beyond serving as one of the mainstays of global recovery in this decade, China—India, Brazil and Russia being equally important to the recovery process—matters; its history, and contribution to Western civilization, in addition to having been etched in the fabric of contemporary society far and wide, are now being revived on more acceptable terms globally. Indeed, as one of the ancient civilizations still standing, China has been remarkably successful in redefining itself as a significant player in an essentially Western-dominated world at the start of the twenty-first century (Mitter, 2003). Hence, its presence and growing influence cannot be wished away or minimized.

With respect to the last point, it is instructive that a 2009 CNN poll of Americans found that over 70 percent of respondents perceived China as an economic threat to the US[3] even though China has not only publicly declared that it has no regional or global ambitions but also, more significantly, has been supportive of the US in these difficult economic times; China is now the single largest holder of US debt. As such, China bears examination not only in terms of its perception of self but also, and perhaps more importantly, in terms of how it is perceived by others in context of their own ambitions and vulnerabilities. To this end, a brief historical background is offered as context to the discussion on US-China relationship that followed since the ascension of the ruling China Communist Party (CCP) in 1949.

Historical Background

China's history dates back to more than 4,000 years. It became a united kingdom—the Middle Kingdom—under the Emperor Qin (Ch'in) in 221 B.C. with an imperial system that remained "remarkably" consistent for more than 2,000 years, up to the early twentieth century, until it was overthrown in 1911 (See Kesselman, et al., 1996: 371). It is one of the very few civilizations that can point to some form of continuity dating back to before the common era (B.C.E.), having survived the ravages of time and, of course, conquests.

The Middle Kingdom, to be sure, has shrunk in size, but it looms large in terms of history and culture, both of which continue to define the Chinese personality and relationship with non-Chinese, despite the trappings of modernity. This continuity of culture is credited to several interrelated factors. First, what is today's structure of government in most Western capital—a President or Prime Minister, and small groups of advisers—and proclaimed as constituting an effective system of national government, was in place in China "long before the strong monarchical states of Europe took form in the seventeenth century" (Kesselman, et al., 1996: 371), and certainly centuries before there was a United States of America, or the unification of India under British rule (Misra, 1990) as the largest democracy.

Second, Chinese agricultural having benefited from advanced techniques for its time, including irrigation and multi-cropping which were copied by the modern world, became the mainstay of the Chinese empire; commerce and transport were equally highly developed for the time, as was smelting. Studies on the development process during the Song period, as noted by He Ping (2002: 26), "have implied that imperial China was at one point economically much closer to modernity than other societies." For example, the link between the imperial officials and the peasants was the landlord, not unlike the manorial system of England, with one discernible difference: there were over one million small villages functioning as separate entities in consort with flourishing urban centers: Hangzhou with a population of over a million people was deemed the largest and grandest city in the world in the thirteenth century. This system served to hold the empire together in relative peace and prosperity until the middle of the nineteenth century.

Third, the teachings of Confucius (c. 551–479 B.C.E) that stressed social harmony, righteous behavior, and deference to one's elders informed the official ideology and served to perpetuate the established order. Confucianism permeated Chinese psyche and became the essence of Chinese in much the same way as individualism has become the essence of American, as discussed in chapter four. As observed by Kesselman, et al. (1996: 372), "Confucianism was basically a conservative orthodoxy that served to justify and maintain an autocratic state, a patriarchal culture and a stratified society." And this was at a time when the rest of the world was undergoing religious and social upheaval, as evidenced by the Inquisitions in Europe and the Christian Crusades that plagued Europe for centuries.

The depth and breadth of Confucianism manifested in China's ability to withstand foreign influence throughout most of its history. For example, while China had been invaded by the Mongols in 1279 and Buddhism had been introduced as a foreign influence, neither was able to dislodge Confucianism as the primary orthodoxy; rather, such intrusions were absorbed by Chinese culture. As observed by Kesselman, et al., (1996: 373), "they were changed more by China than they were able to change China." Indeed, early Christianity failed to take hold in China because of the depth of Confucianism and, to some extent, the presence of Buddhism (Seo and Takekawa, 2006: 224).

Finally, in addition to the factors discussed above, China was the dominant political and military power in that part of the world, imparting its cultural values to its near-abroad, with the possible exception of those south of its border who were mainly influenced by Hinduism (Pye, 1981: 218). As a result, Japan, Korea, and Vietnam incorporated many aspects of Confucianism into their social system while the South Asian states showed a preference for Hinduism and Buddhism (see Wang 2005).

But, as many are quick to point out, China's influence has not always been for the good of the region. The transforming power of Confucianism led to a false sense of security which derived the belief that all non-Chinese were "barbarians" and, therefore, any challenge from the outside could be met by the Middle Kingdom—which was regarded as the center of civilization (He Ping, 2002: 19)—without altering its basic way of life. This was largely true until around the late eighteenth century when a combination of internal and external factors began to shake the foundation of the imperial system. Moreover, its attempts at subverting non-communist governments in the region in the early twentieth century put it at odds with its neighbors who were by this time under Western colonial influence. Hence, as observed by Shambaugh (2005: 1): "When the PRC [Peoples Republic of China] behaves . . . as a non-status quo power, it only became more marginalized from the principal actors and central dynamics of the region." This lesson has been well learned by the China of the twenty-first century as evidenced by its growing influence for the betterment of the region and the wider world.

Convergence of External and Internal Challenges

As noted above, throughout most of its history, foreigners and foreign influences in China were "sinicized" by Chinese culture. This was no less true for the Manchu who founded the Qing (Ch'ing) dynasty in 1644, than it was for the conquering Mongolians in 1279. However, the Qing dynasty though largely successful in maintaining China's political stability during its reign was faced with the convergence of internal and external challenges not encountered since the Mongolian invasion. As turned out, both were devastating to dynastic rule and consequently to the political and social stability of the then longest surviving empire. China, like many before it, seemingly made an enemy of change itself.

With respect to external challenges, China's self-imposed isolation served as a major contributor to its demise as an empire as did the arrogance of its imperial rulers. From having minimal contact with Europeans, China had a narrow perspective of European progress in terms of industrial development and military technology; the latter owing much to borrowed Chinese technology brought back to Europe by Marco Polo and others.

While the Chinese reveled in their cultural power and used gun powder for celebration, the Europeans weaponized the latter and embarked on building empires of their own (Diamond, 2005). As a result, China found European colonizing forces too powerful to repel and was "forced to open its borders to foreign merchants, missionaries, and diplomats on terms dictated by Britain and other Western powers" (Kesselman, et al., 1996: 372) which it now perceives as entitling it to "special treatment in the present" (Mitter 2003: 208). Particularly humiliating to the Chinese was Britain's notion of free trade which took the form of forcing Opium on the Chinese in exchange for their tea. So humiliating was the defeat of the Chinese in the Opium War (1839–42) that modern filmic interpretations served the political propaganda machinery of the CCP (Karl, 2001).

As if ordained, internal struggles added to the challenges to the Qing dynasty. Corruption, economic stagnation, and population explosion and, of course, Western influence, fuelled the Tai-ping rebellion of 1850–1864 in which over 20 million people were killed. The result was the beginning of the end of imperial China. China was parceled-off among the Western powers: Hong Kong was "leased" to the British in consequence of the "unequal treaties" imposed upon the Chinese by an imperial Britain; and control of trade was almost entirely in the hands of foreigners up to 1997.

Peoples Republic of China

The Qing dynasty, and hence the Middle Kingdom, passed into history in 1911 when the Republic of China was established with Sun Yat-sen as its first president. China, for all practical purposes, was knocked off its historical stability-rocker. Sun was deposed by Yuan Shikai who died in 1916. Leaderless, conflict and disintegration defined early twentieth-century China. Warlords fought for control while Western powers capitalized on the chaos.

The CCP was established in 1921 as an inspiration derived from the *Bolshevik* triumph in Russia in 1917. With the advice of the Soviets, coalitions were formed between the CCP and the Nationalist Party headed by Sun who regained the leadership of it after the death of Yuan. The objective of the coalition was to free the country from the domination of the warlords and to re-establish unity. However, Chiang Kai-shek who succeeded Sun in 1925 conspired with some of the remaining warlords to destroy the CCP and to consolidate power under his leadership in 1927. The result was the 'Long March' in 1934–5 by the remnants of the defeated CCP of mainly peasants led by Mao Zedong, himself a peasant, whose belief in the revolutionary potential of the peasantry became the rallying cry and thus catalyst for the establishment of the People's Republic of China (PRC) in 1949.

The year 1949 was a turning point for many countries, not least of which was China. Mao Zedong who was elected CCP Chairman in 1943 became the first President of communist China, having defeated the US-backed Nationalist Party of Chiang Kai-shek. Prior to that, the CCP gained national support from the people by demonstrating its ability to successfully mobilize resistance to Japanese occupation (Kesselman, et al., 1996). It was also during this period that the peoples of Southeast Asia began to take notice of China, often in terms contrary to what Washington intended (Peck 2006; Chung 2005; Pye 1981).

The PRC's Early Geopolitics

China's geopolitics was anything but exemplar for more than two decades after 1949. Indeed, its relationship with its neighbors for most of the latter half of the twentieth century had been one of discontent, suspicion, and curiosity engendered by its widely perceived "dual revolutionary and peaceful coexistence image" (Pye, 1981: 221). At the same time, it was drawing ever so closer to its neighbors, partly in consequence of America's aggressive unilateralism in trade in the 1980s, and partly in consequence of building an economic infrastructure that fosters closer economic cooperation within the region (Garver 2005). Hence, as observed by Wang Gungwu (2005: 187), "'China fever' seems to be replacing 'China fear' and many look forward to the new 'strategic partnership' and Free Trade Area being forged between ASEAN and China."

China, to be sure, had to purge from its historical memory the notion that it was the hierarchical center around which the world was organized (see He Ping 2002): Serving as the final platform for other Asian countries' exports to the West since the 1990s has contributed greatly to instilling an understanding of cooperativeness with its neighbors (Ohashi 2005). Moreover, many now regard economic cooperation with China as essential to their strategic interest, as the Prime Minister of Singapore sought to remind President George Bush in 2008.

In terms of global politics, most Americans have forgotten China's role in the Vietnam War. Chinese paranoia vis-à-vis a potential Soviet dominated Southeast Asia motivated a less than cooperative approach with North Vietnam in its struggle with the US in South Vietnam. While the Soviet Union was the main supplier of arms to North Vietnam through China, the Chinese provided food and advice, with the latter often viewed as contrary to the interest of North Vietnam. Hence, as observed by Pye (1981: 228): "throughout Hanoi's war the Chinese argued for strategies which the Vietnamese saw as demeaning and not what they wished to hear from a friend and ally." Moreover, the invitation first, by Secretary of State Henry Kissinger, and later by President Nixon to Beijing in 1972, was perceived by Hanoi as the ultimate betrayal.

Clearly, China saw supporting US Asia policy and forging diplomatic relations with it as being in the best interest of China even though this meant alienating Hanoi who was perceived as firmly in the camp of the Soviets and thus a bridgehead for Soviet domination in the region. The Chinese saw the Soviet challenge to the US as an opportunity to extract concessions on arms sales from the US by offering some form of security cooperation with it. Such, an arrangement found support from the Carter administration but ran into the Reagan administration's distrust of, according to Talbott (1981: 89), "countries which do not share America's basic values, political philosophy, and social structure."

Notwithstanding these several setbacks to China's early confused policy towards its neighbors, it is significant that during this learning period and having benefited from the wisdom of India and the experiences of the Southeast Asians, whose approaches to international relations were better informed in consequence of their exposure to colonialism, China became less of a bully in the region and more of an influence for the betterment of its neighbors. Moreover, Chinese intellectualism began to exercise an ameliorating influence on domestic policy and international relations. As a consequence and as part of the awakening process, then, China began to realize the importance of closer relationship with its neighbors to its own development and national security interests. Indeed, despite their mutual suspicion of each other and early border skirmishes, China and Russia "have cultivated a loose *entente* against the US" (Buzan, 2004: 156). This cooperation has since been strengthened in response to US invasion of Iraq in 2003. It received a boost from the proposal by the Bush administration to erect a defensive shield in Poland and Czechoslovakia which the Russians perceived as a potential threat to their security.[4]

The PRC and Other Developing Countries

It should be noted that during this period China's policy towards other developing countries was one of economic assistance predicated on the political rather than on economic development: assisting socialist governments to overcome reliance on their former colonial masters as many of them were ideologically inclined to do (Dator 2006: 126). It was this policy that concerned the Eisenhower and Johnson administrations and informed US Asia policy for much of the period until 1971 (Peck, 2006).

After 1971, what started out as a generalization of its own experience as the model for other developing countries in the 1960s morphed into advice that stressed country-specific conditions and needs as a result of lessons drawn from other countries experiences in the 1970s (Harding, 1981: 276). In addition to Harding's observation, this changed-approach to international relations by China could be attributed to its own experience of learning from the US. Recall, that in the early 1970s, President Richard Nixon opened America to Chinese scholars and enterprise managers willing to learn new techniques. In addition, as the world's largest importer of copper and steel, and a significant importer of iron ore, aluminum, and other raw materials, China has contributed to the increasing firmness of world commodity prices which benefitted developing countries exports.

Ebb and Flow in US–China Relations

In the eyes of succeeding US administrations, China was, and still is, a communist country, and like the former Soviet Union, is viewed through a different ideological prism by the West, often suspiciously so in consequence of its growing influence in Asia (Dillon 2007: Ikenberry 2004). Moreover, US concerns are informed by its immediate post-World War II interaction with the ruling CCP since 1949.

The CCP not only successfully defeated the US-backed Nationalist Party of Chiang Kai-shek, who found a safe haven on Taiwan, but also intervened in the Korean War. With respect to the latter, China's intervention was intended to preserve at least part of North Korea as a buffer; in actuality, it resulted in thwarting President Truman's objective of unifying Korea as a democracy (Halprein 2004: 183). In addition, in negotiations with the US on Korea and Indochina, the PRC disarmingly stressed as policy the peaceful coexistence with its neighbors in Asia whilst the American expectation was for a display of, according to James Peck (2006: 180), "inherent hostility to the requirements of the global order" upon which Washington's Asia policy turned.

US hostility towards China was hardly contained during the 1950s and 1960s. As James Peck (2006: 179) tells it: "The intensity with which Eisenhower sought to isolate China dominated his strategic, ideological, and economic policies in Asia from the very beginning." Moreover, Secretary Dulles, in pursuing a policy of deterrence, threatened to "use nuclear weapons to discourage aggression at all levels." (Gaddis 2004: 226). This overt threat did not end with the armistice in Korea in 1953 but rather became a permanent feature in language emanating from Eisenhower and Dulles, and directed primarily at China. As Bundy (2004: 88) observed:

> In two later crisis [following the Korean War], over the offshore islands of
> Quemoy and Matsu in 1955 and 1958, Eisenhower used both open references
> to nuclear weapons and visible deployments of nuclear-armed forces to under-
> line the risks Mao was running.

Given this antagonistic policy-approach to China, Secretary of State John Foster
Dulles allegedly refused to shake hands with Zhou (Cho) Enlai in Geneva in
1954 as part of the scripted "tactics" for the Geneva meeting which were: "The
US should . . . endeavor to stimulate the communists to the adoption of harsh
negotiating tactics and inflexible positions" (Peck, 2006: 181) so as not to reach
an agreement with them and to make them appear hostile in the eyes of the
world (see Talbott, 1981). But as Peck tells it, the tables were turned: "The Chinese seemed peaceful; the United States, warlike. Zhou Enlai seemed flexible,
willing to negotiate; Dulles, rigid and hard-line."

Eisenhower's China policy found support with the Johnson administration
despite President Johnson's insistence that he would not heed "those who urge
us to use our great power in a reckless or casual manner" (quoted in Gaddis
2004: 226). One of those urging the use of America's hard power was James
Thompson Jr. In a March 1, 1966 memorandum captioned *"Some Propositions
on a China Strategy"* (quoted by Peck, 2006: 180) he writes:

> If Communist behavior is such that tensions in the Far East are substantially re-
> duced, most Asian countries, except Nationalist China [Taiwan], Korea, and
> Vietnam, would probably cautiously relax their present suspicions of Peiping
> and move gradually toward broader contacts and normal diplomatic relations
> with Communist China. This, in time, would enlarge Peiping's [Peking's] abil-
> ity to influence these countries. . . . Any softening on the part of the U.S. would
> have extremely serious consequences.

It was not until President Nixon visited China in 1972 that US-China relations began to warm, culminating in formal diplomatic relations in 1979. Evidently Panda diplomacy—Ling-Ling and Sing-Sing—proved to be a workable
approach for the Chinese: Seeking to block what appeared to them to have been
the threat of Soviet hegemony in the region by the holding-out of China as a
potential market for American-made products, proved to be a winning strategy
for both parties. Even then, the two countries continued to view each other with
suspicion fuelled by extremists on both sides. Indeed, prior to turning his attention to the Soviet Union, presidential candidate Ronald Reagan criticized the
Carter administration for normalizing relations with the PRC and held out the
possibility of re-establishing relations with Taiwan which, of course, roiled the
Chinese. The Chinese accused Reagan of wanting to turn back the clock (Salo-
mon 1981: 4). Moreover, the inscrutable nature of the Chinese was perceived as
too costly and time consuming for those in the Reagan administration who thrive
on instant gratification. Hence, US attention was directed at societies that were
more in keeping with its own or to countries falling within its sphere of influence such as Japan, Taiwan, and South Korea, for example.

Given the twelve years of Republican administration since the 1980s, US–China relations reached its lowest point in 1995. Indeed, America's relentless criticisms of China's human rights record and its alleged influence in staging the Tiananmen Square protest in 1989[5] served to prompt President Deng Xiaoping to declare in September 1991 that the conflicts between the two countries rose to the level of "a new cold war." These sentiments were articulated by President Jiang Zemin in August 1995: "Western hostile forces have not for a moment abandoned their plot to Westernize and divide our country" (quoted in Huntington, 1996: 223).

For its own strategic reasons, the US did nothing to allay the increasing animosity expressed by China's leaders and scholars during this period. Indeed, the US openly sought to assert its own influence in the region by permitting the Taiwanese President to come to America and hosting him, despite China's protests. Additionally, selling 150 F-16s fighters to Taiwan, opposing China's entry into the WTO, and accusing it of exporting weapon-technology and military components to Iran, added to the tension between the two countries. The Clinton administration also dispatched Secretary Warren Christopher to tell the Chinese what was expected of them by a Democratic President and Congress; the Secretary returned a much enlightened diplomat.

The Hong Kong Paradox

As the handover of Hong Kong drew near, China began to prepare the West for a smooth process, knowing full well that the event would be used as an opportunity to highlight the difference between communism as practiced by China and capitalism as practiced by the West by emphasizing Hong Kong's unrivalled economic and financial success as a British colony. As Chow (2001: 222) tells it:

> This new narrative of global capital with its revealing ambiguities about democracy is the place where the otherwise ideologically competing—and seemingly incompatible—forces of U.S. imperialism, British colonialism, and Chinese nationalism coincide.

Indeed, Hong Kong was not only the last of the British colony of any significance; it evidences global capitalism at its very best as a result of British rule, not to mention native ingenuity and a Confucian work ethic. The continuation of its economic prosperity thus became the focus of UK and US administrations, not fully realizing that, as Chow (2001: 222) observed: "like Britain and the United States, with their considerable trade interests in the Far East, the PRC, too, in spite of its overt ideological 'difference' is now a giant investor in Hong Kong businesses."

Not surprising, then, the idea of "one country, two systems" became the mantra of the PRC which, ironically, could not be disputed for the simple reason that Hong Kong as a democratic colony is an oxymoron. Hence the paradox in

Secretary Albright's pronouncement: "We will be watching to see that the Hong Kong of tomorrow is like the Hong Kong of today." prompting Chow (2001: 222) to ask rhetorically, "Since Albright's words mean that even though it is officially no longer a colony, it need not advance any further politically so that it can remain the "same" as it was in 1997?"

The UK, of course, played its swan song with much pomp and bravado. The Chinese, on the other hand, heard it as the last call and played down the lecture from outgoing Governor General Chris Patten, emphasizing its "one country, two systems" formula for incorporating the island economy into China in seeming appeasement to an emotional UK. To the Chinese, however, the sun will never again rise on the British Empire in East Asia and that was all that mattered. The doom and gloom predicted by China-watchers did not occur if only because in the years preceding the handover, China began to lay the ground work for a smooth transition, fully realizing that Hong Kong was its access to Western capital, technology, and markets.

Hong Kong continues to be an important entry point into China for Western capitalism. Westerners cannot get enough of China in the twenty-first century. Indeed, most dispassionate analyses portray China as the basis for continued growth in Western economies and counsel navigating the shallows and moderating expectations[6] in the early years. But for most Americans and others with the fever of empire still in their blood, it is a bitter pill to swallow. Hence, Gerald Segal's provocative question, "Does China matter?" is itself an acknowledgement that, for policymakers in the West, it seemingly does, and, therefore, is a reality even though it would be better for an enlightened world that it should not be as perceived (Buzan and Foot, 2004: xi). Put another way, does being number one matter?

On the other side of the coin, in terms of historical time lines, the memory of China's humiliation attendant the Opium War—the carving up of the Middle Kingdom by Western powers—and the betrayal by the Nationalist Party led by Chaing Kai-shek still burn in the belly of CCP-led China. Such historical memory manifests in the PRC's relationship with the West on the one hand, and in the attitude of the West to a culture it never fully understood nor was able to subdue, on the other hand. And a twenty-first century West knows it, despite attempts to portray nineteenth- and twentieth-century Chinese development history in terms of "insufficient modernization, incomplete modernity, and or aborted modernism" (Karl, 2001: 238).

Also, contrary to Western expectation, the "liberal rhetoric of resistance" of the liberal intellectuals has yet to impinge on the admitted "oppressiveness" of the CCP which, it is argued, "comes from its [CCP's] determination to ensure social stability as a necessary precondition for economic modernization" (Zhang, 2001: 338). Evidently, liberal intellectuals in China still find compelling the argument that the whole is greater than the sum of its individual parts. Not what the capitalist world-economy needs since, as observed by Leslie Sklair (1995: 45-48):

> Global capitalism does not permit cultural neutrality. Those cultural practices that cannot be incorporated into the culture-ideology of consumerism becomes oppositional counter-hegemonic forces to be harnessed or marginalized, and if that fails, destroyed physically.

Moreover, as we are reminded by the events in the Middle East, the US has neither the patience nor the time to be accommodating of Confucian ideology, or any other for that matter, in its quest for continued hegemony.

US impatience and the influence of Western capitalism notwithstanding, Confucianism still exerts an overwhelming influence in socio-economic and political thought in China, and manifest most forcefully in its approach to modernization, and supported, confusingly to Western observers, by the liberal intelligentsia, (Zhang, 2001: 338). Not to be unkind, the Japanese, on the other hand, lost their essential Japanese identity primarily on reaching their "true potential" as defined in Western ideological terms. This is not to say that the next generation of Chinese would not go the way of their Japanese counterparts.

China matters then, not as a direct economic rival to America or the West which informs Western intellectual discourse and thus policy. Rather, China matters because Confucianism is perceived in the West as a challenge to Western ideology; but it is a challenge only to those who continue to hold to the nineteenth century notion that China needs to be "transformed . . . to follow the path of reform towards marketization, plurality and even democracy" (Yahuda, 2004: 10).

The PRC and Economic Reform

In the West, economic reforms are first adopted as national policy, with implementation as the necessary follow through along prescribed methods, such as, for example, in welfare reform in the US where, as Weaver (2000: 258) observed: "states often adopted innovations before their efficacy in changing behavior or incomes had been demonstrated." Similarly, reforms in developing countries influenced by Western ideology tend to have processes adopted as policy only to discover their inappropriateness, as demonstrated by privatization (Chang 2006). Reforms in China, on the other hand, mirror the process in a laboratory or of a clinical trial: "gradual and incremental, without any detailed 'blueprint' guiding the process" (Prasad and Rumbaugh, 2004: 2). Such an approach allows the Chinese to experiment with an approach, fine tune it, and then apply it to the country at large once efficacy has been established.

While the Chinese approach is frustrating to US policymakers and practitioners whose expectations are for an American approach, it allows the Chinese to control the socioeconomic disruptions that attend reforms that have not been fully thought through (Fukuyama 1999). It also provides time to construct appropriate institutional support for full and effective implementation, having benefited from the experiences of its neighbors.

A good example of the Chinese approach is the experimentation with Special Economic Zones as a way of gradually introducing market concepts, borrowed technology, and foreign capital. The development effectiveness of this approach is contrasted most appropriately with the several failed privatization of state-owned enterprises in developing countries pursuant structural adjustment following the Debt Crisis of the mid 1980s and carried out under the auspices of the IMF and World Bank (Chang 2006).

Early Reform Program

Given the approach to economic reform outlined above, there are five distinct phases to China's reform program. The first phase centers on the decentralization of farming. Like the Soviet model of collectivized agriculture, China's commune system, which increased access to social services and was responsible for some large-scale infrastructure projects, proved to be one of the weakest links in China's command economic system in the absence of any incentive to the workers. Consequently, production levels in 1977 remained at 1957 levels. Hence, in early 1980s, Deng Xiaoping supported the move of production control away from the collectivized system to a "household responsibility system" (the first phase) by contracting out farmland to individual families who took full charge of production and marketing of their crops. As a result, agricultural production grew at six percent or better in the 1980s (Prasad and Rumbaugh 2004; Kesselman et al., 1996).

The knock-on effects of increased agricultural production manifested in improved living standards for farmers, and more significantly, in support of Deng's efforts to expand and modernize China's industrial production. As told by Kesselman, et al (1996: 390), the Chinese countryside was transformed by a rural industrial revolution (the second phase), "that, in speed and scope, is probably unprecedented in the history of the modern world."

The "township and village enterprises" (TVE) that formed the backbone of this revolution were relatively small-scale rural factories run by local governments outside the control of the central government and accounted for more than 25 percent of the country's industrial output. Needless to say, such autonomy brought its own problems: corruption and power struggle, and, at times, even defiance of the central government. But the TVE also provided competition to the state-run enterprises and drove the marketization process from 1978 to about 1996. Many of the TVE were later privatized by way of "restructuring." with many TVE managers and employees becoming owners in joint-stock cooperatives.

Concurrent with the reforms in the rural areas, huge investments were taking place in the heavy industry sector as phases three and four. Informed primarily by ideas and knowledge brought back from the several visits to the US by Chinese leaders and enterprise managers, China's "Big Push" industrialization strategy that signaled the demise of a purely socialist system began to take hold after 1979 on a phased-in basis as discussed above. Indeed, after 1972, investment as a share of GDP grew from just over 25 percent to about 43 percent in 1994, before falling back to just under 40 percent in 2004 (Naughton, 2007: 57). As a result, between 1952 and 1978, industrial output grew at an annual rate of 11.5 percent, with industrial production accounting for 44 percent of GDP by 1978. New industries were created, with some encouragement given to private-sector development, thus giving rise to a new enterprise class just about the same time British Prime Minister Margaret Thatcher was in the process of transforming the UK's socioeconomic structure. Agricultural production during the same period as a share of GDP declined from 51 percent in 1952 to 28 percent in 1978 (Naughton, 2007: 56).

With the reorientation away from a primarily agrarian social structure to an industrially-based economy, China was ready to take the next step: Phase five. Phase five, of course, speaks to Deng Xiaoping's decision to integrate China into the global economic system and in particular into the Asian region (Shambaugh 2005). This phase required restructuring the role and function of government, gradually subjecting the economy to competition, and increasing the enterprise, social and financial reform processes as precursors to admittance to the WTO at the end of 2001. The preparation process served to expand China's economic growth further between 2002 and 2005 (Ohashi 2005). Interestingly, while the reform experience of China shows that markets work and should be the underlying strategy of development, according to Naughton (2007: 7): "[it] provides no support for the argument that, since the market is a superior mechanism, the full panoply of market institutions should be set in place as quickly as possible in as many realms as possible." Indeed, China was the exception to the rule simply because of its approach to reform, as noted above.

Social Issues

As agricultural production shrank, rural labor migrated to the towns and cities, seeking non-farm occupations, thus requiring even greater investment in manufacturing industries. However, with about 50 million "transient" workers in the towns and cities, and an unemployment rate of between eight and ten percent (Naughton, 2007: 186–7), the increasing pressures on urban housing and social services became major concerns for the central government. Crime, prostitution, drug abuse, homelessness, and other social ills were beginning to plague city managers and the Chinese leadership. It is this concern that has forced Chinese officials to become more export oriented and to target investments to job creation. Thus, as observed by Alan Blinder of Princeton University: "China must export like mad to grow like mad to give production work to the hoards of people migrating from the country to the cities."[7]

China in the Twenty-first Century

China's economic growth and influence in the twenty-first century could be likened to a super tanker which once in open waters is propelled by its own momentum. It is a momentum that is clearly creating geo-economic and geopolitical challenges—both in its forward motion and in its wake—to the long-established international economic and political order established by the West. It is also a perceived source of concern for the US whose dominance since the end of World War II has never really been challenged by any other country. For example, China produced more cars than the US in 2006, and its economy has been growing at least three times faster than the American economy, with an unprecedented 11.1 percent growth rate in the first quarter of 2007. At this rate, Goldman Sachs reportedly expects China's GDP, at market exchange rate, to surpass America's GDP by 2027, and is likely to become number one on purchasing power parity (PPP) basis within four years;[8] and this was before the 2007-08 financial crisis that shook the American economy to its foundations. Moreover, China's quick recovery from the fallout of the 2007-08 financial crisis speak to its ability to adapt to changes in the global market place in short order;[9] it speaks also to the existence of endemic constraints in the American economic model, requiring fundamental changes over an extended period of time and at a heavy cost to its GDP.

Apart from the fear factor of an economically-strong and growing China, there are positive externality arising from China's continued economic growth. China's demand for resources from other countries has served to raise commodity prices in developing countries. Moreover, China's energy demands have fostered new economic ties with many of the Pacific-rim countries, including Australia. In the case of the latter, it is instructive that the Australian company, Resourcehouse Ltd. has struck a $60 billion, 20-year agreement to supply coal to China Power International Development Ltd.; a contract reported by the BBC as rising to the level of once in decades or even in a century opportunity.[10]

In addition, Southeast Asian countries and Japan have seen their exports to China increased at unprecedented rates in consequence of a China policy that allows export-oriented foreign investment enterprises (FIE) to import production facilities as well as parts and components for assembly, fully exempt from customs duties (Ohashi 2005). Hence, from a total export–import perspective, China FIE trade ratio for 2001 shows exports at 50.1 percent and imports at 51.7 percent (Ohashi 2005, 82). In addition to exemption from customs duties, FIE are eligible for rebate of domestic value-added taxes on their exports.

As a result of incentives offered to FIE, China's nominal trade with the world has increased at unprecedented rates. For example, Japanese exports to China increased from 3.9 percent of total exports in 1980 to 13.6 percent in 2003, South Korea's from zero percent in 1980 to 20.5 percent in 2003, Singapore's from 1.6 percent in 1980 to 7.0 percent in 2003, Philippines's from 0.8 percent in 1980 to 12.0 percent in 2003, Indonesia's from zero in 1980 to 7.4

percent in 2003, and India's from 0.3 percent in 1980 to 6.4 percent in 2003 (Rumbaugh and Blancher, 2004: 11). Even exports from the EU increased from 0.8 percent in 1980 to 4.2 percent in 2003. As a consequence of the increase in imports from almost all its trading partners, China runs negative bilateral trade balances with most of these trading partners while reporting trade surpluses with the US and the EU. Indeed, for selected Asian countries and the US and EU, China's (including Hong Kong) trade deficit increased from US$4.0 billion in 1997 to US$35.0 billion in 2003 (Rumbaugh and Blancher, 2004: 11).

But the Southeast Asian countries are not the only countries to benefit from a growing China. As a result of its export drive, China's trade with the EU increased in May 2007 by 29.0 percent over May 2006 to US$129.9 billion, and by 18.2 percent with the US to US$115.2 billion over the same period. The EU is now China's biggest trading partner. It also experienced 15.1 percent increase in trade with Japan for a total of US$91.2 billion. Nonetheless, of concern to the US is that, whilst exports to China increased by 19.1 percent, imports increased by 28.7 percent with a trade deficit of $22.5 billion for May 2007. That trade deficit has since shrunk to US$10.9 billion in January 2010[11] but remains a concern of the US. However, dispassionate analyses suggest that, while China's trade surplus with the US has been increasing ever since, it is primarily because it serves the American economic interest to do so. Without cheap Chinese imports, inflation would be a major concern in the US (see also Chapter Eight).

From the above quoted data, it is clear that China serves as the final assembly platform for many of the Southeast Asian countries and runs trade deficits with them in consequence; nevertheless, such trade deficits do not enter into discourse on China's trade surpluses with the US and EU. That this is so is perhaps because both the US and the EU approach their trade imbalances with China from self-serving discrete perspectives, notwithstanding that the benefits do not accrue entirely to China. With respect to this latter point, it is instructive that James Fallows of the *Atlantic Monthly* found that for every US$1,000.00 item produced in China by an American firm, only about US$100.00 remain with the Chinese; the balance of US$900.00 stays with the US company doing business in China.[12]

Clearly, the power of the lobby in the US ensures that US-China trade relations are kept at a confrontational level if only to benefit the domestic producer. In this connection, consider this observation by Adam Smith (Campbell & Skinner, 1976: 475):

> In the restraint upon the importation of all foreign commodities which can come into competition with those of our own growth, or manufacture, the interest of the home consumer is evidently sacrificed to that of the producer. It is all to the benefit of the latter, that the former is obliged to pay that enhancement of price which this monopoly almost always occasions.

China's new Geopolitical Role

Beyond economics, the importance of China to an effective international relations framework is underscored by its ability to get the 'Six-party Talks' regard-
ing North Korea's nuclear weapons program restarted when others had all but
given up. But, while China's ability to persuade the North Koreans is deemed
acceptable from the perspective of the US, to the extent that it seemingly serves
America's interest at the front end, there are implications that are deemed less
acceptable to the US and the West when taken in context of the increasing influence of China. In other words, it would have been preferable for China to have
failed.

One such implication is the reaction of other Asian states to China. As remarked by Zhuang Jianshong, from Shanghai's Jiaotong University: "I don't
think it would be an exaggeration to say that most Asian countries now look to
China more than they look to the US."[13] This is quite a contrast to the China-
Southeast Asian relationship of the 1960s and 1970s as discussed above.

Zhuang Jianshong is not alone in this view. Although the US has a superior
defense capability in the region, and, under the Bush administration, was actively seeking to strengthen strategic relations with countries such as the Philippines, South Korea, Singapore, and even Indonesia, according to Professor Ross
of Boston College: "China is the shadow covering the entire region."

In addition to its obvious influence in Southeast Asia, China has improved
its relations with India, as evidenced by India's Prime Minister Vajpayee's visit
to Beijing in June 2003 and the quiet diplomacy in which both are engaged to
resolving the Sino-Indian boundary (Lampton 2005). The growing cooperation
in trade between China and India is also indicative of a closer tie between the
two leaders in Asia. China's relationship with Pakistan also is being maintained
at a cordial and respectful level (Musharraf, 2006), without jeopardizing its improving relationship with India. As observed by Zhang, (2005: 51), China's
main concern is to ensure a working relationship with the major powers in the
region, "so that China will never again become isolated and encircled by great
powers."

However, China's growing influence in the region is not entirely of its own
making. Indeed, it is being aided by the mistakes in US foreign policy not only
towards Southeast Asia, as evidenced by US reaction to the 1997–8 Asian financial crisis and its neglect of ASEAN, but also by its tendency to unilateralism as
evidenced by its actions in the Middle East. As remarked by the Malaysian
Prime Minister, "Mr. Bush has a different agenda and the Muslims know it." In
this connection, it is worth noting the little-reported agreement of the Southeast
Asian countries to "pool" their foreign currency reserves in the event of a repeat
of the 1997–8 speculative frenzy that befell the currencies of four of their members. Whether or not such pooling translates to a formal monetary union remains
to be seen.

Challenge to Entrenched Western Dominance

But, eclipsing US and the West economic dominance is not the only concern for US policymakers of an emerging China. As China's massive industrialization takes hold, its demand for raw materials, to be sure, has changed the dynamics of international trade, creating pricing pressures for certain commodities while providing increased opportunities for marginal suppliers especially in developing countries, thus creating a shift in relationships. Moreover, in addition to stimulating scale-production of raw materials and other manufacturing inputs in other developing countries, China's growing investments in these countries' production processes have allowed it to forge new political and economic alliances, with the potential to serve as catalysts to reducing the income inequality gap between rich nations and the developing countries. It is a role that is new to China, a role it undertakes willingly and with a level of confidence rooted in its history past and present; but it is a role that is fraught because China represents change to the capitalist world system.

Threat or Opportunity?

Despite its benefit to global prosperity, China's emergence is perceived not as benignly as the Chinese leadership hoped it would be, but rather as a significant threat to entrenched Western economic and security interests in general, and to US dominance, in particular. To be sure, outside of the crisis in the Middle East, there is no other contemporary issue more talked about than the perceived challenges posed by China in the twenty-first century, and for good reasons. For example, further underscoring China's momentum is the revelation by the WTO that China has surpassed the US in exports in the second half of 2006 and has overtaken Germany as the world's number one exporter in 2008.[14, 15] Additionally, China is also poised to overtake Japan as the second largest economy in the world within the next five years.

As revealed by the CNN poll quoted above, the anxiety over China's emergence as a potential economic rival to the West is becoming increasingly manifest: Such anxiety finds outlet in academic papers and in economic and financial presentations and policy proposals. Indeed, the rhetoric of the US Congress is unmistakably anti-China, calling as it does for tariffs and other forms of protection against Chinese imports in response to complaints from corporate contributors and constituents affected by the increasing competition from Chinese products. Evidence, Congressman Duncan Hunter's accusation that, "China is cheating on trade."[16] Yet, as Secretary of the Treasury, Henry Paulson, points out in his discussion with Charlie Rose on April 23, 2007, trade helps to keep inflation rates down in America and contributes to American economic prosperity.

As well recognized in dispassionate analyses, faster growth in China and other developing economies, such as India and Brazil, will benefit the American economy, not harm it, and, moreover, help to sustain it at a level that has been reached prematurely. In addition, as pointed out above, China serves as an export platform for many countries, including the EU and Japan, and, in that functionality, creates wealth for its trading partners while creating jobs for the millions that immigrate to its cities. In addition, the consequential wealth-creation in other countries benefits the US to the extent that it provides markets for American goods and services.

Despite these obvious long term benefits, what former Secretary Paulson and the intellectual capitalist class would have preferred, given the overleveraging of assets and the dollar (discussed in the earlier chapters), however, was faster liberalization of China's financial markets. Indeed, the introduction of competition in China's financial sector would likely have raised the current interest rate on savings from two and a half percent to above five percent. Such a move would not only have served to increase Western access to approximately US$2.0 trillion of Chinese savings but also would have resulted in an increase the income stream to Chinese savers who in theory would have had more to spend on Western goods and services. But as Paulson, and before him John Snow, observed, the Chinese will not be pushed. Ingrained in Chinese culture is the belief that there is a time for everything and everything in its time; it has served the Chinese well for over 2,500 years.

Given its history, China has yet to subscribe to the notion that promoting individualism would bring its millions in the countryside out of poverty. In fact, the American experience in the twenty-first century is far from a recommendation and indeed must give pause to countries like India and China. It is also instructive that China's commitment to job creation for its massive work force is tied to its high savings rate with which its consistently high economic growth rate is positively correlated. In this connection, it is worth noting that, foreign direct investment (FDI) as a share of GDP began to decline gradually to just under three percent in 2005 (Naughton, 2007: 404), consistent with a greater reliance on internally-generated savings while maintaining an acceptable growth rate. It is also noteworthy that, in 2005, Hong Kong, Taiwan, and Macau accounted for 35 percent of FDI in China whilst the combined investment from the US, EU and Japan accounted for 15 percent (Naughton, 2007: 403). Clearly, China is pursuing a self-generated growth policy premised on its past wealth accumulation and massive foreign currency reserves.

Beyond trade issues, despite its impressive transformation to a market economy, China is still being regarded as the last bastion of communism after the disintegration of the Soviet Union in 1991, such is the inflexibility in labels. As such, China, in the minds of most US lawmakers, replaced the Soviet Union in terms of being a target for America's democracy imperative. In this latter connection, the divergence in perspectives could not be greater.

China sees democracy as country-specific in a pluralist world whose diversity must be respected as a "very important feature of the world."[17] To this end, according to the Chinese Ambassador, while recognizing the need for providing guidance to the parties in Sudan "to come to terms through peaceful negotiations." China considered the problems in Sudan as internal. Former President

Bush, on the other hand, saw the world through the prism of idealism and resolved to proselytize freedom and democracy: "The best hope for peace in our
world is the expansion of freedom in all the world."[18]

It is further instructive that China considers sanctions not ends but means
and, in the opinion of the Chinese Ambassador, if not used properly can be
counterproductive.[19] This has been made quite obvious in its refusal to agree
with the proposal to impose extreme sanctions against Iran.

China's possession of nuclear weapons and one of the largest standing ar-
mies in the world with a declared policy of invading Taiwan should it declare
independence adds to the concerns of the US. Moreover, constant reminding of
China's role in the Korean and Vietnam Wars further serves to reinforce attempts to demonize it, and every so often, to reaffirm a US China policy of containment, despite disclaimers to the contrary.

In addition to US concerns is the announcement by the British Prime Minister in 2007 that the UK will reintroduce the use of hard power as an option to its
international relations framework. Such change in policy must be seen as partly
motivated by China's modernization of its military and its achievements in
space. The revelation that the UK had in the past considered using nuclear
weapons against China does nothing to allay historical fears nor do labels such
as: "a huge challenge to the United States"; "yellow peril"; "totalitarian regime";
and "ambitious." many of which are derived from a position of waning economic competitiveness and influence in world affairs.

Specific US Concerns

US concerns appear to center not only on China's enviable economic growth
rates that are more than three times that of the US—deemed unsustainable by
most Western observers for over two decades—but also on its expanding political reach beyond its near-abroad. Indeed, China's exercise of soft-power in the
region renders existing US China policy of containment ineffective; and its no-
strings-attached investment policy are being widely received in Africa and Latin
America and are perceived as impacting America's influence in these regions.

With respect to Latin America, as observed by Representative Nita Lowey:
"We are witnessing a reversal of the several political and economic gains made
over the last several decades . . . . China is becoming a major player in the energy sector."[20] China, to be sure, has increased it presence in Latin America,
concluding economic ties with Brazil, Venezuela,[21] and others who have grown
suspicious of the America that has been revealed to the world since March 2003;
in addition, many developing countries are opting for less stringently-
conditioned European Union aid as a replacement for US aid.

This expanding reach of China is financed by its growing trade surplus and
its foreign exchange reserves estimated to be US$3.0 trillion in 2009 over which
the West has little or no control. While, therefore, many commentators have
focused on the US trade deficit with China, from a foreign policy perspective the

concern is really about China's increasing ability to exert influence in the resource-rich developing countries in Africa and South America. Over the decades, China has been building solid economic relations with these countries
based on a declared policy of mutual respect and non-intervention, as noted
above. In this latter regard, the Chinese approach predicated as it is on a *quid
pro quo* relationship contrasts strikingly with a system of asymmetrics that defined the core-periphery relationship or a North/South divide (Peck 2006: 224–
5) with which developing countries are all too familiar in their transactions past
and present with the West.

China's growing appetite for resources to fuel its economic growth to be sure
requires that it sources its needs through the international market place and,
where necessary, through bilateral cooperative agreements. As a consequence,
its demands serve to render the long-serving Western core-periphery model of
resource transfer obsolete, especially with respect to oil and other basic commodities, resulting in increased cost of raw materials to Western production centers. In this regard, the increase in price for commodities is seen as benefitting
many developing countries, especially those African countries that see China's
economic expansion as a path out of poverty.

In addition to trade issues, China appears to be unresponsive to US pressure
on human rights and other issues of governance, offering its own priorities constructed around its self-determined national economic and security interests. As
emphasized by the Chinese Ambassador to the United Nations (UN) in Geneva
to Carrie Gracie of the *BBC* on "Hard Talk" in August 2006, "China does not
need any advice on its internal affairs from anyone nor is it a threat to any other
country." This perspective has been reiterated by Ambassador Zhou Wenzhong
in 2007.

With respect to the question of being a threat to its neighbors, as if to allay
any fears of border disputes with them, Ambassador Zhou Wenzhong reiterated
China's respect for history and for its existing borders with, for example, Russia.[22] Indeed, Russia's Ambassador to the UN Vitaly Churkin unequivocally
confirmed that all border issues with China have been "completely resolved,
completely settled" and that the two countries are pursuing their common economic and strategic interests bilaterally and internationally. These agreements
notwithstanding, former National Security Adviser to President Carter, Zbig-
niew Brzezinski, drawing from the well-entrenched Western perspective of
China, sees Russia as needing to join the West as a form of protection against
China.[23] But Ambassador Churkin sees China–Russia relationship as "a very big
political and cultural friendship in every way."[24]

As would be expected, the Europeans have not been far behind with their
own concerns which for now center mainly on trade issues but which have not
risen to a level to prevent them from seeking investment opportunities in China.
Indeed, US companies have been playing catch-up with the Europeans in the
'gold rush' of the East. Some US companies, *Google*, for example, have even
rebutted attempts by US politicians to impose their political agenda upon it so as
to gain a foothold in the China market. Google has since threatened to pull out

of China, seemingly no longer respectful of Chinese rules and regulations as valid to its politically-informed agenda.

While Western investments are welcomed in China, they are received cautiously, especially since the 1997–8 Asian financial crisis. To the extent investments are "foot-loose." they are perceived as fuelling a speculative bubble not unlike that witnessed in the East Asian countries in the years just before the 1997–8 financial crisis. As noted in Chang (2006), that crisis had its roots in the global reach of Western investors and an over-dependence on short-term investment flows to finance economic growth. It is thus a credit to the Chinese government to have recognized the consequence of speculative capital inflows and to seek to control their impact on the Chinese economy despite protestations from the US. Indeed, it is to everyone's long-term economic interests that the Chinese economy be not subjected to the disruption that attended the 1997–8 Asian financial crisis and the American derived financial crisis of 2007–8.

The Strain on US Foreign Policy

Curiously, President Bush was one of the first to betray a link, albeit obliquely, between China's emergence and the crisis in the Middle East. Recall his unscripted remark that China's energy demands are putting a strain on US foreign policy. Also, in his meeting with President Lula da Silva of Brazil on March 8, 2007, he again pronounced on the energy demands of China. On that occasion he added India to the equation and stressed the need for developing alternative energy sources—not for export to the US however, but for Brazil's domestic consumption—so as to reduce the pricing pressure on the US.[25]

The strain on US foreign policy, as we have witnessed, manifested most blatantly in the invasion of Iraq and in the propping-up of despotic regimes friendly to the US and the West in contradiction to the expressed US policy of spreading democracy and freedom. In addition, the looming self-fulfilling prophesies of confrontation with Iran designed arguably to preempt an alliance between it and China—the Confucius–Islamic connection of Samuel Huntington (1994), if you will—are all too revealing. Moreover, when considered in context of the long-term objective to contain China, the well-publicized arguments for Israel's right to exist or to defend itself is arguably no more than an over-played geopolitical card, albeit an important card in context of Middle East politics.

Given the above, as with its Middle East policy since 2003 the former Bush Administration's China policy must be seen necessarily in context of its declared policy of "preventive" actions, and, arguably, rooted in Huntington's notion of a clash between the US and China reaffirmed to some extent by Niall Ferguson.[26] Indeed, the inevitability of such a clash as perceived by Huntington and Ferguson is cast in terms of China's emerging challenge as discussed above and its resolve to defend its national sovereignty and historical heritage while the US, initially buoyed by the exercise of its presumptive "moral authority" under George Bush, though locked in an ideological war of its choosing in the Middle East, is propelled necessarily by the territorial imperative. This is an unavoidable conclusion made more immediate when considered in context of the Bush doctrine of preemption, which, when taken as a whole curiously exposes an almost discernible grand strategy for containing China. It is, therefore, no accident that the BBC, in a commentary on the crisis in the Middle East, should highlight China's role in Africa and its increasing energy demands as the basis for implying that the real conflict is still to come.

Jaw-boning and Fear-mongering

This heightened and growing anxiety of the US over China's emergence is further reflected in the visit to China in 2005 by the then Treasury Secretary John Snow, with follow-up visits by his successor Henry Paulson and by Chairman Ben Bernanke in 2006 and 2007, and Secretary Geithner in 2010. These visits were designed principally to express US concerns over the growing US-China trade imbalance, perceived as it were to be the consequence of an undervalued Chinese currency, and to jaw-bone corrective actions from the Chinese. They were also intended, according to Secretary Paulson, to persuade the Chinese to speed up their reforms and to liberalize their financial sector. But, as the collapse of the US financial system in 2008 revealed, they were no more than attempts to stem the inevitable collapse of the US financial system.

Even if Chinese cooperation were forthcoming, the contradiction in US foreign and defense policies operated to negate such cooperation. For example, while the Treasury Secretary and the FED Chairman sought to gain concessions from the Chinese, Secretary of State Rice was unabashedly engaged in promoting the US administration's take on China's hegemony as an imminent danger to the region. In addition, the then Secretary of Defense, Donald Rumsfeld's contribution took the form of direct questions and pronouncements on China's increase in military spending; both were seen as attempts to contain China by stimulating fears in its neighbors and are reminiscent of the Eisenhower policy of containment without isolation in the 1950s.

President Bush's visit to India and engaging in what was perceived as inconsistent with the international nuclear non-proliferation treaty (NPT) by entering into a nuclear cooperation agreement—approved by the US Congress in 2006—as part of a broader strategic agreement with a country that is not a party to the NPT is also indicative of reviving Eisenhower's China policy of containment. Equally telling was the silence of the US administration and indeed the US news media in general on the failed test launch of an intercontinental ballistic missile by India just days after North Korea's failed attempt to test its long-range missile on July 4, 2006, was roundly condemned.

Clearly, up until the failure of Israel to dislodge Hezbollah in 2006, US policy towards China was less than accommodating or warming. Indeed, despite the rhetoric, the Bush administration's policy could be perceived as indirectly aggressive to the extent that it openly sought to encircle China through strategic alliances in the region in hopes of completing the containment by gaining control of Middle East oil and strengthening Israel's position in the region. But, as is being played-out, rather than contain China, the Bush administration's Middle East policy of aggressive unilateralism, now widely perceived as a failure, has served to strengthen ties between Russia and China.

The Huntington Factor

One of the first to express concern over China's emergence is Samuel Huntington (1996: 313). His perception of an emerging China as, "the biggest player in the history of man" whose "assertiveness" in the region "would be contrary to American interests as they have been historically constructed" cannot be ignored, and, arguably, has served to inform the presumptive Bush administration's grand strategy to contain China (Chang 2008). Indeed, Huntington's perspectives undoubtedly resonated with an essentially neoconservative US administration in a world that has been largely constructed on dominance and economic determinism (Dator 2006; Adem 2004). But it is a world now in turmoil in consequence of an America that had been taken down the path of militarism by an intelligentsia—the Vulcans—who were clearly seduced by notions of absolute power.

Not unexpectedly, then, when viewed through the lens of Huntington's (1994) perspectives and resultant polemics that have come to inform twenty-first century discourse, China's growing influence in regional and world affairs necessarily conjure fear and distrust by the West. Adding to the China-phobia in the US, is the increasing US trade imbalance with China which in 2008 stood at US$280 billion. In addition, China's growing foreign currency reserves, estimated to be over US$3.0 trillion in 2009, and its use of such reserves to either acquire energy properties around the world or invest in energy production facilities in other countries, and its refusal to side with the US and the West in their bid to impose punitive sanctions on North Korea and Iran feed the China-phobia. Hence, according to Niall Ferguson, "China is becoming more assertive; a rival not a partner... "When China's economy is equal in size to that of the U.S., which could come as early as 2027 . . . it means China becomes not only a major economic competitor - it's that already, it then becomes a diplomatic competitor and a military competitor."[27]

China and the Middle East Crisis

Given the heightened anxiety over China's emergence, then, there is the nagging suspicion the invasion of Iraq and consequential play-out of self-fulfilling prophesies there and elsewhere in the region were largely the results of the initial stage of a grand strategy to contain China gone awry; to this observer, it was a strategy that arguably had as its ultimate objective the containment of China's economic growth and growing influence through controlling its access to Middle East oil (Chang 2008). Indeed, when viewed through the prism of the *Clash of civilizations*, China's increasing energy demands to fuel its rapidly-growing economy, according to Huntington (1996: 240), "are likely to impel it to expand its relations with Iran, Iraq, and Saudi Arabia, as well as Kazakhstan and Azerbaijan." and, thus, must be of concern to the West in general and the US in particular.

Since Huntington's observation, Iraq, of course, was invaded by the "Coalition of the willing" in March 2003 on the basis of a perceived threat to world peace by the Saddam Hussein regime purportedly in possession of WMD, thereby coincidentally eliminating one of the potential China alliances identified by Huntington. In addition, Kazakhstan and Azerbaijan have been openly courted by the US—much to the displeasure of the then Russian President Putin—while schemes to control Central Asia have been and still are proffered by others.

With respect to a China–Iran alliance envisaged by Huntington, Iran's claims of pursuing nuclear energy for domestic use is yet another opportunity to thwart such an alliance. Indeed, despite denials to the contrary by the Iranian government and, as with the invasion of Iraq, no supporting evidence—just suspicions of intent—of a nuclear weapons program, the US administration supported by the UK, France, and Germany, have labeled Iran's uranium enrichment program as a precursor to the production of nuclear weapons, and through successive UN resolutions have effectively issued ultimatums to Iran to stop such enrichment or face sanctions. Thus, for the time being, any possible China-Iran alliance is on hold.

Despite attempts to block alliances as perceived by Huntington, China has been able to forge other alliances. For example, in January 2006 the Chinese government secured cooperation agreements on energy with the King of Saudi Arabia on his historic visit to China. As a follow-up, in August 2006, similar agreement for the supply of oil was entered into with Venezuela. China is also tapping into Cuban gas reserves which must be of further concern to the US. As noted earlier, an Australian firm has reportedly entered into an agreement to supply China with coal worth US$60.0 billion over twenty years.

Comparative Foreign Investment

As is now well recognized, China is using its vast foreign exchange reserves to invest in energy producing countries in Latin America, Africa and beyond. Indeed, its investment in the energy sector in Iran is in defiance of US declared restrictions imposed on third countries. But much like US restrictions on third country investments in and trade with Cuba, its restrictions on Chinese foreign investment is largely ineffective. Moreover, many countries have come to the realization that short of its military power, America is, in the phraseology of Jagdish Bhagwati, evidencing "diminished giant syndrome." In addition to its declining share of world trade, its share of world GDP declined from 40.3 percent in 1950 to 21.8 percent in 1980 and further still in the 1990s despite attempts to stem the decline through bilateral and regional trade agreements, and, of course, quantitative restrictions. Also, the US is now the world's biggest debtor nation with a national debt estimated to reach US$17.1 trillion in the next ten years, the servicing of which is estimated to reach US$800 billion annually.

China, on the other hand, is growing at a phenomenal rate, even in the face of economic downturns in the major industrialized countries attendant the 2007–08 financial crisis. Its economy has increased ten-fold in the last 20 years, and, before the 2007–08 recession, there was no letting up in its export drive. As recognized by Alan Blinder of Princeton University, "China must export like mad to grow like mad." In this connection, it is on the treadmill of economic growth which, unfortunately, is regarded by many Americans as eclipsing America's hegemony. And, notwithstanding that China's export drive is America's continued low-inflation rate, many would rather just have it all by seeking to contain China through the exercise of condign power. As observed by Ikenberry (2004: 324):

> The United States will not seek security through the more modest realist strategy of operating within a global system of power balancing, nor will it pursue a liberal strategy in which institutions, democracy, and integrated markets reduce the importance of power politics altogether.

China's Modernization of its Military

As is becoming clear, there is increasing concern over China's modernization of its military notwithstanding that the US, Russia, and indeed the UK, are also upgrading their weapon systems. As former President Clinton remarked, the change over to diesel-powered submarines by the Chinese navy allows them to run deeper and become less tractable. The shooting down of one of its own satellites by laser in early 2007 has also raised concerns at the Pentagon. Joint military exercises between Russian and Chinese forces further raised red flags at the Pentagon, even though they were in keeping with what is considered normal defensive exercises, not unlike those of the US battle groups in the Persian Gulf.

Clearly, the Chinese unlike the Japanese are not intimidated by US or Western fire power despite being no more than a "middle power." It is for this reason that there is concern over China's developing capability in space. It is also for this reason and the perceived potential for a "Confucian–Islamic connection" that the West led by the US is seemingly deeply committed to preventing Middle-East Arab countries and, more especially, Iran from acquiring nuclear weapons. When examined in context of the Eisenhower China policy, and variants thereof since then, these actions suggest a continuation of the policy of containing China into the twenty-first century, albeit by way of economic containment. However, the opportunity for a "showdown" with China, as debated and summarized in the June 1966 Long Range Study by the US State Department, has passed with China's acquisition of advanced technology and the modernization of its military well on its way.

China's Normative Power

According to Johns Hopkins University's David Lampton (2005: 317), China's "normative power" is growing in consequence of a posture that speaks to "economic engagement, security assurances, opposing superpower domination, championing a level playing field for developing countries and being economically successful." This perspective is shared by John Ghazvinian (2007) whose account of the African experience speaks of a "Beijing Consensus" which stands in contrast with the Washington Consensus of the 1980s and 1990s that speaks to private-public partnerships and liberalization of economies in developing countries[28] (see also Ghazvinian 2007). It is a posture that resonates with many in Asia and the developing world, and one that contrasts most strikingly with the doctrine of preemption and the archaic core-periphery paradigm that heretofore served the developed Western economies; it is also one that is more likely to be embraced as the more acceptable of the two by an informed pluralist world.

Notwithstanding this contrast in approaches which many Chinese emphasize, China, contrary to US rhetoric, regards the US as the world's sole superpower and a source of advanced technology and, of course, market for its products. Hence, according to Zhang and Tang (2005), China's power diplomacy is oriented necessarily towards the US first, and to the region thereafter. Be that as it may, China's posture on championing a level playing field for developing countries and opposing superpower domination is deemed incompatible with the capitalist world system, and thus has elicited criticisms from the West who, having written off over US$40.0 billion of developing countries' debts in 2006, believe that there should be some strings attached to Chinese aid to developing countries. But from the Chinese and developing countries' perspectives, there needs to be a paradigm shift with respect to foreign aid; from the long-established centre–periphery framework to one that is fully supportive of sustainable development and is respectful of indigenous cultures.

In light of the above, until the US reorients its policies from dominance to leadership, there will always be concerns over China's role in a changing world order.

NOTES

1. Yueh, L., "China can be engine of growth." *BBC NEWS*, http://news.bbc.co.uk/go/pr/fr/-/2/hi/business/7676957.stm, October 20, 2008
2. Mcdonald, J., "China exports show trade recovery on track." *Associated Press*, http://finance.yahoo.com/news/China-exports-show-trade-apf-4119920176.html?x=0&sec=topStories&pos=9&asset=&ccode=
3. "Most Americans see China as economic threat: Poll." http://news.yahoo.com/s/afp/20091117/ts_alt_afp/chinausdiplomacyeconom
4. Heintz, J., "Russia test-launches new ICBM." http://news.yahoo.com/s/ap/20070529/ap_on_re_eu/russia_missile_test

5. Buchanan, P., "McLaughlin Group." *PBS.org*

6. See "Come in number one, your time is up." *The Economist*, April 14, 2007, p. 12

7. "Charlie Rose." PBS.org, 26 April, 2007

8. "Come in number one, your time is up." *The Economist*, April 14, 2007, p. 12

9. "China looks to its own consumers." BBC, http://news.bbc.co.uk/go/pr/fr/-/2/hi/business/8006029.stm, April 18, 2009

10. Ducet, L. "News Hour" *BBC NEWS,* February 6, 2010; see also "Australian firm strikes $60B coal deal with China." *Associated Press*, February 6, 2010

11. Mcdonald, J., "China exports show trade recovery on track." *Associated Press*, http://finance.yahoo.com/news/China-exports-show-trade-apf4119920176.html?x=0&sec=topStories&pos=9&asset=&ccode=

12. J. Fallows interview with Jeffery Brown, "News Hour." *PBS.org*, June 25, 2007

13. Geown, K., "China challenges US at apec forum." *BBC NEWS*, http://news.bbc.co.uk/go/pr/fr/-/2/hi/asia-pacific/6150406.stm ; November 15, 2006

14. "China leapfrogs Germany." *BBC News*, http://news.bbc.co.uk/go/pr/fr//2/hi/business/7829230.stm, January 14, 2009

15. Klapper, B.S., "WTO: 'China overtakes U.S. in exports." http://news.yahoo.com/s/ap/20070412/ap_on_bi_ge/wto_china

16. "Iowa Republican Fundraiser and Straw Poll." *C-SPAN*,, 11 August, 2007

17. Zhou Wenzhong, China's Ambassador to the US, "Chinese Developing International Relations." Watson's Institute for International Relations, Brown University, *C-SPAN 2,* March 22, 2007

18. Excerpt from the President's Inaugural Address in January 2005.

19. Zhou Wenzhong, China's Ambassador to the US, "Chinese Developing International Relations." Watson's Institute for International Relations, Brown University, *C-SPAN2*, March 22, 2007

20. 2008 State Department & foreign Operations Spending' House Budget Committee, www.appropriations.org , *C-SPAN*, March 21, 2007

21. "Chavez: China to devote $20B to Venezuelan projects." *Associated Press,*http://finance.yahoo.com/news/Chavez-China-to-devote-20B-to-apf2343826544.html?x=0&sec=topStories&pos=3&asset=&ccode=

22. Zhou Wenzhong, China's Ambassador to the US, "Chinese Developing International Relations." Watson's Institute for International Relations, Brown University, *C SPAN2*, March 22, 2007

23. Brzezinski's interview, "Charlie Rose." *PBS.org*, June 15, 2007

24. Interview with Charlie Rose, "Charlie Rose." *PBS.org*, July 7, 2007.

25. NPR News, *National Public Radio*, March 8, 2007

26. Task, A., "US Empire in Decline; on Collision Course with China." *Newsmaker*, October 20, 2009

27. Ibid

28. Ghazvinian, J., 'Book TV', *C-SPAN 2*, March 27, 2007

Chapter Eight

Targeted Revaluation: A Double-edged Sword?

As discussed in Chapter Two, one of the instruments in the tool box of American policymakers, the guardian of Western capitalism, is what I call targeted revaluation. The idea behind the theory of targeted revaluation is to avoid a general devaluation of the domestic currency as a means to reducing trade deficits and indeed budget deficits; it is pursued if such deficits were perceived as primarily resulting directly and or indirectly from the competitive advantage of a specific rival.

According to the theory, targeting the competitor's currency for revaluation should result not only in the correction of the trade imbalance with the competitor—the classical trade theory premised on devaluation—but also in a general reduction in the competitor's exports to third markets. In other words, the expected effect would be the equivalent of slowing the export-led economic growth of the competitor from the revaluation; only in this case, it is not by way of choice as presumed in economic theory, but rather by imposition from a rival pursuing its self-interest. Moreover, the country seeking the revaluation of its competitor's currency should be able to continue to benefit from its imports of cheap products from other low-cost producers with which it has a positive trade balance or on which it must rely for the supply of essential raw materials such as, for example, oil and other natural resources, without having to expend more of its own resources for them.

Clearly, the presumption of targeted revaluation—a manifestation of aggressive capitalism—is that the country seeking the revaluation would be able to redress its trade imbalance by taking advantage of its targeted competitor's expected loss of competitiveness, as suggested in game theory. Furthermore, the resultant expected reduction in the competitor's foreign exchange earnings should, again in theory, limit its ability to influence third countries geopolitically as well as geo-economically. This latter expectation has become an imperative of the Western economies in consequence of the emergence of the BRIC countries, more specifically China, in the last decade; their demands for resources, in addition to increasing the pricing pressures on the developed economies, have fostered a new geo-economic relationship with other developing countries which, in turn, is perceived as contrary to the interests of the Western economies led by the US. Indeed, the emergence of Asia as a direct challenge Western economic dominance has been the concern of the Western dominated and controlled Bretton Woods institutions since the early 1980s.

Prior to the rise of Asia as a challenge to Western dominance, the greatest challenge to the West was the elimination of Islam; this it sought to do by a process of conquest, conversion, and incorporation. As observed by Arnold Toynbee (1948: 186–7):

> This concentric attack of the modern West upon the Islamic world has inaugurated the present encounter between the two civilizations. It will be seen that this is part of a still larger and more ambitious movement, in which the Western civilization is *aiming at nothing less than the incorporation of all mankind in a single great society, and the control of everything in the earth, air, and sea* which mankind can turn to account by means of modern Western technique [emphasis added].

Since Toynbee's observations of the Westernization imperative vis-à-vis Islam, Israel has been added to the equation on the side of the West, and, for a while, gave the West a distinct if not overwhelming advantage in this historical conflict between Christendom and Islam (Chang, 2008). However, as I see it, on the other side of the equation must be added China, which has emerged on the world scene in the last decade and which is now, in consequence, regarded as posing an even greater threat to the Westernization imperative than Islam; hence, the need to restrict China's influence at all cost has become an imperative of the US as the guardian of the capitalist world-economy (Chang 2008). But, as discussed in Chapter Seven, since the US has little or no direct leverage over China, it is forced to find other ways of containment, including changing the rules of international trade to its advantage, albeit in the short term.

While short-term fixes resonate with a particular subset or subsets, those fixes that are the product of manipulation of the established rules of the game often redound to the long term disadvantage of their perpetrators, for two reasons. The first, is that such contrivances serve as perverse incentives to high-cost and inefficient producers who, in addition to contributing to the misallocation of resources, become even more dependent on intervention, as evidenced, for example, by the perpetual propping-up of the domestic textile and clothing industries in the US and EU, and the US steel and sugar industries; it is also evidenced by the collapse and rescue of the domestic auto industry that was sheltered from competition by a series of trade barriers. Second, short-term fixes elicit countervailing actions that are often more difficult to counter legitimately within established international economic frameworks and law.

Given the above observations, before getting into the discussion on the slippery slope of targeted revaluation, it is necessary first, that the theoretical basis for international trade, that is, comparative advantage, be reviewed, and second, that the issue of exchange rates be placed in its proper historical context.

The Law of Comparative Advantage

As formulated by the English economist David Ricardo (1772–1823), trade between countries occurs as a result of the comparative advantage each has in relation to the other in the production of certain goods and services. While in many cases trade is premised on absolute advantage by reason of the uniqueness of the product and resource endowment, in general, it is premised on the availability of and easy access to one or more of the factors of production that are basic to the production process as reflected in the relative cost to produce that product. Hence, natural resource endowment, abundance and availability of cheap labor, capital formation, advanced technology, and entrepreneurial skills, have a role in varying degrees in determining absolute or comparative advantage.

Clearly, countries with an abundance of labor would have an absolute advantage in producing labor-intensive products while highly industrialized countries would be operating at a higher level of development (see Rostow, 1961) and are therefore likely to have a comparative advantage in the production of capital-intensive goods. Therefore, the more technology-advanced countries would have an even greater advantage in manufactured goods by bringing such advanced technology to bear on the production processes, as was the case of the US and the EU up to around the 1980s; indeed, it could be said that the US and EU at one point in time enjoyed absolute advantage in the manufacture of capital-intensive products.

Irrespective of whether a country has an absolute advantage or a comparative advantage, it will, as the theory goes, continue to enjoy such advantage in the production of a specific good until its marginal cost of production is equal to the marginal cost of production of its nearest competitor. Production beyond this point would put it in a state of disequilibrium, in which case, the producer would be at a comparative disadvantage vis-à-vis other producers, which could include the country over which it initially had a comparative advantage.

A state of disequilibrium is signaled when the marginal cost of production exceeds the marginal revenue from trade as measured by the world market price of the product or products; it is reached either through exhaustion of endowed finite resources; increased cost of imported raw materials; higher domestic labor costs; high energy costs; and reduced domestic savings. When disequilibrium is reached, the country must make fundamental structural adjustments to restore equilibrium, as was the case with most developing countries in the late 1970s and 1980s. In the case of the advanced industrialized countries, on the other hand, history tells us they have been able to devise ways to delay the onset of disequilibrium which include: colonization of resource-rich countries; establishing a center-periphery relationships with lesser developed countries; the imposi-

tion of tariffs on imports; the payment of subsidies to high-cost domestic producers; and later, the imposition of non-tariff barriers on cheap imports, as evidenced by voluntary export restraints and unilateral trade sanctions as embodied
in the US Trade and Tariff Act, 1974. In addition, many countries have resorted
to their superior economic and military powers to control access to vital resources, especially by weaker countries; this is especially so when a state of
disequilibrium is reached and comparative advantage has given way to contrivance as the basis for trade.

Countries operating on the edge of their contrived advantage are thus prone
to trade imbalances—especially with those countries whose cheap products help
to keep domestic inflation low—when the props to their trade advantages are
removed and the inputs to production reflect their true costs, as is the situation in
which the US finds itself in the twenty-first century. Furthermore, trade imbalance is quickly reached when unrestrained access to vital resources, such as oil,
is controlled by their legitimate owners, as evidenced by the formation of the
Organization of Petroleum Exporting Countries (OPEC) in 1960; the increase in
the price of oil (from a low of US$4.00 a barrel) since the Arab oil embargo in
1973, has been a significant contributor to America's perpetual trade imbalance
since the 1980s.

In addition to the dismantling of some of the artificial props to comparative
advantage, chiefly, colonialism, the rapid industrialization of East Asia during
the last quarter of the twentieth century further served to erode both comparative
and contrived advantages of the Western industrialized countries that had become complacent; most of them felt secured in their prowess at negotiating trade
agreements on favorable terms, and in their ability to bring their influence to
bear on the decision-making process at international organizations such as the
United Nations, the WTO, the IMF, and the World Bank.

Exchange Rates: Historical Context

Floating exchange rates came into being in the early 1970s in consequence of
the perceived constraints of the gold exchange standard; its proponents argued
that the world would be better off in terms of economic welfare if trading nations were not held to paying for their imports with gold converted at the fixed
price of US$35.00 per ounce to which they agreed back in 1934; theories were
therefore developed to authenticate and generalize floating exchange rates.
However, the real reason for the switch was that the US found itself as the greatest debtor nation in the world after WWII, and the only way to get out of its
debt-overhang was to devalue its sovereign debt, converted at a gold-exchange
rate of US$35.00 per ounce, by inflating the price of gold.

With the price gold shooting up to US$800.00 per ounce soon after the
adoption of floating exchange rates, debts that were incurred at the gold-
exchange rate of US$35.00 per ounce disappeared almost in the twinkling of an

eye; in other words, those creditors holding US Treasury IOUs that were converted at a gold exchange rate of US$35.00 per ounce, received the equivalent of less than $0.05 in the dollar in terms of gold.

Clearly, moving from the gold-exchange standard to floating exchange rates was the logical next step forward from the adoption of the gold-exchange standard in 1934. The basic argument was the same: trade, according to its proponents, needed to be expanded, and settlement in gold was not only cumbersome, it was also a slight to the trading regime premised on integrity; but, so too were the real underlying reasons and, of course, the outcome, which was to get the US out of debt. Both incidents evidenced the extent to which powerful nations would seek to change the rules of the game to get out of sticky situations.

Up until the mid 1980s, floating exchange rates worked for the US. However, it was not long before the US found itself back into a similar debt situation: It was incurring budget deficits to fund its quest for hegemony under Ronald Reagan; at the same time, indulging in over-consumption, and building an economy from external borrowings. It was also overleveraging its trust with the wider world while accessing world resources by overleveraging the Dollar which had become, by reason of the size and strength of the US economy, the accepted currency for international settlement since floating exchange rates were adopted in 1972. Furthermore, the modernization of the German and Japanese economies had taken its toll on the US economy; Germany had during this period displaced the US as the number one export nation in the world, with Japan a close third. East Asia was also on the move, growing at more than twice the rate of the OECD countries as depicted in Figure 4.1.

Clearly, the empirical evidence up to mid 1980s served to validate the theory of international trade premised on comparative advantage, as envisaged by David Ricardo; and, since this was to the disadvantage of the dominant industrialized countries, the theory of comparative advantage had to give way to the new notion of competitive advantage, contrived to protect the existing advantage of the Western economies. As a result, what was considered comparative advantage in one period, and in one place, soon morphed into human rights violations at another place, and in another period; production standards and other high-minded stipulations of the importing country had to be met by the exporting country. And, if those were not enough to raise the cost of production of the exporter, tariffs and quantitative restrictions were imposed by the importers.

As discussed by Bhagwati and Patrick (1990), tariffs and quantitative restrictions were taken to their limits in the last quarter of the twentieth century; but they soon became an embarrassment to their practitioners and, therefore, had to be phased-out gradually, and, then, only through rancorous negotiations.

With a phase-out of tariffs, and to some extent quantitative restrictions, the need for a new approach to containing the competitiveness of the BRIC countries and East Asia became a US imperative, if not a West imperative, as evidenced by the resort to targeted revaluation which is a form of currency manipulation.

Currency Manipulation

Currency manipulation, strangely enough, is a function of floating exchange rates; it was first introduced by the US in the late 1980s in response to its trade imbalance with Japan. According to the then Harvard economics professor, Lawrence Summers, effecting a 10 percent devaluation in the Dollar would do more for the US economy than a 10 percent reduction in imports or a 10 percent increase in exports. However, rather than devalue the Dollar, it was found that it was preferable, for reasons explained below, to target the Japanese Yen for revaluation simply by suggesting to the currency market that the Yen was undervalued while simultaneously professing a strong Dollar policy for general consumption. But, while the Yen increased in value in response to intervention in the currency market, the trade imbalance with Japan remained; even so, targeted revaluation has since been made an aspect of US trade policy, hence the push to have the Chinese float the Yuan.

What is curious with this new approach to trade, that is, targeted revaluation, is that a country's foreign exchange earnings, and thus reserves, have now been made targets for readjustment by those who have squandered their own resources and savings pursuant instant gratification and geopolitical dominance, and now are reluctant to bear responsibility for their profligacy; moreover, by any measurement, this approach is tantamount to socializing international trade within the framework of free-market capitalism, which is a philosophical contradiction.

The Slippery Slope of Targeted Revaluation

Despite the theoretical benefits to be had from targeted revaluation, this theory is turned on its head when the country seeking to pursue revaluation of a competitor's currency does so from a position of weakness. As defined here, weakness is not only what exists internally but also what is manifested externally; in the case of the US, this includes the obvious inability to export consumerism as a way of life, and to effect substantial changes to the targeted rival's economic structure and, thus, the relative strength of the rival. In this regard, the issue becomes one of determining whether indeed the sea is full and the current serving. It also includes the not so obvious: inability to achieve declared geopolitical and geo-economic objectives as well as a susceptibility to manipulation from within the ranks.

For the above reasons, targeted revaluation is only for the strong; it is certainly not within the capacity of weaker developing countries to engage in such a practice. Indeed, as the structural adjustment experience of the 1980s and 1990s evidence, developing countries exist as a laboratory for proving-in economic dogma, in this case, to validate the notion that devaluation of the domestic currency serves to revive flagging economies through expenditure-switching (see Fischer & Easterly, 1990). That the outputs of the countries which are forced to devalue their domestic currencies are gobbled up at confiscatory prices by those whose currencies are kept artificially high precisely for that purpose, is incidental to the high-minded purpose of development aid and preferential trade agreements. Strong, however, is also relative, which brings me to the specific case of US–China relationship and the slippery slope of pursuing targeted revaluation of the Chinese currency at this point in time.

As discussed in Chapter Two, the US is seeking a revaluation of the Chinese Yuan on the grounds that the Yuan's peg to the US dollar is too low, thus giving China a competitive advantage over the US in bilateral trade as well as in third markets. There is no disputing this assertion, although maintaining a relatively low value of one's currency is a practice learned as show above; equally, however, a country's currency can also be made to appear undervalued by external contrivance as discussed below.

In addition to the above, there are other factors at play that operate to the detriment of the US dollar and the US economy as a whole. First, despite its charges of unfair trading practices by its trading partners, the US, like those that have gone before it, has essentially priced itself out of several of the markets it once had a competitive advantage; the internal cost structures of many US producers have placed them in unsustainable and indefensible positions in a global competitive environment. These conditions have given rise to unilateral trade sanctions by the US, as authorized by the Trade and Tariff Act, 1974, as amended to include Super 301 (see Bhagwati & Patrick, 1990). While such sanctions were successfully employed as strategy in the 1980s and 1990s, they are now met by countervailing sanctions. In other words, many developing countries are empowered by their own development since the mid 1980s and, having learned to play the game (Stiglitz, 2002), by their own sense of strengths and weaknesses; as such, they are responding increasingly with like sanctions. Indeed, like the spread of information technology, US trade strategies have become decipherable, as opposed to transparent, thus leveling the playing field to the consternation of the largest and most powerful economy in the world.

Second, given the shift in focus of the US economy from traditional manufacture to financial services since the mid 1980s, it follows that the US must rely increasingly upon lower-cost producing countries to feed, clothe, and entertain its masses while its highest 20 percent of income earners indulge in wealth accumulation and conspicuous consumption in keeping with Thorsten Veblen's *Theory of the Leisure Class.* In this model, the US will always experience a negative trade imbalance; it matters not that today it is with China; yesterday it was with Japan; and tomorrow it will be with some other low-cost producing country. Therefore, that the US should at this point in time seek to have the Chinese currency revalued is clearly not because of its trade imbalance with China; rather it is because the US wants to contain China because, unlike its relationship with Japan, it has almost no control over the direction of China's politics or economics.

To maintain its hegemony and thus access to needed resources to feed its voracious appetite for wealth accumulation, the US must bring other international actors under its control, failing which, it must work cooperatively even with those it considers foes so as not to implode. Knowing this, it would not be unreasonable for China to seek the removal of special restrictions attached to its membership of the WTO in a *quid pro quo* arrangement for a managed revaluation of its currency; that is, for China to be held to the rules of the game, the rules must be applied *in toto* to all members of the WTO and not from a reductionist and self-serving perspective as heretofore. It is therefore telling that Secretary Geithner's visit to China in April 2010 has been interpreted by Harvard's Julian Chang as signaling one of "cooperation" to the Chinese. The Europeans have long recognized that Western dominance peaked with the self-generated economic liberalization of the Middle East in the 1970s, despite the recruitment of Israel to the Westernization cause; that the West has been in the decline since then with the rise of Asia; and, that the US, having doubled-down on Iraq in 2003, is now struggling to stay in the game as principal.

In support of the above perspective and returning to the politics of international economics relations, consider the empirical evidence with respect to the failure of successive revisions of the precursors to the Multi-fiber Arrangement (MFA), and indeed the MFA, governing the importation of textile and clothing into the US since the 1960s (Goto, 1989). The evidence speaks to the slippery slope of self-serving short-term attempts at stemming erosion of competitiveness without addressing causality. Briefly, the Short-term Arrangement (STA) and the Long-term Arrangement (LTA) governing the importation of textile and clothing, the precursors to the MFA, were designed to protect the US textile industry by restricting Japanese exports of textile and clothing into the US and Europe; continuation of these arrangements were later made a condition precedent to Japan's entry into the General Agreement on Tariff and Trade (GATT), the predecessor to the WTO. While Japan's exports of textile to the US fell from 63 percent of total US imports in 1958 to 26 percent in 1960 in consequence, the void was quickly taken up by Hong Kong whose share of US imports rose from 14 percent to 27.5 percent (Tussie, 1987: 76). Hong Kong was later succeeded by other lower-cost producing developing countries as the US and the EU sought to restrict imports from Hong Kong further, and, later, from successive lower-cost producing countries, by changing the rules of the game. Meanwhile, the increasing cost of production of textiles and clothing in the US, and in the EU, required not only extensive farm support from the government but even greater restrictions on textile and cotton imports to the point of flagrant violation of the rules, ergo MFA III and IV, prompting this observation by Diana Tussie (1987; 73):

> GATT has been intended to provide the framework for the smooth expansion of international trade on the basis of comparative advantage and international specialization. Yet the description of a disrupted market rested precisely on the refusal to admit lower costs as a reason for the growth of trade.

In addition, in his *Economic Report of the President to the Congress* in February 1991, President George Herbert Walker Bush was obliged to make this observation:

> The continued existence and increasing restrictiveness of the global management of textile trade has eroded the confidence of many developing nations in the GATT system. . . . One of the goals of the United States and other nations in the Uruguay Round is to phase out the policies that currently control textile and the clothing trade.

Third, targeting the Chinese Yuan for revaluation does very little to correct America's trade imbalance; it merely allows the US to continue to import more from low-cost producers other than China, as the experience of textile and clothing evidenced. This it must do in order to maintain some semblance of competitiveness in world markets since imports from low-cost producing countries, including China, help to keep labor costs in the US from increasing by keeping inflation down. Hence, as posited by Wu Xiaoling, a former central bank vice governor, "the root cause of the problem was not a cheap yuan, but the relatively low cost of labor and resources in China."[1]

For these reasons, a reduction in imports from China will have to be met by an increase in imports from other low-cost producers if inflation were to be contained; more than that, the void will be filled by other low-cost producers as the US fails to curb its consumption of imports. Simply put, then, the US is not obliged to buy cheap Chinese-made goods; it also does not need any country's permission to impose punitive tariffs; its trade history is replete with unilateral trade sanctions (Bhagwati & Patrick, 1990). The difference between then and now is that imposing sanctions in the twenty-first century from a position of weakness comes at a cost ordinary Americans are ill prepared to shoulder.

Fourth, as recognized by the FED Chairman, Ben Bernanke, "consumer spending is the mainstay of the US economy."[2] It accounts for over 70 percent of GDP. Moreover, US exports is a paltry 12 percent of GDP compared with Germany's 47 percent of GDP; and, that this is so, has more to do with the American culture of consumerism than with China's trade practices or the value of its currency. Clearly, the US needs to reorient from a consumption-driven economy to an export-oriented economy, what economists refer to as expenditure-switching. This requires a general devaluation of the dollar, not just a revaluation of the Chinese Yuan, so as to realign the real exchange rate in favor of the export sector (Fischer & Easterly, 1990; Edwards, 1989; Dornbusch, 1988). In addition, given the high propensity to consume in America, any currency devaluation—vis-à-vis a particular country's currency or a general devaluation— needs to be accompanied by other measures to bring about a reduction in aggregate demand so as to have the export-dividend derived from currency depreciation reflected in a reduction to the current account deficit; it must also be prepared to export what is demanded, not what it wants to export for strategic reasons, a complaint that has been voiced repeatedly by the Chinese.

Also, devaluation of the dollar means that a larger proportion of domestic resources will have to be devoted to servicing external debts. Such cost is estimated to reach US$800.0 billion annually in less than ten years. The danger here is a further increase in external borrowings to service the debt when what is required is an increase in savings; there are numerous accounts of developing countries falling into just such a debt-trap in the 1970s and 1980s (Nashashibi, et al., 1992). In other words, the US is faced with precisely the same conditions several developing countries faced in the 1970s and 1980s (World Development Report, 1989). The only real difference is that, whereas high commodity prices combined with negative real interest rates in the 1970s (Krugman, 1988) encouraged deficit financing in developing countries, in the case of the US in the last two decades, it was the overleveraging of an increasingly overvalued currency combined with easy access to a pool of foreign savings attendant overleveraging of assets that encouraged the external financing of a ballooning national debt, including the bailout of Wall Street.

Fifth, there is no guarantee that the initial benefits derived from a revaluation of the Yuan would be sustainable. Indeed, there is every chance American triumphalism and complacency would prevail, as was the case of the "Big Three" Detroit motor companies' so-called victory over Japanese exports in the late 1980s and early 1990s. During that period, the Japanese Yen was targeted for revaluation. While growth of the Japanese economy was stymied for most of the 1990s in consequence, its trade surplus continued throughout this period.[3]

Sixth, a revaluation of the Chinese Yuan could redound to the benefit of the Chinese economy given the size of its domestic market, which is still at an embryonic stage, and its abundance of labor. Indeed, that the Chinese government injected US$586 billion into the domestic economy in 2009 as a cushion against the shock from a reduction in exports to the Western economies in recession suggests countervailing measures to a forced revaluation of their currency;[4] this it did, not by borrowing but by drawing down on its reserves. Moreover, any revaluation of the Chinese Yuan vis-à-vis the Dollar would reduce the cost of needed raw materials that are priced in Dollar; the Japanese experience of the 1990s speaks to this contention.

Last but not least, unlike the US that is debt-laden, China's huge foreign currency reserves and dollar-denominated assets could be used to continue its economic growth even in the face of sanctions; it will, however, have less to invest in US treasuries which, in turn, will reflect in higher debt cost to the US as it seeks additional foreign borrowings to finance its recovery program. Additionally, under these relatively different conditions, it would be a poor policy choice if the US forced a revaluation of the Yuan for short-term objectives; the Chinese could use its reserves to drive up commodity prices thereby putting pricing pressure on already high-cost producers in the US and the EU. Clearly, then, as recognized by several analysts and economists, forcing a revaluation of the Chinese currency at this point in time would not lead to any material improvement in the US trade balance. Furthermore, such an outcome would require continuous revaluations of the Chinese currency to the point of making it a substitute currency, and this is not what US policymakers would want happen in the current climate of distrust, even by friends and allies.

Finally, the US has changed, almost in the twinkling of an eye, from being the greatest post WWII creditor country of the world to being the greatest debtor country of the world; and, in spite of its traditional aversion to communist entanglements, the US has been driven, by the necessity to rescue capitalism, to seek funding, from China, for its burgeoning budget deficit. As observed by Congressman Ron Paul in 2007, "the US is borrowing US$2.5 billion a day, most of which is coming, unbelievably, from the Chinese."[5] Since then, China has become the single largest holder of US sovereign debt notwithstanding that it is trimming its holdings of US treasuries.[6]

Clearly, then, targeted revaluation of the Yuan is not without its risks, especially when the country targeted is also your banker. The cover page (and story) in the February 6, 2010, issue of the *Economist Magazine*, captioned "Facing up to China," is telling. In addition, there is perhaps a lesson to be drawn from this 60 year old caution by Arnold Toynbee (1948: 198) with respect to the West's complaint against the Turks:

> The victim of our censure might retort that, whatever he does, he cannot do right in our eyes, and he might quote against us, from our own scriptures: 'We have piped unto you and ye have not danced; we have mourned to you and ye have not wept.'

A Word about Asset Bubbles

Contrary to popular belief, assets bubbles are not naturally arising from market forces; rather, they arise from manipulation of the market. The overleveraging of assets is a function of revaluation of these assets in keeping with the principle of "mark to market"; and, in the absence of appropriate financial regulation, is the primary causes of asset bubbles, as evidenced by the US experience of the last decade, especially in the housing market. Hence, the belief that asset bubbles could be exported to China from a revaluation of the Yuan is rooted more in wishful thinking than in reality. Moreover, given that the Chinese economy is still largely state-centric; promoting assets bubbles in China is more likely to reverberate to the disadvantage of the Western economies.

While one of the consequences of the revaluation of the Japanese Yen in the late 1980s and early 1990s was asset bubble, it is highly unlikely that a revaluation of the Yuan would have similar results. Unlike Japan of the 1980s, China has yet to reach the stage of diminishing marginal returns, and any reduction in the price of needed resources will benefit its growth, that is, increase the level of real output, in the short term; this is Keynesian economics; it is how the US developed its powerful economy decades ago; and it is a clear means by which China can grow its economy from within, given its less-than full-employment condition. Hence, it is instructive that the Chinese Premier, Wen Jaobao, while acknowledging that "there has been a large drop in exports" asserted at the same time that, as a result of China's stimulus package, "Investment growth has accelerated, consumption has increased quite rapidly and domestic demand continues to rise."[7]

Moreover, because China is not constrained by the wrangling of special interests groups, it has been able to target its stimulus package for swift results. As a result, its economy grew by 10.7 percent in the last quarter of 2009, and over 12 percent in the first quarter of 2010, prompting the government to raise the reserve requirement of the commercial banks—another form of preventing asset bubbles—notwithstanding that inflation is well within acceptable levels.[8]

The High-stakes Game of Trade

Clearly, the game of trade is far more complex than is commonly understood; and the US has perfected the art of asymmetric trade relations. Consider, for example, the assertion by Chinese Commerce Minister, Chen Deming, that one of the main causes of the US trade imbalance with China is "U.S. restrictions on exports of certain goods to China, such as high-tech items that could have both civilian and military use."[9] As argued above and in *Territoriality and the Westernization Imperative* (Chang, 2008), restricting the export of advanced technology to countries like China is a form of containment however you slice it; it is an effective strategy when such countries have cost structures that can only be improved to the disadvantage of the more developed countries whose competitive advantage has peaked and whose returns on capital investments are diminishing. In other words, countries like Japan in the 1980s and the BRIC countries in the twenty-first century must be contained, and when they break out, they must run the gauntlet that includes the charge of under-valued currencies, as was the case with Japan in the late 1980s, and is now the case with China; and, that is because there is more to international trade than increasing world economic welfare as first envisaged by David Ricardo.

Building on Toynbee's observation quoted above, in addition to restricting US exports of high technology only to friends and allies, trade is being used as a geopolitical weapon. In the particular case of China, the restriction of access to US technology, as charged by the Chinese Commerce Minister, when taken together with the joint US–EU complaint in 2008 that China is imposing a tax on certain environmentally-damaging materials, albeit needed for production in the West (see page 80), reveals the extent to which trade policies, as enforced by the WTO, are designed not to promote free trade or fair trade but rather to protect the capitalist world-economy and thus world dominance by the West. In this latter regard, as documented in the *United Nations, Human Development Report, 1995*: "The world has become a global financial village.... But the poorest 20 percent of the world's people have benefited little from the increased globalization of economies. In world trade, their share is only one percent (Todaro, 1995: 497)." In the same vein, the IMF observed in *World Economic Outlook, 1997*: "A large part of the developing world has yet to reap the benefits of globalization: many countries have continued to lose ground."

Balance of Payments Accounting: Measurement Issues

In addition to asymmetric trade agreements, it is clear that the old approach to Balance of Payments accounting has lost currency as an accurate measurement of bilateral trade flows in the twenty-first century. As constructed, the current approach to balance of trade on current account does not fully capture the real purpose of international trade and settlement that was necessary prior to the introduction of floating exchange rates or to the increasing resort to outsourcing and the extensive use of lower-wage countries as export platforms. In terms of the latter, the composition of international trade has been radically altered by the outflow of production resources and flow-back to the home country of products that have been outsourced to a lower-cost producing country; hence, the system of accounting for trade needs to be revised to reflect not only this changed dynamic in international trade and settlement in the twenty-first century but also in the interest of fair play.

While the use of export processing zones (EPZ) became vogue in the 1970s and 1980s primarily as means to access the abundance of lower-cost labor and other resources at their sources, such practices have trade and currency-valuation implications for the more advanced developing countries, such as China, in the twenty-first century. Consider, for example, the production of textile and clothing that have been largely transferred from the industrialized countries to the lower-cost producing countries in Asia and South America, as discussed above. The manufacture and exports of textile and clothing is still a major source of foreign exchange earnings for many developing countries, including China, despite the myriad of tariffs and non-tariff barriers imposed by the US and EU against their imports. However, given that a good proportion of textile and clothing from China is primarily in consequence of outsourcing by American and European companies for return to the home country's domestic market, very little in terms of value-added is retained by China, as discovered by James Fallows of the *Atlantic Monthly* (see page 119). For this reason, only that portion of the value of the final product retained should be treated as export for the purpose of computing bilateral trade balances, in this case, with China.

In addition to functioning as a source of cheap labor for Western companies, China functions as *de facto* EPZ for countries such as Japan, Malaysia, Singapore, Taiwan, and South Korea (see page 118). Therefore, like an agency or consignment arrangement in which revenues are shared between principal and agent, exports by the host country that are directly attributable to outsourcing must be shared between the home country and the host country in proportion to the benefits derived from this particular type of arrangement; it matters not that the production facilities are located in the country of final processing, that is, the exporting country, or that the exporting country is the beneficiary of foreign capital investment; what matters is the proportion—the value-added—that remains with the host country. In other words, only the value-added portion of the product should be used in any accounting for trade between the two countries. To this end, imported inputs for final processing in a *de facto* EPZ should be treated as direct off-sets against the associated exports that are effectively on behalf of third countries; put another way, there must be a high proportion of "local content" to qualify the product as the output of the country of final processing. This is not novel, it is one of the primary clauses of the North American Free Trade Association (NAFTA); it was devised to prevent Japan from using Mexico as an export platform to the American and Canadian markets; hence, for products to qualify as "Made in Mexico," there had to be 70 percent local content. Therefore, given the existence of this precedence and the notion of equity in trade, the same criterion should be applied to determining balance of trade surpluses of countries that are used as export platforms, that is, there has to be at least 70 percent local content for the product to be considered as export of the country of final processing.

Conclusion

As argued above, targeted revaluation is, at best, a short term tool of questionable value to the user; indeed, it could redound to the disadvantage of those who seek to invoke it from a position of weakness, and the US is in a position of weakness not experienced since the Great Depression of the 1930s. Moreover, it is questionable whether the charges of currency manipulation can be supported by the facts, especially given that the Chinese economy is still largely state-directed, and currency transactions are conducted primarily by the state.

Equally important to the issue, is the contention that without the above-proposed revisions to Balance of Payments accounting, countries, in particular the US, that are ramping up foreign investments—direct and indirect—in low-cost producing countries or are increasingly taking advantage of lower labor costs and the absence of costly regulations in foreign lands, will almost always report negative balance of trade with those countries with which they have such arrangements or which are being used as export platforms by third countries. I would further argue that since cross-border investment flow has become one of the defining characteristics of international trading relations in the twenty-first century, the income derived from such flow is as much part of the global trade dynamic as the cross-border flow of goods and services, and, therefore, should be treated as one and the same when measuring so-called trade imbalances. Also, given that American corporations do not pay taxes on foreign earnings until such earnings are repatriated to the US and treated as income, such earnings are likely not reported as inflows for Balance of Payments accounting purposes until they are repatriated, in which case, holding income overseas serves to have a distorting effect on the Balance on Current Account.

In the light of the above, and looking past the convenient rhetoric of an undervalued Chinese currency, that the US has been experiencing trade imbalances since the mid 1980s speaks to a change in the international trade dynamic occasioned by globalization; it is a dynamic that not only promotes the use of EPZ but also emphasizes outsourcing of production and flow-back of finished products; thus, it is a dynamic that goes to the root of the existing Balance of Payments accounting methodology as argued above. What is more, given that the US imports over 80 percent of its energy at an average price that is now more than ten times the price that existed prior to the Arab oil embargo in 1973, it follows that such increase in energy costs would be reflected in a deteriorating trade balance for countries operating at the margin. Indeed, the evidence suggests that, since the 1980s the US's perennial trade deficits on current account are largely derived not just from the high costs of imported energy but also from the loss of competitiveness of industries that are heavily energy-dependent and, thus, long before China became a major exporter to the US and EU.

Clearly, the issue of trade imbalance is not as straight forward as before the introduction of floating exchange rates. In addition to the negative impact of higher energy costs upon the US balance on current account, taking the approach to Balance of Payments accounting suggested above would most likely reveal that the current US trade imbalance with China is exacerbated not only by American companies outsourcing to China but also from third countries' use of China as an export platform for their exports to the US. Indeed, the trade data emanating from China for the first quarter of 2010 confirm this dynamic. For example, although China experienced a trade surplus of US$9.7 billion with the US for the month of March, it reported an overall trade deficit of $7.24 billion for the same period, and clearly speaks to factors other than exchange rates at play.[10] Under these conditions, seeking a revaluation of the Chinese currency must be seen for what it is: an economic tool with geopolitical implications; but, in this case, one that has not been fully thought out. It is therefore instructive that China's President Hu Jintao should insist with President Obama that:

Detailed measures for reform would [be] considered in the context of the world's economic situation, its development and changes as well as China's economic conditions. It won't be advanced by any foreign pressure. . . . Renminbi appreciation would neither balance Sino-U.S. trade nor solve the unemployment problem in the United States.[11]

Clearly, the lessons from the Japanese experience of the late 1980s and early 1990s, and from the 1997–98 Asian financial crises, have not been lost on the Chinese or, indeed, BRIC generally; their willingness to defend their currencies and other investment instruments against short-selling has effectively closed that window of opportunity to international currency speculators who pursue profits in weakened states. Moreover, as the contradictions in US trade and for-

eign investment policies, as highlighted by the Chinese as constraints to bal-
anced trade between the two countries, become issues for negotiations, targeted
revaluation becomes less defensible, more so in an era of globalization and an
inappropriate Balance of Payments accounting system. Be that as it may, desperate times require desperate measures. Without floating exchange rates there
can be no currency speculation, which is a function of international financial
liberalization, and without currency speculation, there can be no market intervention by the more powerful international actors whose *de facto* control of the
foreign exchange markets provides them with yet another tool to minimize the
economic challenges from the emerging economies. It thus remains to be seen
whether the Chinese are capable of holding their ground in the face of the self-
interested support for targeted revaluation that is forthcoming from the EU and
the IMF.

NOTES

1. Yao, K., & Buckley, C., *Reuters*, http://news.yahoo.com/s/nm/20100405/bs_nm/us_
   china_usa_yuan_1, April 5, 2010
2. "U.S. Economic Outlook," House Financial Services Committee, *CSPAN*, February
   16, 2007
3. Baston, A., "Risks fuel China's resolve on Yuan," *The Wall Street Journal*, February
   16, 2010
4. "China looks to its own consumers," *BBC NEWS*, http://news.bbc.co.uk/go/pr/fr/-
   /2/hi/business/8006029.stm, April18, 2009
5. "Campaign 2008," Iowa Republican Fundraiser and straw poll, *C-SPAN*, August
   2007.
6. Crutsinger, M., "China trims holdings of Treasury securities" *Associated Press*,
   March 15, 2010
7. "Campaign 2008," Iowa Republican Fundraiser and straw poll, *C-SPAN*, August
   2007.
8. "Stocks swoon after China brakes lending again," *Associated Press*, http://finance.
   yahoo.com/news/Stocks-swoon-after-China-apf-985550292.html? February 12, 2010
9. Wong, G., "China warns US against sanctions over Currency," *Associated Press*,
   March 21, 2010
10. Kurtenbach, E., "China's $7.24B March trade deficit 1st in 6 years" *Associated
    Press*, http://finance.yahoo.com/news/Chinas-724B-March-trade-apf195908372.
    html?x=0&sec=topStories&pos=1&asset=&ccode= April 10, 2010
11. "China's Hu rebuffs Obama on yuan," *Associated Press*, April 13, 2010

Chapter Nine

Biting the Bullet:
A Concluding Perspective

There comes a time in every country's history when it must face its own demons. It is a rite of passage to becoming a great nation and to escaping the "diminished giant syndrome," if you will. Based on the foregoing, it should be evident that the US is at a crossroad. The choice it makes, as noted earlier, is an existential one, for, as observed by Heraclitus (c540–c548 B.C.), "the road up and the road down are one and the same." Hence, it is a choice that must be made within the next few years with wisdom and the fortitude to carry through notwithstanding the initial costs in terms of its perception of self or indeed in terms of its inflated and morally insupportable and unsustainable way of life. This it must do, not just for the betterment of those who believe in the promise of the US Constitution, but also for the survival of the idea that there could be such a thing as one nation comprising peoples of disparate ethnic groups, indistinguishable from one another despite obvious manifestations of difference. To these ends, it needs to overcome the temptation to exploit the weaknesses of those who come in droves seeking fulfillment to the promise of a better life, not necessarily for themselves but for their children and grandchildren. Most of all, it needs to rehabilitate itself from an addiction to greed. How it does these things depends crucially upon its willingness to move from a state of denial to one of accepting the evidence, to embracing the rules of the game, and to biting the bullet, none of which is new to the American experience; rather, most are commonly found in well-run businesses and, more especially, in sports.

In sports, whether it is football, baseball, basketball, or any other team sport, the manager or head coach knows that reversing an unacceptable record comes first and foremost from recognizing weaknesses within the team and organization, and to making the necessary adjustments; it does not come from seeking to alter the rules of the game nor from maliciously interfering with another team's successes. This willingness to effect changes from within without fear or favor has proven to be most effective in reversing fortunes; and it is ingrained in the American spirit of fair play in sports. It is thus within this spirit of self examination, fair play, and biting the bullet that the following discussion on the several issues is offered.

The Job-creation/Budget Deficit-reduction Paradox

The great debate in the US in 2010 centers around job-creation and budget deficit reduction, around rather than on, because it is a contradiction to have both during a severe recession or near-depression, more so, when there are external imbalances.

Taking the last point first, economies get into trouble as a result of the willingness of foreigners to finance trade deficits; such willingness encourages inaction with respect to adopting appropriate adjustment policy-measures. For decades now, the US has been running saving-investment imbalances predicated on its ability as a highly industrialized country to attract foreign capital (Masson & Mussa, 1995). Hence, with an inflow of foreign capital, the trade imbalance is likely to continue without any expenditure-reducing action taken. This leads to greater external imbalance as a result of deteriorating terms of trade to the extent that imports remain at the same level or greater whilst exports continue to decline as a result of a declining real exchange rate. This has been one of the main causes of the Debt Crisis experienced by the developing countries in 1982. At the extreme, the Bolivia experience of the early 1980s well exemplifies the macroeconomic consequences of expansionary fiscal policies that include extensive external debt financing.

While the US situation is not nearly approaching that of Bolivia, or even the current budgetary problems of Greece, there are similarities with respect to underlying causality. Abstracting from America's ability to lean on its friends and allies to purchase certain goods and services, such as advanced weapons systems and other defense-related systems, thereby slowing the decline of its share of world trade, the US is experiencing a deteriorating real exchange rate as evidenced by its increasing trade deficit on current account. Its external debt is also increasing as noted above, supported primarily by an over-valued currency. As estimated by some economists, the national debt will reach US$17.0 trillion in ten years or about 140 percent of GDP when the unfunded portions of Social Security and Medicaid are added. When private debt is taken into account, America's debt burden is estimated to be as high as 800 percent of GDP; this is higher than the debt load found in most of the developing countries whose economies have had to be restructured in the 1980s under the auspices of the IMF and World Bank.

As it is in 2010, both the government and the private sector are competing for foreign financing. This would eventually lead to a crowding-out of foreign participation in the private-sector if the government continues to borrow externally to finance its budget deficit. Moreover, over the decades of restructuring in accordance with cutting-edge ideas, such as catering to "competitiveness-enhancing foreign direct investment"[1] many of the major developing countries have been able to attract foreign investments away from their traditional havens. This tendency is represented by the relatively greater increase in the outflow foreign direct investments (FDI) which now largely find their way to those countries that offer the best conditions for profit maximization with limited risk in a globalized economy (United Nations, 1998). Indeed, as observed by the United Nations Conference on Trade and Development (UNCTAD) "the clustering of economic activity, infrastructure facilities, access to regional markets and, finally, competitive pricing of relevant resources and facilities" (United Nations, 1998: 35) are the determinants of FDI location; and the BRIC countries are ahead of the curve. This trend in FDI outflow is evidenced by the then President Bush's efforts to reassure foreign investors that America welcomes foreign investment. In more direct terms, according to the then Treasury Secretary, Henry Paulson: "We just want to make it very clear that we welcome foreign investment and it is vital to our economic strength going forward."[2]

Crowding out becomes a real problem when foreign participation has been substantially reduced and both government and the private sector must compete for funds internally. Any such competition would push interest rates up to levels that could force curtailment of some private-sector investment as the level of idle money balances is reduced, the classic case of crowding-out. While it is possible that high interest rate might attract foreign financing back into the game, increase in debt-service costs would become an issue for the government, as was the case with Greece's bond offer: As reported, while the five billion Euro 10 year syndicated bond offer was over-subscribed, the interest rate was 6.4 percent, twice that paid by Germany, thus reflecting the increased risk attached to Greece's sovereign debt and adding substantially to debt-service costs. The solution, as imposed by the IMF and World Bank in such situations in developing countries, is structural adjustment. The literature is replete with the experiences of developing countries, from the largest to the smallest.

Structural Adjustment

Structural adjustment as supported by the IMF and World Bank in the 1980s and early 1990s requires expenditure-switching policies with very little regard to the social consequences in the short term. Thus, in addition to a reduction in government expenditure, taxes have often had to be increased even at the expense of employment; increase in unemployment was looked upon as the necessary short-term price of realignment, that is, until the private sector, more precisely, the export sector, regains its competitiveness. Job-creation under these conditions is incompatible with a policy of budget deficit reduction in the short-term.

Therefore, while tax-reduction could possibly serve as an incentive for private-sector investment in job-creating private-sector projects, the loss in tax revenues would add to the deficit in the short-term; at best, it merely transfers public funds to the private sector by way of tax reduction and other tax incentives without the government having any say in how such funds are spent. The idea that increase in payroll tax revenue would result from job-creation in the private sector is not unique to private-sector investment; one would expect an increase in payroll taxes irrespective of whether employment was private-sector derived or public-sector derived.

In addition to the approaches adopted by the IMF and World Bank during the 1980s, the experience of Argentina in the wake of the 1994–5 Mexican economic crisis offers lessons from which to draw. Not only did Argentina receive external funding but it was also subjected to an effective monitoring regime. Given the hundred of billions of dollars the government has invested in several entities, such as AIG, General Motors, Fannie Mae, and Freddie Mac, it could institute a monitoring regime not unlike the surveillance activities employed by the IMF during the 1994–5 crisis. The idea, of course, is not only to protect the government investment in these entities but also to ensure that the past mistakes are not repeated.

Tax Increases

As indicated above, according to conventional wisdom, in addition to expenditure reduction by the government, taxes will also have to be increased. While this has been par for the course in developing countries accessing the IMF/World Bank's structural adjustment facility (SAF) and enhanced structural adjustment facility (ESAF), it is a polarizing issue in twenty-first century America. Indeed, the extreme view is that tax reductions, not tax increase create jobs. Proponents of this theory point to the increase in jobs under Ronald Reagan in the 1980s as evidence; they also hold that government should not be involved in businesses that are better run by the private sector. While this is economics orthodoxy, the situation in the US is anything but normal. Without substantial infusion of liquidity by the government, recovery would likely be prolonged; more than that, the recession could even be deeper, feeding on itself as more and more jobs are lost to business closures.

Those who seek tax reduction does so on the basis of the expected political gains to be had from such a policy. Without tax increases, the government could be forced to dispose of its interests in those companies—AIG, General Motors, Chrysler, Fannie Mae, Freddie Mac, and others—it rescued by way of equity purchase, just as developing countries were compelled to privatized state-owned or state-managed enterprises, irrespective of social consequences. Based on the experience in developing countries, forcing the government to divest its holdings in the above-mentioned companies would likely destroy the political base of the Democratic Party, to the extent that it is anchored in organized labor, without significantly reducing the public debt or even the budget deficit. In addition, the government would also have to reduce its social impact ameliorating programs which the political right considers anathema to capitalism but which now account for 75 percent of the income of the lowest 20 percent of American households (see Table 6.1).

While many consider the latter proposition unconscionable in the light of the growing income inequality in the US as depicted in Table 6.1, reduction in social programs or an increase in taxes are two of the several choices facing the US at the crossroads. In this regard, it is noteworthy that many European countries and Canada have managed to grow their economies without having to abandon the less fortunate members of their respective societies. Moreover, many of them consider a progressive tax system as being in the national interest; but then, the Europeans and Canadians are by and large not challenged in ways Americans appear to be challenged. In addition to which, opportunities for personal growth in these countries have largely transcended social and other barriers that are still present in America, if latently so.

Tax Cuts, Leakages, and Waste

Although tax increase is an option for the US, it should come after and not before redressing the misallocation of resources arising from the extension of the Bush tax cut in 2008 and from the existence of tax loopholes to corporations. According to Senator Kent Conrad, 71 percent of the benefits of the Bush tax cut went to those earning over US$400,000 a year. In addition, the tax gap that exists between what is actually collected and what should be collected is estimated to run in the hundreds of billions of dollars annually; according to the Internal Revenue Service, the gap was US$345 billion in 2001. In addition, many US corporations are registered in off-shore tax havens so as to shelter their foreign-earned income from US taxes. Hence, as found by Christopher Helman of *Forbes*,[3] the tax as a percentage of income paid by many top US corporations is less than that paid by the average income earner in the US. This is because many US corporations, such as General Electric, are able to shelter their foreign income by offsetting losses incurred from domestic operations and also by holding such foreign income overseas for as long as possible without having to pay US taxes on them.

Adding to the budget deficit is what many regard as corporate welfare. The US spends about US$70.0 billion annually on subsidies of one kind or another, mainly in support of inefficient and uncompetitive industries. Given that such subsidies are for the most part inefficiently employed, the government could tie future payments to performance standards in the hopes of increasing the competitiveness of recipient industries; the South Korea experience speaks to the effectiveness of this approach to subsidies. Moreover, the US should seek to discontinue subsidies that can only be justified on the basis of relevance to political campaign contribution. For example, it is an inefficient use of resources when the price of gasoline at the pumps is 52 cents per gallon higher because of a tax on imported ethanol imposed to protect US corn growers.

Closing these revenue leakages will go a long way toward reducing the budget deficit. In addition, cutting back on military operations overseas, and reducing the waste in Medicare and Medicaid, according to Jeffrey Sachs,[4] should save the government about four percent of GDP. Indeed, when the various savings from Sachs's estimates are added up, they are close to the amount required to service the debt.

Infrastructure

Infrastructure has been long recognized as essential to economic growth. Indeed, over the last two decades, the building of an efficient infrastructure network—created assets, if you will—has been largely responsible for the growth in investment flows to the BRIC countries as noted above. It has also accounted for the shift in competitiveness to these countries. Also, as observed in lesser developing countries (LDC), there is a positive correlation and mutually reinforcing relationship between infrastructure spending and GDP growth. This relationship has been emphasized by lending agencies and underpinned development loans to LDC since the late 1980s in keeping with this finding (African Development Bank, 1999; World Bank, 1994).

In the case of the US, however, this relationship between infrastructure spending and GDP growth has been lost on policymakers over time. Indeed, as the US moved away from an industrial-based economic model to a service-oriented economic model—the new economy—attendant deregulation, infrastructure spending, other than private investment in the power and telecommunications sectors, as a percentage of GDP declined. The result in 2010 is a decaying public infrastructure that, if the experiences of the lesser developing countries in the 1970s and 1980s are generalized, would result in further decline in US competitiveness and massive budget deficits.

In this harsh economic environment, however, the US government has the opportunity to redress its decaying public infrastructure and to rejuvenate its flagging industrial and manufacturing sectors. With high unemployment, infrastructure projects could provide the required catalyst for sustainable economic recovery. Moreover, rather than pay unemployment benefits in the hopes for a quick turn-around in the private sector, the unemployed could be working on such public-funded projects, with unemployment benefits that would have been paid out used as an offset to the wages paid for such work. While such an undertaking would add to the budget deficit in the short-term, it should be looked upon as an investment in the future as public infrastructure is rebuilt across America, and US competitiveness in its traditional industries is restored. The Civilian Conservation Corp (CCC) created by President Theodore Roosevelt in the 1930s provided employment to three million unemployed Americans during the depression years; it evidenced addressing the challenges from within, drawing upon Americans' sense of duty to self, family, and country.

Failing a rebuilding of its economic infrastructure, the US will find itself engaging in monetary gimmickry in hopes that the competition would falter and that the financial services sector would be restored to its former glory. Meanwhile, those economies that have paid the requisite attention to fundamentals would be in relatively stronger positions than ever before. Reinforcing this perspective are reports that the Asian economies have been largely unaffected by the 2007–8 financial crisis that swept through the Western industrialized countries.[5] Furthermore, as expressed by the OECD, growth in the Asian economies appears to be the way out for the "feeble West."[6] Evidently, the lessons that attended the 1997–8 Asian financial crisis were not lost on them.

Positive Externalities from Environmental Protection

The US has for too long taken a half-hearted approach to the issue of environmental protection. The main reason for this is the strength of special interest groups, as evidenced by the 14,000 lobbies in Washington D.C. Many have argued that imposing stiffer environmental protection regulations on American companies puts them at a competitive disadvantage vis-à-vis countries that are low-cost producers which also do not have to comply with such regulations.

While there is no denying that requiring higher pollution control standards from American companies has a cost component, it is also true based on the evidence that environmental protection has positive externalities, including employment opportunities in new industries that would have to be created to service such needs. However, in a society in which reductionism and existential ideologies reign supreme, such positive externalities are not considered relevant unless they accrue directly to the benefit of the industries affected. Yet, many other countries have been able to respond positively to the need for stiffer environmental protection regulations when the whole is viewed as more important than the sum of its parts.

Despite the obvious benefit in terms of reduced cost of healthcare nationally from pursuing a cleaner environment, over 365,000 manufacturing plants in America consume vast quantities of fresh water and are allowed to pollute the rivers, streams, and lakes. Indeed, according to a report of the Environmental Protection Agency (EPA), over 40 percent of America's estuaries, rivers and lakes contain phosphates, asbestos, mercury and nitrates making them unavailable to common use such as fishing or swimming while posing considerable health hazards in consequence.

During the first decade of the twenty-first century, the petroleum industry backed by the US auto industry was able to stymied efforts to reduce carbon emissions by reason of its influence in Washington. Yet, according to some studies, reducing carbon emissions could contribute up to 2.4 percent growth to GDP;[7] but rather than take the long-term perspective implicit in adopting specific quantitative limits on carbon emissions, many companies have pushed for a cap and trade regime. The argument advanced by the proponents of cap and trade is that they will be disadvantaged vis-à-vis countries such as China and India who would not be held to the same standards. Therefore, by allowing them to purchase "emission rights" from other countries, mainly the developing countries, they would be able to cap emissions to agreed levels without losing competitiveness to the emerging countries.

In addition to cap and trade, many companies have recently advanced the idea of buying trees in the rain forests as a means to continuing to conduct business as usual. The argument in this case is that since trees contain a certain quantity of carbon, protecting them from being harvested is tantamount to reducing carbon emissions, and, as such, the savings in emissions should accrue to the benefit of the owners of the trees. They further claim that the benefit is two fold: carbon reduction and protecting the rain forests.

Clearly, both cap and trade and the buying of trees in the rain forests are nothing more than contrivance; they are designed primarily to avoid addressing the issues of carbon emission by the highly-industrialized countries whose prosperity came at the expense of the environment. Yet, by changing the production methods and dependency on fossil fuels coupled with a simultaneous reduction in consumption of the world rain forests, both the environment and the rain forests would be saved. Also, from an international relations perspective it is time the major developed countries take responsibility for bringing the world to the tipping point of environmental catastrophe, and instead of seeking to transfer costs onto the developing countries by way of contrivance, help them to make better choices based on the mistakes that have been clearly made by those that went before them in pursuit of wealth accumulation.

The Twin Pillars of Development and Social Cohesion

In addition to the debate on job-creation and budget deficit reduction, there are two other debates raging in the US on equally fundamental issues. The first, and perhaps the more ideological, centers on healthcare in America; the second, centers on Education. Yet, for most developed and developing countries, both are considered fundamental to human development and social cohesion and thus are taken for granted as basic human rights. For the US, however, they are issues at the cross road and are seemingly driven not by concerns for the human condition but rather by concerns for individualism and economic ideology. Therefore, examined in this section are healthcare and education from the perspective of their contribution to development and social cohesion. Also examined are the concerns from an American sociopolitical and economic perspective.

Healthcare

As mentioned in Chapter Five, the major donor countries and international agencies have made the provision of adequate healthcare a condition for grants and soft loans to developing countries, more specifically to those seeking relief under the Enhanced Highly Indebted Poor Country (EHIPC) initiative sponsored by the IMF and World Bank. As such, since 1996, participants seeking debt forgiveness under the IMF/World Bank-sponsored programs were required to submit a Poverty Reduction Strategy Paper (PRSP) that includes access to adequate healthcare as policy. It is therefore ironic that the US as one of the donor countries should lag other less-rich countries in this vital measurement of human development.

Despite spending more per capita than any other developed country, the US lags the Scandinavian countries and Japan in life-expectancy. Moreover, 45.7 million Americans (over 15 percent of the population) are without access to healthcare in a country in which healthcare accounts for over 16 percent of GDP, almost double that of other developed countries. No other developed country expends so much on healthcare while at the same time excludes so many from what is considered a basic human right, such is the power of the healthcare lobby in the US.

As observed by the former US Comptroller General, David Walker: "If there is one thing that could bankrupt America, it is healthcare. It's not just eating up the federal budget, it is eating up state budgets, and it's eating the budgets of the private sector enterprises."[8] In addition, according to President Obama, "total out of pocket costs [for Americans] have increased by almost 50 percent."[9] As seen through the eyes of former President Clinton, the American healthcare system, as presently configured, is spotting the competition ten to sixteen percentage points in trade. None the less, in opposing President Obama's healthcare-reform initiative and the inclusion of a public option in the equation, the industry spent US$263 million on lobby in the first seven months in 2009[10]—compared with approximately US$100.0 million in 1994 against the Clinton initiative—even in the face of declining American competitiveness attributed partly to rising healthcare costs.

With respect to former President Clinton's observation, the disadvantage to US industries is reflected not only in the almost doubling of healthcare costs in America relative to the cost in other countries but also in the opportunity costs associated with a relatively unhealthy work force, as reflected in lost man days from illnesses of one kind or another.

Clearly, the majority without healthcare coverage is to be found in the lowest 20 percent of income earners comprised mainly of Black and Hispanic Americans. Recall, as discussed in Chapter Five, 24.5 percent of Black Americans and 21.5 percent of Hispanic Americans live in poverty and are without access to adequate healthcare. In contrast, healthcare for low-income families in other OECD countries is provided under a universal healthcare system which is considered anathema to middle- and upper-class American notion of freedom of choice. Yet, there is no conclusive evidence to suggest that Americans are healthier or enjoy a higher quality of life than citizens of other countries either by reason of that option or as a result of the higher expenditure on healthcare. Indeed, as noted earlier, Americans rank tenth on the United Nations' happiness scale, behind several countries with substantially smaller GDPs and less GDP per capita.

In terms of choice, the notion of the rational fool, to be sure, is aptly evidenced by the extent to which consumer choice is influenced by healthcare providers and the pharmaceutical industry, especially with respect to those products that target an ego-centric America, such as, for example, sexually-related products, as observed by Harvard Professor, Michael Sandel, in his *2009 Reith Lectures*.[11]

The current healthcare system in America is considered by affluent middle and upper class Americans as one of the two remaining pillars of the "traditional approach" to human development that defined a pre-1964 America. Hence, President Obama's proposal to reform the American healthcare system has run into a brick wall of special interests represented on both sides of the isle. Many have argued the cost burden of reform whilst the main argument has been ideological, with defenders of the existing system recycling old arguments to discredit other healthcare systems that are still proving their viability. Therefore, like the 1994 healthcare debate between President Clinton and the Republicans, President Obama and the Republicans could hardly be further apart on this issue.

At the extreme right of the debate are Chairman of the Republican National Committee, Michael Steele and Republican Senator Jon Kyl. Michael Steele stresses the freedom of choice as inviolable:

> Obama-Pelosi wants to start building a colossal, closed healthcare system where Washington decides. Republicans want and support an open healthcare system where patients and doctors make the decisions.[12]

But, as reiterated by the President and his team, those who are already covered under existing private insurance plans will not have their choice of provider affected. Rather, they are likely to benefit from the reform initiative that seeks to remove "pre-existing condition" as a basis for refusing health insurance coverage under private insurance plans. According to the President, a recent report this year shows 12 million have been discriminated against because of pre-existing condition.

The so-called "Blue dog" group of House democrats also objects to the President's proposal, stressing the concerns of "middle-class Americans." In so doing, their position suggests the existence of a third political party situated within the framework of the Democratic Party. Their concern centers on the potential of raising "middle-class taxes" to pay for extending healthcare coverage to lower-income Americans. Moreover, middle-class Americans are more likely covered by employer-provided health insurance plans and are thus afraid of losing their choice and of being taxed on employer-provided benefits. This group for all practical purposes, then, sees itself closer to the capitalist ideology and comes down on the side of inequality. However, as Obama sees it, "it's a contest between hope and fear."

For clarity, the American middle class is considered to be concentrated in the third and fourth 20-percent (one-fifth) groupings of households on the GINI income distribution as depicted in Figure 5.1 above. They account for 14.5 and 22.9 percent of total household income in 2006 respectively compared with 12.0 percent for the lowest 40 percent of households in America. Therefore, as the group bearing the greatest share of the tax burden, their self-interest dictates that government transfers to lower income groups be minimized.

Cost as Scapegoat

In terms of costs, Senator Jon Kyle charged: "They [Democrats] propose to pay for this new Washington-run healthcare system by dramatically raising taxes on small businesses owners."[13] But, as often stressed by President Obama, there is no intention to raise taxes on small business owners earning less than US$250,000 a year. Furthermore, the projected cost of the proposed new health-care system does not differ substantially from estimates made by the previous administration: In February, 2007, the Bush administration released a report that shows healthcare costs are expected to double to US$4.1 trillion over the next decade, up from US$2.1 trillion in 2006.[14]

In seeking to justify rising healthcare costs in the US, industry lobby continue to advance the arguments that the US carries the burden of research and development for the rest of the world—considered "free riders"—and that the long waits for certain medical procedures experienced in other countries are absent in the US. With respect to the first, the amount and quality of research in the practice of medicine and in innovations in the US, to be sure, are second to none. The US continues to lead the world in biotechnology research and development; but the rewards associated with such leadership are also significant to the winners. Moreover, such research is not driven by concerns for humanity as much as they are driven by the profit motive in a capitalist world economy.

In terms of convenience, there is no denying that the long waits experienced in other countries are not present in the US. The waiting lists for certain surgical procedures in Britain and Sweden, for example, would be unacceptable to Americans accustomed to near-instant response to their surgical needs. But such delays are not necessarily inevitable with a universal healthcare system. Often, the delays can be attributed to the limited availability of highly specialized and costly equipment in contrast with an over supply in the US which is a major contributing factor to the high cost of healthcare in America. Hence, as charac-terized by the London newspaper, *The Daily Mail*, America is "the land of the fee" when it comes to healthcare.

Masking the high cost of healthcare in the US is the system of employer-provided private insurance plans and the government-sponsored Medicare program. As observed by *New York Times* columnist, David Leonhardt,[15] the healthcare system is paid for by medical insurance premiums and Medicare taxes deducted from our paychecks. As a result, the costs for tests and medical procedures, the main sources of revenue for doctors and hospitals, are not seen by the employee. Few Americans therefore make the connection between waste at the delivery end with the high costs of healthcare which effectively are borne by the employees either directly from higher payroll deductions or indirectly from lower wages. Hence, the incentives are for more tests and medical procedures and not for preventative medicine.

In addition to creating revenues, tests and procedures are ordered for protection against malpractice suits. According to *PricewaterhouseCoopers' Health Research Institute,*[16] unnecessary tests and procedures add over US$210 billion a year to healthcare costs. Republicans argue that costs associated with avoiding malpractice liability could be reduced by capping malpractice awards.

But unnecessary tests and medical procedures are not the only source of waste in healthcare in America. According to the most recent Pricewaterhouse-Coopers' report, another US$210 billion is wasted on inefficient claims processing. As reported, many providers spend about 40 percent of their revenues on filling out complicated claims forms, charging that there are as many different forms as there are insurers. The process also takes its toll on reimbursement turnaround time since insurers are predisposed to dispute tests and procedures. The solution, according to Susan Pisano of America's Health Insurance Plans, is for standardizing the system, using technology which would have to be adopted by hospitals and doctors, with appropriate rules information-sharing.

Yet another source of waste is the overuse or inappropriate use of the emergency room. Again, as PricewaterhouseCoopers' inquiry finds, the problem lies this time with the patient. Many patients ignore their doctor's advice only to end up in the emergency room which costs about ten times the cost of a visit to their primary provider. Such misuse of the emergency room adds another US$12 billion a year to unnecessary healthcare costs.

Finally, healthcare is a US$3.0 trillion industry and as noted earlier accounts for over 16 percent of GDP. Even at one percent profit, the industry is highly lucrative. Hence it will resist any attempt to change its status as a private-sector-controlled system. To this end, many consider the administration's proposed reform of healthcare as the first step to socialized medicine notwithstanding assurances to the contrary from the President. The alternative, as they see it, is to address directly the needs of those who are currently without healthcare. Even then, opposition comes from all sides; according to one of the hosts of CNBC's morning program, "everybody wants to cover 30 million people without covering the cost side first." Hence, as at the date of writing, the Obama healthcare reform plan has gone the way of the Clinton healthcare reform plan; on this occasion, not because it is novel to the American experience or lacks credibility but rather because, as recognized by President Obama, he did not give it the attention it deserved.

Lessons Past

When taken in context of past efforts, indeed commitment, to providing universal electricity and telecommunications services to Americans, the arguments against universal access to healthcare is spurious. Not only was the government permitted to direct tax dollars to help defray the cost of the infrastructure but it was also allowed to tax low-cost users a "universal service fee" or "access charge" that went towards supporting the provision of service to those residents living in high-cost areas. What is noteworthy is that the providers were made responsible for the collection and utilization of and accounting for these access charges as part of the rate-making process.

While universal access to electricity and telecommunications services were ideas rooted in mid-twentieth century concerns for the human condition, the idea of taxing recipients of employer-provided health insurance benefits is anathema to the endless accumulation of capital in twenty-first century America.

Education

As depicted by the 2008 Human Development Index for education, the US ranks 19, not only behind most of the major industrial countries but also Cuba which is ranked 13. On top of the HDI for education is Australia, with South Korea (7); Slovenia (18) Lithuania (19); and the UK (28).

Clearly, despite the rhetoric, education in the US has not received the priority it deserves. As revealed by the data, the government is culpable in the absence of awareness and leadership. As observed by Derek Bok (1996: 90):

> Levels of productivity throughout the industrialized world will come to depend more and more on the basic ingredients of investments, education, and training. It is here that the United States lags behind in ways that our traditional approach cannot readily overcome.

What is significant about Derek Bok's critique is that it was published over a decade ago with information that reflects the state of education two decades ago. Yet, as revealed by the UN's index on education in 2008, the US rather than improving on its standing appears to be advancing to the rear. This observation is supported by the several tables drawn from OECD Indicators 2008 Education at Glance[17] referenced below.

First, "Table A3.1 Graduation Rates in Tertiary Education (2006) for first time Graduates" sets the tone for other indicators: Iceland ranks highest with a graduation rate of 62.8 percent followed by Australia (59.1%); Finland (47.5%); Denmark (44.6%); the Netherlands (43.0); Sweden (40.6%); Italy (39.4%); UK (39%); Japan (38.6%); OECD average (37.3%); and US (35.5%) which is below the average for the OECD.

Second, it follows that the US ranks high amongst OECD countries in incompletion rate in tertiary education. Indeed, as shown in Figure 5, Incompletion Rates in Tertiary Education (2005), the US had an incompletion rate of 53.0 percent—second only to Italy of the OECD countries—of those entering tertiary institutions which was considerably higher than the OECD average of 31.0 percent and well above Japan's 10 percent; Denmark's 15.0 percent; France's 21.0 percent, and Germany's 23.0 percent.

Figure 9.1

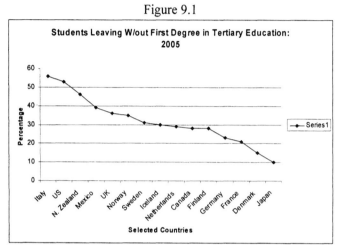

Source: OECD. Table A4.1 (www.oecd.org/edu/eag2008).

Third, the number of science graduates per 100,000 employed 25-34 year old in 2006 puts the US below the OECD average of 1,694. As shown in the OECD table A3.6, South Korea leads the way with 3,863 per every 100,000 employed 25-34 year olds (more than double that of the US). France has 2,706; Australia 2,622; Ireland 2589; Finland 2,335; New Zealand 2,330; UK 2,290; Sweden 1,716; Japan 1,612; Denmark 1,484; Germany 1,425 and the US 1,368.

In terms of upper secondary education, according to the OECD (Table A1. 2a), 97 percent of 25–34 year olds in South Korea and 82 percent of Irish 25-34 year olds now have an upper secondary qualification, versus 37 percent and 41 percent respectively in 1976. Less spectacular but equally indicative of progress in the filed of education are the comparative data for the following countries: the Chez Republic 94%/84%; Canada 91%/76%; Sweden 91%/73%; Finland 90%/63%; France 82%/52%; UK 76%/61%; and Germany 84%/79%. In contrast, the US has shown no improvement during this period, maintaining an 87%/87% level. Indeed, a more recent study on student assessment performance published in 2010 showed the US ranking 25 out of 30 countries, with Norway ranking number 1.

Despite the relatively high ranking in the measurement on upper secondary education for the US population as whole, recent surveys on education in America show 43 percent of Hispanic-Americans, and 25 percent of Black-Americans are without a high school diploma. In contrast, only 15 percent of White-

Americans are without a high school diploma. At the very least, therefore, many countries have caught up with the US and, in the case of South Korea, the Chez Republic, Finland, Sweden, and Canada, have surpassed it since 1976.

The relatively low ranking of the US in almost all of the indicators on education has in part been attributed to its approach to its funding of education. For example, according to the OECD data for 2007, Education at a Glance 2008 (Annex 3 EAG 2008), the US spends 1.0 percent of GDP on upper secondary education. In comparison, as a percentage of GDP, Canada ranks highest amongst the OECD countries with 3.6 percent, followed by the UK with 2.9 percent; France (1.5%); Finland (1.4%); Norway (1.4%); South Korea (1.4%); Sweden (1.3%); Denmark (1.3%); and Japan (0.9%). While the disparity is a function of relative size of GDP rather than the commitment to education, when translated to a per-capita measurement, the disparity is even greater. This latter point is made clearer when the use of public funds is considered.

In the case of the US, the financial burden of tertiary education has been transferred to students; federal support to higher education had been reduced gradually over the last 20 years while the cost of education has been increasing, forcing students to incur greater student loan debts in pursuit of higher education. The consequence is an increasing gap in the graduation rate between high-income (55 percent) and low-income groups (14 percent) as lower-income students find the cost of higher education prohibitive, thereby accounting for the high rate of incompletion as depicted in Figure 5.

In terms of public expenditure on education, on the other hand, primary education in the US accounts for 9.4 percent of total expenditure whilst tertiary education accounts for 3.5 percent. As such, the US ranks above the OECD average of 9.0 percent and 3.0 percent for primary and tertiary education respectively. Indeed, of the countries named above, only Iceland (12.3%/3.4%); Ireland (10.7%/3.3%); and Denmark (9.3%/4.5%) rank higher than the US in terms of public expenditure on education. Moreover, the redirection of funds from the basic three "Rs" (reading, writing and arithmetic) to emphasizing the availability of technology in the classroom does more for feeding into the capitalist model of wealth accumulation than for educating the majority of American secondary school students; in other words, the classroom has become a market for technological products.

The above said, it has to be realized that education is not an end but a means to wealth accumulation in a capitalist world-economy, more especially in the US; but, as recognized and articulated by Derek Bok, levels of productivity will become more and more dependent on education as a basic ingredient; also, as observed by Chang (2008: 128): "With minorities accounting for one-third of the population at the end of 2006, and expected to comprise over 50 percent of the population by 2050, if not sooner, cut-backs in public funding of education portend even greater erosion of US competitiveness." The implications for the future of America and, in consequence, for the wider world, cannot be ignored; with respect to the later, I am again reminded of Father Bryan Hehir's expression of concern (see page 12).

Of course, some might argue that what matters is not the amount spent on education but rather how it is spent and, indeed, how much of it is wasted. To be sure, one of the arguments advanced for the low performance of American secondary school students is the unequal distribution of funding to the schools. In this regard, it is instructive that the Chancellor of the District of Columbia Public Schools, Michelle Rhee, proposed, as an aspect of her continuing reform program for the District school system, a Professional and Development Resource budget for 2010 that reflects an increase of 400 percent over 2007. Such increase will target "higher standards and real results in student achievement"[18] as objectives. However, based on the intense opposition to reform—both from within and without—that confronted Michelle Rhee in the early stages of her tenure as Chancellor, a quick turnaround in the American primary education system is highly unlikely. Chancellor Rhee, it should be noted, had the unfailing support of a strong and unwavering Mayor which support is clearly absent in many other school districts around the country.

It is thus a curiosity that despite the apparent superior support for education, the drop-out rate at American tertiary institutions is second only to the drop out rate for Italy, as shown in Figure 9.1 above. Clearly, there are causes other than the absence of public support for education. In this connection, many have argued that the incentives are for instant gratification—conspicuous consumption—and therefore, pursuing a four-year college degree is seen as consumption-deferred which, for many, is too high an opportunity cost. In retrospect, it is perhaps what Brink Lindsey's critique was all about. On the other hand, it is possible that staying out of poverty does not accommodate the sacrifice in time and lost income opportunity that must be made to attend college, even though there are tangible rewards on completion, as measured by the income differential between a high school graduate and a college graduate. Perhaps a more realistic explanation is the commercialization of college education in America; many ill-prepared secondary students and adults are encouraged to pursue a college education if only because they are able to access the Federal student loan program which has become a major source of income for the "for profit colleges."

In terms of education as a contributing asset to growth, the South Korean experience is unequalled. South Korea had no doubts about the importance of education to its economic development. As well documented by the World Bank and others, a well-educated work force was one of the main catalysts that propelled South Korea to being one of the top ten industrialized countries in the world (Amsden, 1989). Indeed, as shown in Figure 4.1, its growth rate for the period 1965–89 exceeded that of all of the major established industrialized countries in the world. This awareness of the importance of education has received renewed support, as revealed by the OECD data cited above. But, again, South Korea's commitment to national development and social cohesion is deeply rooted in its culture and history.

A Final Thought

As we come to realize that the present crisis is anchored not in traditional market economics but more in our total embrace of aggressive capitalism since the 1980s, the need to become less ideological has risen to the level of an imperative. We need, as the Librarian of Congress, James Billington, exhorts, "to get back into developing the qualities of judgment, wisdom, and imagination that are internally generated and not defined by somebody else's picture on the screen." We need to recognize that we have become the victims of our own game theories; that we, in form and substance, validate Jonathan Swift's satire if only we would listen to ourselves and to see ourselves as the world sees us.

How we get back to that aspect of the American experience, the nurturing experience, for the most part, depends crucially upon how disposed we are to the rigors of dispassionate examination of self, and to effecting a paradigm shift from selfishness to sharing. Such a shift in perspective requires overcoming Cooley's *looking-glass self*; it further requires abandonment of consumerism predicated on narcissism; it requires embrace of humility and a rejection of dominance. We need to prove Thucydides perspective of 2,400 years ago, wrong in the twenty-first century; we need to break the cycle of historical determinism.

The US is the only country in over 2000 years that is in a position to do just that, not because it is the most powerful country in the modern world—the Persians, Greeks, Mongols, Chinese, Romans, Egyptians, and several others were equally great and powerful for their respective times; but they are no more as empires—but rather, as observed by Arnold Toynbee (1948: 38–9), "we are not doomed to make history repeat itself; it is open to us through our own efforts, to give history, in our case, some new and unprecedented turn." To this end, we need to recognize that elected officials in reflecting the desires and phobias of their constituents through the electoral process bring their own aspirations and phobias to policy which could be destructive as well as constructive. Hence, as further recognized by James Billington, it is a process that asks the unimagined questions of our value-system. More importantly, we must bring ourselves to accept the unwelcomed answers, however inconvenient, if we were to give credibility to our unrivaled achievements and our future role in the inevitable pluralist world premised on a system of world government. We further need to recognize and look past the existential explanations of today for a holistic tomorrow.

One way to ensure that history does not repeat itself is to recognize that failure of previous attempts at creating a new manifestation of society— which the on-going American experiment at nation-building is—rather than doom subsequent experiments to fail in their turn, offer them opportunity to succeed through the wisdom that can be gained from suffering, as expressed by Arnold Toynbee (1948: 39), and not from contrivance. In offering this perspective for the salvation of Western civilization, Arnold Toynbee was clearly looking past Homer's pronouncement that, "those whom the Gods wish to destroy, they first make mad." Hence, we need at this juncture of the American experience to effect a change in perspective: from "winning as everything" to accepting failures for their character-building properties. In terms of nation-building, we need to see the forest rather than the trees, and this we must do, for, as further observed by Arnold Toynbee (1948: 39), "as human beings, we are endowed with the freedom of choice, and we cannot shuffle off our responsibility upon the shoulders of God or nature. We must shoulder it ourselves. It is up to us."

Clearly, a reorientation of the American educational system, from its current framework that endemically discriminates against the poor to one that is targeted to raising all levels of education nationally, is paramount. Indeed, we need to see education not just as facilitator of knowledge and thus, control in the hands of a few but, more importantly, as the basis for wisdom of a nation derived from an understanding of the interconnectedness of self to the whole and the importance of the whole to the self. To this end, we need to recognize that when the locus of education is self-fulfillment rather than the betterment of the whole—family, community, country, humanity—it is, I would argue, destructive. In this latter regard, we need to recognize that in the hands of kings who are tyrants or tyrants who become kings, education is as destructive as it can be facilitating of wisdom and greatness in the right hands.

NOTES

1. Competitiveness-enhancing FDI seeks out created assets developed by host countries that offer a well-calibrated and determinants of FDI locations that are sought after by competitiveness-enhancing transnational corporations.
2. "US launches campaign for more foreign investment, http://news.yahoo.com/s/afp/20070510/bs_afp/useconomytrade_070510164110
3. Helman, C., "What the Top U.S. Companies Pay in Taxes," *Forbes.com*, April 2, 2010
4. Sachs, J. *Time Magazine*, February 15, 2010
5. Bajaj, V., and Bradsher, K., "Asia Sails Smoothly through Debt Waters," *The New York Times*, February 8, 2010.
6. "Asia helps feeble West in Global Recovery: OECD," *Reuters*, November 19, 2009.
7. See https://www. climate.yale.edu/seeforyourself
8. Walker, D. "Role of the National Guard and Reserves," Commission on the National Guard and Reserves, *C-SPAN*, June 20, 2007
9. Town Hall Meeting, Grand Junction, Colorado, *C-SPAN*, August 15, 2009
10. Harmon, J., *CNBC*, August 3, 2009
11. "Reith Lectures, 2009 – Markets and Morals," *BBC World Service*, June 9, 2009.
12. Espo, D., "RNC chairman attacks Obama on healthcare." *Associated Press*, July 20, 2009
13. Elliott, P. "Obama defends call for broad healthcare overhaul," *Associated Press*, July 18, 2009.
14. Heavey, S. "Healthcare spending seen doubling in ten years." *Reuters,* February 21, 2007
15. http://marketplace.publicradio.org/display/web/2009/07/22/pm-healthcare/
16. Kavilanz, P., "Healthcare's six money-wasting problems," *CNNMoney.com* http://

finance.yahoo.com/news/Health-cares-six-moneywasting-cnnm3136760791.html?
x=0, August 10, 2009
17. www.oecd.org/edu/eag2008
18. Testimony of Michelle Rhee, Chancellor Meeting of the Council of the District
of Columbia, Performance Oversight Hearing: Proposed FY 2010 Budget. April
9, 2009

Bibliography

Abdel-Malek, A., 1981, "Civilization and Social Theory", Vo. 1 of *Social Dialectics*, London, England: Macmillan & Co

Adem, S., 2005, *Hegemony and Discourse: New Perspectives on International Relations*, Lanham, Maryland: University Press of America

African Development Bank, 1999, *African Development Report, 1999*, Oxford, England: Oxford University Press

Amsden, A.H., 1989, *Asia's Next Giant, South Korea and late industrialization*, NY: Oxford University Press).

Bell, M.W., et al., 1993, "China at the Threshold of a Market Economy", *IMF Occasional Paper 107*, (Washington, DC: IMF).

Bhagwati, J. and H.T. Patrick, 1990, *Aggressive Unilateralism: America's 301 trade policy and the world trading system*, An Arbor, Michigan: University of Michigan Press.

Bhagwati, J., 1988, *Protectionism*, Cambridge, Mass: The MIT Press.

Blejer M., & Chesty, A., 1991, "Analytical and Methodological Issues in the Measurement of Fiscal Deficits. In *IMF Working Paper 90/105*, Washington, D.C.: IMF

Bok, D., 1996, *The State of the Nation, Government and the Quest for a Better Society*, Cambridge, Mass: Harvard University Press.

Borrell, B, & Duncan, R. C., 1992, "A Survey of the Costs of World sugar Policies." In *The World Bank Research Observer*, Vol. 7 No. 2, July, 1992

Bundy, McG., 2004, "The Unimpressive Record of Atomic Diplomacy." In *The Use of force, Military Power and International Politics 6th Ed.*, R.J. Art and K.N. Waltz eds., Lanham, Maryland: Rowman & Littlefield Publishing, Inc., 85–93.

Buzan, B., 2004, "How and to whom does China matter?" In *Does China Matter? Essays in memory of Gerald Segal*, B. Buzan and R. Foot, eds. London: Routledge.

Cardarelli, R., and Kose, A., 2004, "Economic Impact of U.S. Budget Policies", in *IMF Occasional Paper 227: U.S. Fiscal Policies and Priorities for Long-run Sustainability*, M. Mühleisen, and C. Towe, C. eds. Washington, DC: IMF.

Chang, C., 2008, *Territoriality and the Westernization Imperative: Antecedents and Consequences*, Lanham, Maryland: University Press of America

———, 2006, *Privatisation and Development, Theory, Policy and Evidence*, Hampshire, England: Ashgate Publishing Limited.

Chow, R., 2001, "King Kong in Hong Kong: Watching the "Handover" from the USA."
    In *Whither China? Intellectual Politics in Contemporary China*, X. Zhang, ed.
    Durham, NC: Duke University Press, 211–228.

Chunan, P., et al, 1996, "International Capital Flows: Do Short-term Investment and
    Direct Investment Differ?" In *Policy Research Working Paper 1669*, Washington
    DC: World Bank

Chung, J.H., 2005, "China's Ascendancy and the Korean Peninsula." In *Power shift:
    China and Asia's New Dynamics*, D. Shambaugh, ed. Berkeley, California:
    University of California Press, 151–169.

Compton, J.R., 2005, "Shocked and awed: the convergence of military and media
    discourse." In *Global politics in the Information Age*, M.J. Lacy and P. Wilkins eds.
    Manchester, UK: Manchester University Press.

Diamond, J., 2005, *Collapse, How Societies Choose to Fall or Succeed*, New York:
    Penguin Group

————, 1999, *Guns Germs, and Steel*, New York: Penguin Group

Dillon, D.R., 2007, *The China Challenge, Standing Strong against the Military,
    Economic, and Political Threats That Imperil America*, Lanham, Maryland:
    Rowman & Littlefield Publishing, Inc.

Donaldson, T., 1989, *The Ethics of International Business*, New York: Oxford University
    Press

Dornbusch, R., 1988, "Overvaluation and Trade Balance," In *The Open Economy: Tools
    for policymakers in developing countries*, Dornbusch et al (eds), New York: Oxford
    University Press

Dornbusch, R., et al, 1988, Eds. *The Open Economy: Tools for policymakers in
    developing countries*, New York: Oxford University Press

Edwards, S., 1990, "Exchange Rate Misalignment in Developing Countries." In *World
    Bank Research Observer, Vol 5 No. 2*, July 1990

Finger, J. M., 1992, "Dumping and Antidumping: The Rhetoric and the Reality of
    Protection in Industrial Countries." In *The World Bank Research Observer, Vol. 7
    No. 2*, July, 1992

Fischer, S., 2000, "Private Sector Involvement is Important to Reform of Intetnational
    Monetary System." In *IMF Survey, Volume 29, Number 15*, July 31, 2000, (241)

Fischer, S., & Easterly, W., 1990, "The Economics of Government Budget Constraint."
    In *World Bank Research Observer Vol 5, No. 2*, July 1990

Fukuyama, F., 1999, *The Great Disruption, Human Nature and the Reconstitution of
    Social Order* New York: The Free Press, Simon & Schuster.

Gaddis, J.L., 2004, "Implementing Flexible Response: Vietnam as a Test Case." In *The
    Use of force, Military Power and International Politics 6th Ed.*, R.J. Art and K.N.
    Waltz eds., Lanham, Maryland: Rowman & Littlefield Publishing, Inc., 221–246.

————, 2003, "Order versus Justice: An American Foreign Policy Dilemma." In *Order
    and Justice in International Relations*, R. Foot et al., eds., Oxford: Oxford
    University Press, 155 – 175.

Garver, J.W., 2005, "China's Influence in Central and south Asia, Is it Increasing?" In
    Power shift: China and Asia's New Dynamics, D. Shambaugh, ed. Berkeley,
    California: University of California Press, 205–227

Gorbachev, M., 1987, *Perestroika: New Thinking for Our country and the World*, New
    York: Harper & Row

Goto, J. 1989, "The Multifibre Agreement and its Effects on Developing Countries." In
    The World Bank Research Observer, Vol. 4 No. 2, July, 1989

Grandin, G. 2006, *Empire's Workshop: Latin America, the United States, and the rise of the new imperialism* New York: Metropolitan Books.

Griswold, C., 1999, *Adman Smith and The Virtue of Enlightenment*, Cambridge, UK: Cambridge University Press

Halprein, M.H., 2004, "The Korean War." In *The Use of force, Military Power and International Politics 6th Ed.*, R.J. Art and K.N. Waltz eds., Lanham, Maryland: Rowan & Littlefield Publishing, Inc., 181–196.

Hamilton, C., de Melo, J. & Winters, L., 1992, "Who Wins and Who Loses from voluntary Exports Restraints? The Case of Footwear." In *The World Bank Research Observer, Vol. 7 No. 1*, January, 1992

Harding, H., 1981, "China and the Third World." In The American Assembly, Columbia University and Council on Foreign Relations, Inc.

Helleiner, G., 1997, "Capital Account Regimes and the Developing Countries." In *International Monetary and Financial Issues for the 1990s*, Vol viii, New York: United Nations

He Ping, 2002, *China's Search for Modernity, Cultural Discourse in the Late 20th Century*, New York: Palgrave Macmillan.

Huntington, S. P., 1996, *The Clash of Civilizations and The Remaking of World Order*, New York: Touchstone, Simon & Schuster.

Ikenberry, G.J., 2004, "America's Imperial Ambition." In *The Use of force, Military Power and International Politics 6th Ed.*, R.J. Art and K.N. Waltz eds., Lanham, Maryland: Rowman & Littlefield Publishing, Inc., 321–332.

Jenkins, B.M., 2004, "International Terrorism." In *The Use of force, Military Power and International Politics 6th Ed.*, R.J. Art and K.N. Waltz eds., Lanham, Maryland: Rowman & Littlefield Publishing, Inc., 77–84.

Kaarsholm, P., 2006, "States of Failure, Societies in Collapse? Understanding of Violent Conflicts in Africa." In *Violence Political Culture & Development in Africa*, P. Kaarsholm, ed. Oxford, UK: James Curry Limited.

Karl, R., 2001, "The Burdens of History: Lin Zexu (1959) and *The Opium War* (1997)." In *Whither China? Intellectual Politics in Contemporary China*, X. Zhang, ed. Durham, NC: Duke University Press, 229–262 .

Killick, T., 1995, *IMF Programmes in Developing Countries*, London: Routledge

Kesselman, M., et al., 1996, *Comparative politics at the Crossroads*, Lexington, Mass: D.C. Heath and Company.

Keynes, J.M., 1964, *The General Theory of Employment, Interest and Money*, New York: Harcourt Brace Jenovich

Krueger, A.O., 1993, *Economic policies at Cross-purposes: The United States and Developing Countries*, Washington, DC: Brookings Institution.

Krugman, P., 1999, *The Return of Depression Economics*, New York: W.W. Norton & Company.

———, 1988, "External Shocks and domestic PolicyResponses." In *The Open Economy: Tools for policymakers in developing countries*, Dornbusch et al eds., New York: Oxford University Press

Lacy, M.J., and Wilkins, P., 2005, *Global politics in the Information Age*, Manchester, UK: Manchester University Press.

Lampton, D.M., 2005, "China's Rise in Asia Need Not Be at America's Expense." In *Power shift: China and Asia's New Dynamics*, D. Shambaugh, ed. Berkeley, California: University of California Press, 306–328.

Lentner, H.H., 204, *Power and Politics in Globalization*, New York: Routledge

Lewis, W., 1955, *The Theory of Economic Growth*, London: Allen & Unwin

Lin, Yutang 1960, *The Importance of Understanding, Translations from the Chinese*, Cleveland, Ohio: The World Publishing Company.

————, (1949), *The Wisdom of China, An Anthology*, London, UK: Michael Joseph LTT.

Masson, P., & Mussa, M., 1995, *The role of the IMF: Financing and Its Interactions with Adjustment and Surveillance*, Washington, D. C: International Monetary Fund

Mearsheimer, J., & Walt, S., 2007, *The Israel Lobby and U.S. Foreign Policy*, New York: Farrar, Straus and Giroux

Misra, B.B., 1990, *The Unification and Division of India*, New Delhi: Oxford University Press.

Mitter, R., 2003, "An Uneasy Engagement: Chinese Ideas of Global Order and Justice in Historical Perspective." In *Order and Justice in International Relations*, R. Foot et al., eds., Oxford: Oxford University Press, 207–235.

Mohamed, D., 1998, "Statements by Governors." In 1998 Annual Meetings of the Boards of Governors, *Summary Proceedings*, Washington D.C.: The World Bank Group (133-9)

Moore, J., 1986, "Why Privatise?" in Kay, J, et al, *Privatisation and Regulation: The UK Experience*, Oxford: Clarendon Press

Mühleisen, M., 2004, "Overview: Returning Deficits and the need for Fiscal Reform." In *IMF Occasional Paper 227: U.S. Fiscal Policies and Priorities for Long-run Sustainability*, M. Mühleisen and C. Towe eds. Washington, DC: IMF.

Musharraf, P., 2006, *In the Line of Fire, a memoir*, New York: The Free Press, Simon & Schuster.

Nashashibi, et al., 1992, "The Fiscal Dimension of Adjustment in Low-income Countries", *IMF Occassional Paper 95*, April, 1992

Naughton, B., 2007, *The Chinese Economy, Transitions and Growth*, Cambridge, Mass: The MIT Press.

Ohashi, H., 2005, "China's Regional Trade and Investment Profile." In *Power Shift: China and Asia's New Dynamics*, D. Shambaugh, ed., Berkeley, California: University of California Press, 71– 95.

Peck, J., 2006, *Washington's China, The National Security World, the Cold War, and the Origins of Globalism*, Boston, Mass: The University of Massachusetts Press.

Prasad, E., ed., 2004, "China's growth and Integration into the World Economy, Prospects and Challenges," *IMF Occasional Paper 152*, Washington, DC: IMF.

Prasad, E., and Rumbaugh, T., 2004 'Overview." In "China's Growth and Integration into the World Economy, Prospects and Challenges." *IMF Occasional Paper 152*, Prasad, E. ed. Washington, DC: IMF

Pye, L.W., 1981, "The China Factor in southeast Asia." In *The American Assembly, Columbia University and Council on Foreign Relations, Inc.*

Rawls, J., 1999, *The Law of Peoples*, London: Harvard University Press

————, 1971, *A Theory of Justice*, Cambridge Mass: Harvard University Press

Rostow, W., 1961, *The Stages of Economic Growth, A non-communist Manifesto*, London, England: Cambridge University Press

Rumbaugh, T., and Blancher, N., "International Trade and the Challenges of WTO Accession." In "China's growth and Integration into the World Economy, Prospects and Challenges." *IMF Occasional Paper 152*, Prasad, E. ed. Washington, DC: IMF

Sadar, F., 1993, "Privatization and Foreign investment in the Developing world, 1988-92." In *World Bank Working papers,* , Washington D.C.: World Bank

Sansom, G. (Sir), 2004, "Japan's Fatal Blunder." In *The Use of force, Military Power and International Politics 6th Ed.*, R.J. Art and K.N. Waltz eds., Lanham, Maryland: Rowman & Littlefield Publishing, Inc., 153–164.

Segal, G., 1999, "Does China matter?" In *Does China Matter? Essays in memory of Gerald Segal*, B. Buzan and R. Foot, eds. London: Routledge.

Sen, A., 2002, *Rationality and Freedom*, Cambridge, Mass: The Belknap Press of Harvard University Press)

Seo, Y., and Takekawa, S., "Waves of Globalization in East Asia: A Historical Perspective." In *Fairness, Globalization, and public institutions, East Asia and beyond*, J. Dator, et al, eds. Honolulu: University of Hawai'I Press, 219–248.

Shambaugh, D., 2005, "The Rise of China and Asia's New Dynamics." In *Power Shift: China and Asia's New Dynamics*, D. Shambaugh, ed., Berkeley, California: University of California Press, 1–22.

————, 2005, "Return to the Middle Kingdom?" In *Power Shift: China and Asia's New Dynamics*, D. Shambaugh, ed., Berkeley, California: University of California Press, 23–47.

Sklair, L., 1995 2nd ed., *Sociology of the Global Syatem*, London: Prentice Hall Harvester Wheatsheaf

Solomon, R.H., (Ed.), 1981, *The China Factor: Sino-American Relations and the Global Scene*, New Jersey: Prentice Hall Inc.

Stiglitz, J., 2002, *Globalization and its discontents*, New York: W.W. Norton & Co

Sum, N., 2005, "Global financial markets and the ICT revolution: perfect market or (im)perfect domination?" In *Global politics in the Information Age*, M.J. Lacy and P. Wilkins eds. Manchester, UK: Manchester University Press.

Suskind, R., 2004, *The Price of Loyalty: George W. Bush, the White House, and the Education of Paul O'Neill*, New York: Simon & Schuster.

Talbott, S., 1981, "The Strategic dimension of the Sino-American Relationship." In *The American Assembly, Columbia University and Council on Foreign Relations, Inc.* New Jersey: Prentice Hall Inc.

Thatcher, M., 1995, *'The Path to Power'*, New York: Harper Collins Publishers.

Tobin, J., 1998, "Financial Globalization: Can National Currencies Survive?" *Conference Paper, 10th ABCDE*, Washington DC: World Bank

Todaro, M., 2000, *Economic Development*, 7th ed., New York: Addison-Wesley Longman, Inc.

Toynbee, A., 1948, *Civilization on Trial*, Oxford: Oxford University Press

Tussie, D., 1987, *The Less Developed Countries and the World Trading System*, London: Frances Pinter Publishers.

United Nations, 1998, *World Investment Report: Trends and Determinants*, New York: United Nations (UNCTD)

Veblen, T., 1952, *Theory of the Leisure Class*, (Banta, M., Ed) Oxford World Classics, New York: Oxford University Press

Wallerstein, I., 1999, *The End of The World as we know it*, Minneapolis, Minnesota: University of Minnesota Press.

Wang, G., 2005, "China and Southeast Asia, The Context of a New Beginning." In *Power Shift: China and Asia's New Dynamics*, D. Shambaugh, ed. Berkeley, California: University of California Press, 187–204

Weaver, R.K., (2000), *Ending Welfare as We Know It*, Washington, DC: Brookings Institution Press.

Wermuth, L., 2003, *Global Inequality and Human Needs*, Boston: Alan & Bacon

Woods, N., 2003, "Order, Justice, the IMF and the World Bank." In *Order and Justice in International Relations*, R. Foot et al., eds., Oxford: Oxford University Press, 80–102.

Woodward, B, 2006, *State of Denial*, New York: Simon & Schuster.

World Bank, 2005, *World Development Report 2006, Equity and Development*, Washington DC: IBRD/World Bank

———, 2004, *World Development Report, 2005, a Better Investment Climate for Everyone*, Washington, DC: IBRD/World Bank.

———, 1997, *World Development Report 2006*, Washington DC: World Bank

———, 1994, "Infrastructure for Development", *World Development Report*, London, England: Oxford University Press

———, 1989, *World Development Report*, London, England: Oxford University Press

Yahuda, M.B., 2004, "Gerald Segal's Contribution." In *Does China Matter? Essays in memory of Gerald Segal*, B. Buzan and R. Foot, eds. London: Routledge.

Zhang, X, 2001, "Nationalism, Mass Culture, and Intellectual Strategies in Post-Tiananmen China." In *Whither China? Intellectual Politics in Contemporary China*, X. Zhang, ed. Durham, NC: Duke University Press, 315–348.

Zhang, Y., and Tang, S., 2005, "China's Regional Strategy." In *Power Shift: China and Asia's New Dynamics*, D. Shambaugh, ed., Berkeley, California: University of California Press 48–70.

Index

Abdel–Malek, 64
Afghanistan, 16, 18, 69
Arrow, K., 3
Asian financial crisis, 16–17
Atlantic Monthly, 123, 142
Axis of Evil, 47

Balance of Payments, proposed change
    to, 149–150
banks, free checking, 72
"beggar thy neighbor" policy, 10
Benedict XVI, Pope, 62
Bernanke, B., (see also Federal Reserve
    System) 11, 17, 22, 32–34, 44, 99,
    125; on consumer spending, 145
Billington, J., 7, 169
Blair, Tony, 16, 39, 50, 55
bonuses, 94; from TARP, 103
Bretton Woods, 138
Brown, G., 39; in defense of British
    health care system, 96
Bush administration, 5, 17, 23–24, 33–
    35, 36, 49–50; support for Israel,
    50; and South Ossetia, 54; overpaid
    banks, 72
Bush, G.H.W., 55, 145

Cameron, D., 37, 96
Caribbean Basin Initiative (CBI), 21
Chien, Szema, on *Wealth and
    Commerce*, 69

China, 64, 65:
    American perception of, 109;
    challenges to, 111–112;
    Communist party, 110; "Long
    March", 38; and Confucianism,
    110–111, 117; economic progress
    and reform, 119–120; Eisenhower's
    China policy, 114–115, 130, 133;
    financing US deficit, 13–15, 146;
    foreign investment enterprises
    (FIE), 122; GDP growth, 121, 131,
    145; geopolitics, 123; Mao Zedong,
    38; the Middle Kingdom, 110–112,
    118; and the Middle East, 129–131;
    non–intervention policy, 127;
    normative power, 134; Opium War,
    112, 118; Peoples Republic of
    China (PRC), 111–119
Civilian Conservation Corp (CCC), 159
Civil Rights Act, 1964, 65, 73, 89
Clinton, H., 7
collateralized debt obligations (CDO),
    1, 25, 29, 31, 40, 42, 49
Cooley, C.H., 42, 169
Connolly, J., (Treasury Secretary), 8
credit default swaps (CDS), 1, 25, 29,
    40, 42, 49
Cuomo, A., 27

Dante's Inferno, 85
Dickens, C., *Little Dorrit*, 67

District of Columbia Public Schools, 168

Economist Magazine, 147
Enlightenment, 63, 64, 75, 86
"Enron loop–hole", 58
equality–efficiency trade off, 101
Estoppel, doctrine of, 53
Export Processing Zones (EPZ), 149

Fallows, J., 123
Federal Reserve System, 5, 8–9, 16–17, 23, 26, 29, 31–34, 43, 49, 58
floating exchange rates, 9, 140–141, 148
Fosamax, 74
framing, 86
French Revolution, Cho en Lai's comments on, 51

Game theory, 33, 64, 86
General Agreement on Tariff and Trade (GATT), 144–145
Geithner, T., 13, 76 (see also Treasury Secretary); reassuring Gulf Arab states, 13; reassuring China, 104, 143
Gingrich, N., 26, 28; and budget deficit reduction, 60; attack on Sotomayor, 79; embrace of imperialism, 90
GINI coefficient, 94
Glass–Stegall Act, 1933, 31, 76
 repeal of, 58
Gorbachev, M., 54
Gramm–Leach–Bliley Act, 1999, passage of, 58, 76
Great Depression, 24, 26–29, 34, 35, 39
Greece, experience, 9, 154, 155
Greenspan, A., 1, 15–17, 25–28, 31, 34–35, 38, 49, 69, 84
 self–absolution, 41
Greenstock, J., Sir, 71

Health care, 161–163
Hehir, B. Father, 13, 168
Human Development Index (HDI), 90, 102, 103, 106

income inequality, 63, 75, 81, 89; comparison with other countries, 94–97; Lewis's, Arthur, take on, 99–100; in US, 92
infrastructure, 158–159
International Monetary Fund, 7, 11, 13, 17–20, 56, 99, 119; as surrogate, 81
invisible hand of the market, 69–70

Japan,
 GDP, 58; growth rate, 102; rapid industrialization of, 58
Judicial Watch, 27

Keynes, J.M., 61
 Keynesian economics, 28, 34

landmark geopolitical events, 54–56
Lewis, A. (Sir), 100–101
Lilliputians, 43
Lobbyists, 45, 141
Longterm Capital Management (LTCM), 17, 35, 76

Madoff, B., Ponzi scheme, 67
Manifest Destiny, 7, 47, 50–53; civilizing mission, 72; Devine right, 51; revival of, 75
market triumphalism, 26, 30, 32, 44
Marxism–Leninism, 43
Middle East, 45; birth pangs of, 50
moral hazard, 16, 18, 32–33, 35, 76
Multifibre Arrangement (MFA), 58, 144

Nash equilibrium, 66, 86
national income identities, 18–19
nationalization, 25, 33
Nietzsche, F., 62
North American Free Trade Association (NAFTA), 149

Obama, President, 4, 27, 29, 39, 52; attack on, 77–78; administration, 42
"Operation Iraqi Liberation", 12
Organization for Economic Cooperation and Development (OECD), 11, 22, 44, 58, 63, 91, 94, 97, 106, 141, 159, 162, 166–168

Organization of Petroleum Exporting
    Countries (OPEC), 140

Palmerston, Lord, 4, 56, 63, 68,
"pan–European racism", 72
Pareto–efficient, 69
"Pareto–liberty conflict", 71, 77
Paul, R., Senator, 147
Paulson, H., 11, 17, 21, 25, 71, 74, 101,
    125, 129, 147
Pavlov, I, experiment, 66
Pax Americana, 13
Pax Romana, 4, 12, 15
poverty in the US, 95; human poverty
    index (HPI), 103
preemtive strikes, 52–54
Prisoner's Dilemma, 33, 66, 68
Putin, V., 15

Rand, Ayn, 69, 75, 77, 78, 86
rational fool, 3, 68–70
Rhee, M., 168
Rockwell, N., 2
Romney, M., 48–49

Sandel, M.—*Reith lectures,* 74, 85, 162
Shanghai Girls, 68
Smith, A., *Wealth of Nations,* 69
South Africa, 55,
    African National Congress (ANC),
    55; Mandela, N. 55
South Korea, and education, 165, 167;
    GDP, 58; growth rates, 102;
    industrialization, 58
structural adjustment, 155–156
Summers, L., 141
Super 301, 143
Swift, J., 43, 169

targeted revaluation, 11–12, 137;
    slippery slope of, 142–146,
Thatcher, M., 52, and Russia, 54; as
Prime Minister, 81
"too big to fail", 13, 76
Trade and Tariff Act, 1974, 11, 57,
    140, 143
Treasury Secretary, 8, 11, 23, 24–25,
    31, 71, 74, 129, 155

United Nations Commission for Human
    Rights, 74
United Nations Conference on Trade
    and Development (UNCTAD), 155
United Nations survey on happiness, 95
US:
    Achilles heel, 8; American dream,
    97–98; aggressive trade policies,
    20–21; at the crossroads, vi;
    average household income, 97;
    budget deficit, 7, 18, 20–21;
    relationship with China, 49, 114,
    115, 116, 127 129, 144–150;
    decline in world trade, 132;
    biggest (greatest) debtor nation, 18,
    132, 140, 146; hegemony, 30, 47,
    62, 83, 137; haven for ambitions,
    81; ill–advised policies, 42;
    imperial ambitions, 48; labor
    productivity, 22; national debt, 140;
    saving–investment imbalances,
    154; subsidies, 20, 21; tariffs &
    non–tariff barriers, 10, 21–22; tax
    loopholes, 157; trade imbalance,
    154; trade strategies, 143; troubled
    assets relief program (TARP), 27,
    62

Veblen, T., 143
Volker, P., 44
Voting Rights Act, 1965, 65, 89
Vulcan(s), 15, 18, 38, 49, 50, 131

Wages and Hours Act, 1938, 89
Walker, D., 18
Washington Consensus, 31, 39, 43, 56,
    91, 129
World Bank, 7, 13, 18–20, 56, 104–
    106, 119; and income inequality,
    92; and structural adjustment, 155–
    156; as surrogate, 81, 87
World Trade Organization, 10, 117,
    121, 125, 140, 143, 144, 148
Wolfensohn, J., 92

About the author:

Claude V. Chang teaches economics at Johnson & Wales University, Miami, Florida. He served as Secretary to the Treasury of Guyana and as Advisor to the Public Accounts Committee, Guyana Parliament. He is also a former staff member of the *Commonwealth Development Corporation* (British government) and former UNDP consultant to the Guyana Economic Programme Monitoring Unit.

Chang served on several boards, including the Board of the Guyana Central Bank and the Governing Council of the University of Guyana. Chang's private sector experience includes: Group Manager/Assistant Treasurer, *National Exchange Carrier Association* (NECA), NJ; Deputy General Manager, Finance & Administration, *Guyana Telephone & Telegraph Company*; Financial Controller, *Guyana Sugar Corporation*; Comptroller, *Guam Telephone Authority*; Director of Fiscal Services/Interim Hospital Administrator, *Guam Memorial Hospital*, and Assistant Vice President, *CP National Corporation*, California.

Claude Chang is the author of *Territoriality and the Westernization Imperative* (2008); *Privatisation and Development, Theory, Policy, and Evidence*, (2006); and "Commercial Infrastructure in Africa: Potentials and Challenges" *Economics Research Papers No 45*, African Development Bank (1999). He has also contributed a book chapter to: *Leading Issues in Competition, Regulation and Development* (2004), a British government-funded project administered by the University of Manchester.

Breinigsville, PA USA
27 August 2010
244358BV00002B/2/P